IDLENESS, CONTEMPLATION AND THE AESTHETIC, 1750–1830

Reconstructing the literary and philosophical reaction to Adam Smith's dictum that man is a labouring animal above and before all else, this study explores the many ways in which Romantic writers presented idle contemplation as the central activity in human life. By contrasting the British response to Smith's political economy with that of contemporary German Idealists, Richard Adelman also uses this consideration of the importance of idleness to Romantic aesthetics to chart the development of a distinctly British idealism in the last decades of the eighteenth century. Exploring the work of Adam Smith, Jeremy Bentham, Friedrich Schiller, William Cowper, Samuel Taylor Coleridge, Mary Wollstonecraft and many of their contemporaries, this study pinpoints a debate over human activity and capability taking place between 1750 and 1830, and considers its social and political consequences for the cultural theory of the early nineteenth century.

RICHARD ADELMAN is Lecturer in English at the University of Dundee.

CAMBRIDGE STUDIES IN ROMANTICISM

Founding editor
PROFESSOR MARILYN BUTLER, *University of Oxford*

General editor
PROFESSOR JAMES CHANDLER, *University of Chicago*

Editorial Board
JOHN BARRELL, *University of York*
PAUL HAMILTON, *University of London*
MARY JACOBUS, *University of Cambridge*
CLAUDIA JOHNSON, *Princeton University*
ALAN LIU, *University of California, Santa Barbara*
JEROME MCGANN, *University of Virginia*
SUSAN MANNING, *University of Edinburgh*
DAVID SIMPSON, *University of California, Davis*

This series aims to foster the best new work in one of the most challenging fields within English literary studies. From the early 1780s to the early 1830s a formidable array of talented men and women took to literary composition, not just in poetry, which some of them famously transformed, but in many modes of writing. The expansion of publishing created new opportunities for writers, and the political stakes of what they wrote were raised again by what Wordsworth called those 'great national events' that were 'almost daily taking place': the French Revolution, the Napoleonic and American wars, urbanization, industrialization, religious revival, an expanded empire abroad and the reform movement at home. This was an enormous ambition, even when it pretended otherwise. The relations between science, philosophy, religion and literature were reworked in texts such as *Frankenstein* and *Biographia Literaria*; gender relations in *A Vindication of the Rights of Woman* and *Don Juan*; journalism by Cobbett and Hazlitt; poetic form, content and style by the Lake School and the Cockney School. Outside Shakespeare studies, probably no body of writing has produced such a wealth of comment or done so much to shape the responses of modern criticism. This indeed is the period that saw the emergence of those notions of 'literature' and of literary history, especially national literary history, on which modern scholarship in English has been founded.

The categories produced by Romanticism have also been challenged by recent historicist arguments. The task of the series is to engage both with a challenging corpus of Romantic writings and with the changing field of criticism they have helped to shape. As with other literary series published by Cambridge, this one will represent the work of both younger and more established scholars, on either side of the Atlantic and elsewhere.

For a complete list of titles published see end of book.

IDLENESS, CONTEMPLATION AND THE AESTHETIC, 1750–1830

RICHARD ADELMAN
University of Dundee

CAMBRIDGE
UNIVERSITY PRESS

CAMBRIDGE UNIVERSITY PRESS
Cambridge, New York, Melbourne, Madrid, Cape Town,
Singapore, São Paulo, Delhi, Tokyo, Mexico City

Cambridge University Press
The Edinburgh Building, Cambridge CB2 8RU, UK

Published in the United States of America by Cambridge University Press, New York

www.cambridge.org
Information on this title: www.cambridge.org/9780521190688

© Richard Adelman 2011

This publication is in copyright. Subject to statutory exception
and to the provisions of relevant collective licensing agreements,
no reproduction of any part may take place without the written
permission of Cambridge University Press.

First published 2011

Printed in the United Kingdom at the University Press, Cambridge

A catalogue record for this publication is available from the British Library

Library of Congress Cataloguing in Publication data
Adelman, Richard, 1982–
Idleness, contemplation, and the aesthetic, 1750–1830 / Richard Adelman.
p.   cm. – (Cambridge studies in romanticism)
Includes bibliographical references and index.
ISBN 978-0-521-19068-8 (hardback)
1. English literature–18th century–History and criticism.   2. English literature–19th century–History and criticism.   3. Romanticism–Great Britain.   4. Aesthetics, British–18th century.   5. Aesthetics, British–19th century.   6. Solitude in literature.   7. Labor in literature.   8. Idealism in literature.   I. Title.   II. Series.
PR447.A34 2011
820.9′353–dc22
2011002458

ISBN 978-0-521-19068-8 Hardback

Cambridge University Press has no responsibility for the persistence or
accuracy of URLs for external or third-party internet websites referred to in
this publication, and does not guarantee that any content on such websites is,
or will remain, accurate or appropriate.

Contents

Acknowledgements		*page* vi
List of abbreviations		vii
	Introduction	1
1	The division of labour	10
2	Utilitarian education and aesthetic education	38
3	Cowper, Coleridge and Wollstonecraft	68
4	Coleridge's Pantisocracy, *Biographia* and *Church and State*	102
	Conclusion	133
	Epilogue: Wordsworth and Kingsley	141
Notes		173
Bibliography		195
Index		201

Acknowledgements

I would like to express my gratitude to Claire Colebrook, whose encouragement and expertise led me to conceive of and pursue this theme as a research project; to Jim Watt for offering concise and useful comments on early drafts of the first three chapters; to Mary Fairclough, Liz Edwards and Sarah Sheena for their advice, careful reading and help exploring *The Task* and many other texts; and to Peter de Bolla for his comments on the project as a whole. I am also indebted to the Arts and Humanities Research Council for their financial support, and to York's Centre for Eighteenth Century Studies for providing consistently stimulating and informative research seminars. Finally and most importantly I would like to thank John Barrell, whose insight, suggestions and generosity have enriched this study beyond measure.

Abbreviations

'Address'	S. T. Coleridge, 'Address to a young Jack Ass & it's [*sic*] *tethered* Mother' in *Letters*, Vol. 1, pp. 142–3.
Aesthetic	F. Schiller, *On the Aesthetic Education of Man, in a Series of Letters*, ed. E. M. Wilkinson and L. A. Willoughby (Oxford: Clarendon Press, 1967).
Alton Locke	C. Kingsley, *Alton Locke, Tailor and Poet: An Autobiography*, ed. E. A. Cripps (Oxford: Oxford University Press, 1983);
Biog.	S. T. Coleridge, *Biographia Literaria*, ed. J. Engell and W. J. Bate, 2 vols. (Princeton: Princeton University Press, 1983).
C&S	S. T. Coleridge, *On the Constitution of Church and State*, ed. J. Colmer (Princeton: Princeton University Press, 1976).
Chrestomathia	J. Bentham, *Chrestomathia*, ed. M. J. Smith and W. H. Burston (Oxford: Clarendon Press, 1984).
'Coleridge'	A. L. Barbauld, 'To Mr S. T. Coleridge' in W. McCarthy and E. Kraft (eds.), *Anna Letitia Barbauld: Selected Poetry and Prose* (Ormskirk: Broadview, 2002), pp. 142–3.
'Effusion'	S. T. Coleridge, 'Effusion xxxv', in *The Complete Poems*, ed. W. Keach (London: Penguin, 1997), pp. 85–6.
Essay	A. Ferguson, *An Essay on the History of Civil Society 1767*, ed. D. Forbes (Edinburgh: Edinburgh University Press, 1966).
'FM'	S. T. Coleridge, 'Frost at Midnight' in *Coleridge's Poetry and Prose*, eds. N. Halmi, P. Magnuson and R. Modiano (London: W. W. Norton, 2004), pp. 120–3.

Letters	S. T. Coleridge, *Collected Letters*, ed. E. L. Griggs, 6 vols. (Oxford: Clarendon Press, 1956).
Principles	A. Ferguson, *Principles of Moral and Political Science*, 2 vols. (New York: AMS Press, 1973).
Short Residence	M. Wollstonecraft, *Letters Written during a Short Residence in Sweden, Norway and Denmark*, in *The Complete Works*, ed. J. Todd and M. Butler, 7 vols. (New York: New York University Press, 1989), Vol. VI, pp. 237–348.
Task	Cowper, William, The Task, *and Selected Other Poems*, ed. J. Sambrook (London: Longman, 1994).
'Three years'	W. Wordsworth, 'Three years she grew in sun and shower' in *The Poetical Works of William Wordsworth*, ed. E. De Selincourt, 5 vols. (Oxford: Clarendon Press, 1952), Vol. II, pp. 214–16.
TMS	A. Smith, *The Theory of Moral Sentiments*, ed. D. D. Raphael and A. L. Macfie (Oxford: Clarendon Press, 1976).
WN	A. Smith, *An Inquiry into the Nature and Causes of the Wealth of Nations*, ed. R. H. Campbell and A. S. Skinner, 2 vols. (Indianapolis: Liberty Fund, 1976).
Writings	J. Bentham, *The Panopticon Writings*, ed. M. Božovič (London: Verso, 1995).
Yeast	C. Kingsley, *Yeast: A Problem* (London: J. M. Dent and Sons, 1976).

Introduction

William Wordsworth's poems *The Brothers*, published in 1800, and 'Gipsies', published in 1807, both begin with a denunciation from their different speakers of the apparent idleness of the men and women visible to them. This is the 'priest of Ennerdale' in *The Brothers* censuring the 'tourists' (*Brothers*, 16, 1)[1] he can see from his cottage:

> some glance along,
> Rapid and gay, as if the earth were air,
> And they were butterflies to wheel about
> Long as their summer lasted; some, as wise,
> Upon the forehead of a jutting crag
> Sit perch'd with book and pencil on their knee,
> And look and scribble, scribble on and look,
> Until a man might travel twelve stout miles,
> Or reap an acre of his neighbour's corn.
> (*Brothers*, 2–10)

This judgement clearly contrasts vain movement with honest toil. The objects of the priest's attention 'wheel about' 'as if the earth were air' or sit and 'scribble' for the same length of time it would take a man to 'reap an acre of his neighbour's corn'. Such an opposition between work and leisure is further underlined in the poem's second verse paragraph. There we learn that the priest is not simply surveying the scene before him, but is 'Employed' in his 'winter's work' (*Brothers*, 20):

> Upon the stone
> His Wife sat near him, teasing matted wool,
> While, from the twin cards tooth'd with glittering wire,
> He fed the spindle of his youngest child,
> Who turn'd her large round wheel in the open air
> With back and forward steps.
> (*Brothers*, 20–25)

In 'Gipsies', the poem's speaker describes the 'knot / of human Beings' visible to him with rather more indignation:

> Yet are they here? – the same unbroken knot
> Of human Beings, in the self-same spot!
>   Men, Women, Children, yea the frame
>   Of the whole Spectacle the same!
> Only their fire seems bolder, yielding light:
> Now deep and red, the colouring of night;
>   That on their Gipsy-faces falls,
>   Their bed of straw and blanket-walls.
> – Twelve hours, twelve bounteous hours, are gone while I
> Have been a Traveller under open sky,
>   Much witnessing of change and chear,
>   Yet as I left I find them here!
>   ('Gipsies', 1–12)[2]

These lines seem to represent a more aggressive sentiment, and a different type of speaker, than the speech with which *The Brothers* begins. Yet there is something similar about the motif. In both cases the speaker attempts to contrast unproductiveness with a type of activity. Both phrase their comparison around the number twelve: 'twelve bounteous hours', 'twelve stout miles'. More importantly however, in both instances it would seem to be questionable whether the inactivity being censured is really as vain, idle or unproductive as the speaker would have us believe. In the case of the opening of *The Brothers*, the reader acquainted with a poem such as *Home at Grasmere* would not find it hard to imagine wheeling about like a butterfly in the landscape as positive behaviour. In that poem, the poet himself performs such activity and celebrates its effects:

> I sate, and stirred in Spirit as I looked,
> I seemed to feel such liberty was mine,
> Such power and joy; but only for this end:
> To flit from field to rock, from rock to field,
> From shore to island, and from isle to shore,
> From open place to covert, from a bed
> Of meadow-flowers into a tuft of wood,
> From high to low, from low to high, yet still
> Within the bounds of this huge Concave[.]
>   (*Home at Grasmere*, 34–42)[3]

Similarly, were the figure from *The Brothers* the poet himself, or someone like him, one can imagine looking and scribbling being classified as particularly intense and creative activities.

In line with these possibilities, the speaker of 'Gipsies' seems to make the same style of judgement in what might be described as the opposite case. He has been 'a Traveller' 'witnessing' 'change and chear' in much the same way that the tourists in *The Brothers* 'glance along' and 'look'. Yet his movement 'under open sky' seems to qualify him, in his mind, to censure those remaining in one place. The manner in which the objects of the poet's censure are described seems to confuse matters further. In the brief glimpse the reader is shown of the gypsies, they are an 'unbroken knot'. The impenetrability of their world and the invisibility of what they might be doing is all that characterizes them. Thus neither judgement in *The Brothers* or 'Gipsies' can be said to be verifiable. Both poems begin with an enunciation designed to bolster the activity in which the speaker is engaged.

The manner in which *The Brothers* unfolds bears witness to the partiality of the judgement with which it begins. Leonard Ewbank, the figure on whom the priest's attention falls, is neither a 'tourist' nor a 'moping son of idleness' (*Brothers*, 11). By means of dialogue between Leonard and the priest, as well as description by the narrator, it is revealed that Leonard grew up in the valley in which the poem is set, left to go to sea, and is returning to it in an attempt to find his brother. In the case of this one supposed tourist, the priest's accusations turn out to be false. Leonard is not so much idling as making an emotional journey. His appearance of physical inertia – 'tarry[ing]' in the 'churchyard' (*Brothers*, 12) – masks an intense state of mind.

The case of 'Gipsies' is slightly different. The fact that the poem is made up entirely of the utterance of one speaker means that there is no alternative viewpoint to question the indignation we have already witnessed. There is no narrative voice, for example, as there is in *The Brothers*, offering a more impartial commentary on the poem's action. Despite this one-sidedness, however, the poem has been read as undermining, or as ironizing, its own judgements. David Simpson analyses 'the excess of the sublime mood' with which the reader is presented and demonstrates the manner in which it is constructed by reference to Milton's Satan. In this reading, Wordsworth's speaker significantly over-states his case, implying, consequently, 'both a contempt for and an envy of' the gypsies' 'community'. Their 'paradisal society' holds 'the same position for the speaker as do Adam and Eve for Satan'.[4]

The most famous reaction to Wordsworth's 'Gipsies' is the brief account Samuel Taylor Coleridge gives of the poem in the second volume of his *Biographia Literaria*. Occurring amid an account of the defects of Wordsworth's poetry, Coleridge's brief treatment of 'Gipsies' labels it an instance of '*mental* bombast' (Coleridge's emphasis), 'a disproportion of thought to the circumstance and occasion' (*Biog.*, Vol. II, p. 136):

the poet, without seeming to reflect that the poor tawny wanderers might probably have been tramping for weeks together through road and lane, over moor and mountain, and consequently must have been right glad to rest themselves, their children and cattle, for one whole day; and overlooking the obvious truth, that such repose might have been quite as necessary for *them*, as a walk of the same continuance was pleasing or healthful for the more fortunate poet; expresses his indignation in a series of lines, the diction and imagery of which would have been rather above, than below the mark, had they been applied to the immense empire of China improgressive for thirty centuries. (*Biog.*, Vol. II, p. 137)

Coleridge anticipates the basis of Simpson's reading, finding the language in which Wordsworth's speaker couches his case to be almost ridiculously over the mark. By offering a possible rationale for the gipsies' lack of movement, however, this passage could also be said to replicate something like the censure of Wordsworth's speaker. Coleridge is suggesting that the 'repose' of the 'poor tawny wanderers' is understandable and acceptable if it is the case that they had been 'tramping for weeks together through road and lane, over moor and mountain'. Coleridge's siding with the gypsies is conditional on the assumption of their activity at other times, just as Wordsworth's speaker uses their twelve hours' inertia as the rationale for his censure.

There is another resonance to the opposition between activity and repose in 'Gipsies' to which Coleridge's commentary gives access. In defining '*mental* bombast, as distinguished from verbal', Coleridge offers the following observation: 'This, by the bye, is a fault of which none but a man of genius is capable. It is the awkwardness and strength of Hercules with the distaff of Omphale' (*Biog.*, Vol. II, p. 136). Coleridge is referring to Hercules' punishment for slaying Iphitus. Given in bondage to Omphale, the Queen of Lydia, for three years, Hercules was dressed 'in woman's clothes' and set 'to spinning wool with the female slaves'.[5] Applied to Wordsworth's poetry, this image serves to depict the poet possessing mental powers too powerful for many of the situations in which he might find himself. His mind is concerned with subjects too great to be attached to many ordinary situations. In terms of reading his poetry, this is a significant criticism. Attaching the type of thoughts Coleridge considers to be in Wordsworth's mind to a quotidian scene of gypsies or of daffodils (another example the *Biographia* gives) leads to a problematic discrepancy for the reader. A simple subject matter clashes with an interpretation sublime enough to seem convoluted. The reader can only 'sink most abruptly' from the poet's thoughts to the subject of the poem (*Biog.*, Vol. II, p. 137).

Coleridge's mental bombast thus highlights the manner in which physical and mental idleness differ in 'Gipsies'. Describing Wordsworth as disproportionately thoughtful to the scene in which he finds himself positions mental, intellectual activity as a category of even more significance to the poem than physical movement. Hence for Coleridge's 'man of genius', travelling 'under open sky' and witnessing 'change and chear' operate euphemistically. It is the poem's second stanza that unpacks this euphemism most clearly. Immediately following the speaker's exclamatory comparison of his movement and the gypsies' inertia, the reader is shown the product of the speaker's contemplation:

> The weary Sun betook himself to rest.
> – Then issued Vesper from the fulgent West,
>   Outshining like a visible God
>   The glorious path in which he trod.
>   ('Gipsies', 13–16)

Whilst the speaker may appear to have been simply walking in the open air, the rhetoric of these lines and the kind of perspective they imply represent the intense thoughts the Wordsworthian persona has in the most quotidian situations.[6] An everyday twilight scene is transformed into a grandly dramatic event in the speaker's mind. The evening star does not simply rise or appear as the sun sets, it is 'issued' 'from the fulgent West'. Likewise, the star is not seen as reflecting the light of the sun, but 'outshin[es]' its 'glorious path' like 'a visible God'. The personification and poetic diction against which Wordsworth had railed in the Preface to the *Lyrical Ballads* are deployed here as markers of an internal world more intense than the quotidian nature of the poem's setting.

Leonard Ewbank's tarrying in the churchyard masked an internal reality and an emotional journey. The speaker of 'Gipsies', similarly, strives to demonstrate the intensity of mental activity his leisurely walk conceals. For Coleridge to describe Wordsworth as a 'tourist' in 'Gipsies', consequently, is not to degrade him in the way the priest of *The Brothers* used that term. Travelling in the poem signifies intellectual occupation. It is for this reason that the poem's speaker considers the gypsies to have no task and to be idle. The poem constructs a scheme of behaviour in which movement implies mental activity while inertia equates to both physical and intellectual idleness. The fact that such intellectual activity is characterized by the second stanza's highly wrought language, additionally, means that the poem represents the difference between mental and physical exertion along the lines of the relative intensity of each experience. While the gypsies are idle, the speaker is the opposite of such a state.

His activity and productivity are represented by the grandiloquence of his language. He is in a state of intense and god-like activity in comparison to the inertia of the gypsies. One need not feel guilt over one's lack of occupation, if one's intellectual work is as significant and as impressive as the movement of the 'Heavens' ('Gipsies', 23). The play of poetic energies, in this portrait, is activity par excellence.

The currents and categories of thought I have picked out in *The Brothers*, 'Gipsies' and Coleridge's reaction to the latter are the subject of the present study. 'Gipsies' and *The Brothers* both depict idle contemplation as a category invisible from certain perspectives but central to both poetic composition and human life more generally. The realm of intellectual activity, in all these examples, possesses an intensity of experience beyond anything offered by physical exertion. On the surface of things, in the two poems, occupation and movement imply a level of activity over and above that of wandering, tarrying and idling. Yet these three texts all contend in their different ways that significant activities take place in states of apparent inertia. Coleridge constructs a portrait of Wordsworth's mind intensely at work in even the most quotidian situations. 'Gipsies' depicts the poetic task as akin to the movement of the stars even in an apparently mundane walk. And *The Brothers* explodes the equation of physical leisure and intellectual idleness. All three texts make the distinctions between activity and idleness, and labour and leisure, central to their development and import.

This study argues that behind these distinctions and oppositions there lies a tapestry of discourses, literary, philosophical, educational and economic, in which the relation of activity and idleness was explored in the decades around the turn of the nineteenth century. It aims to pick out some of the main threads in that tapestry. The first chapter of this study investigates the political economy of Scottish Enlightenment philosophers Adam Smith and Adam Ferguson. It explores the model of the 'division of labour' that Smith and Ferguson use to explain the progress of society from primitive to polished states. In both philosophers' hands the division of labour relies on the idea that man has always naturally been inclined to labour and to trade for his own subsistence. Ferguson's *Essay on the History of Civil Society* of 1767 and Smith's *Wealth of Nations* of 1776 both describe the workings and manifold outcomes of these twin activities. My analysis is interested in the appearances made by a notion of repose or idleness in these systems as well as in Smith's earlier *Theory of Moral Sentiments* (1759). The chapter seeks to demonstrate that idleness and contemplation hold a pertinence for Smith and Ferguson's thought that neither philosopher can negate, despite their various tactics for doing so.

The second chapter follows on from the theme of the division of labour by exploring two seemingly opposed systems of education that frame their ambitions around that model of societal organization. Jeremy Bentham's utilitarian education strives to supply the division of labour with useful workers, while Friedrich Schiller's notion of aesthetic education sets itself in opposition to the effects advanced specialization has on a working population. The chapter focuses on Bentham's penal thought in his *Panopticon Letters* of 1791; his more directly educational thought in the *Chrestomathia*, published in 1815; and on Schiller's philosophical treatise *On the Aesthetic Education of Man* of 1795. My inquiry into these models is again interested in the importance they assign to contemplation and to repose. In this instance both Bentham and Schiller orientate their educational aims around the category of idle thought. For Bentham the idle individual is prey to a kind of nebulous malaise that will sap his or her ability to labour. For Schiller labourers untutored in how to contemplate the world around them will become stunted and lopsided, able only to work at their repetitive tasks rather than interact with their fellow men.

The study's third chapter moves from philosophical and educational systems to a consideration of a string of literary accounts of human capability that can be placed in dialogue with the texts of the previous two chapters. William Cowper's *The Task* of 1784, Samuel Taylor Coleridge's 'Frost at Midnight' of 1798 and 'Effusion xxxv' of 1795, and Mary Wollstonecraft's Scandinavian Letters of 1796, all depict idle thought as especially potent, but as the site of specific physical dangers to the individual. The chapter demonstrates that this series of accounts anticipates the parameters of Schiller's thought but might also be described as offering a significantly more in-depth analysis of aesthetic contemplation. In this sense the English thought of this period is not to be seen as following behind the German theory of which Schiller is a representative, but as exploring comparable terrain in a slightly different manner.

The final chapter of this investigation looks at Coleridge's thought in more detail. In addition to the Schiller-like trajectory of thought in 'Frost at Midnight' and the 'Effusion', Coleridge's interests before these poems together with his philosophy after them amount to a consistent and sustained interest in the parameters of idle contemplation. The chapter thus considers the Pantisocracy scheme planned out by Coleridge and Robert Southey, which aimed to set up a society of communal property and labour in Pennsylvania. It goes on to explore the various strands of thought in the *Biographia Literaria* (published in 1817) that come together in Coleridge's definition of poetic capability. And finally it examines the manner in which Coleridge's last major work, *On the Constitution of Church and State* of 1829, attempts to offer the fruits of poetic idleness to a community at large. The chapter considers the connections to be drawn between Coleridge and Schiller's thought, seeking to demonstrate the closer parallels between *Church and State* and the *Aesthetic Letters* than between the *Biographia* and that work.

The study ends with an Epilogue considering the afterlife of the Coleridgean and Cowperian model of aesthetic contemplation at the midpoint of the nineteenth century. In his first two novels, *Yeast* (1848) and *Alton Locke* (1850), Charles Kingsley mounts a series of arguments against aesthetic consciousness, founded in a series of allusions to Wordsworth's 'Three years she grew in sun and shower' (1800). The epilogue considers these arguments alongside John Stuart Mill's *Autobiography* (1873), and the connections that work makes between aesthetics and politics, in order to assess the resilience of the late-eighteenth-century model of aesthetic contemplation two decades after Coleridge's *Church and State*. It finds significant affinities between Mill's simplified version of aesthetic psychology and the parameters of Kingsley's critique.

The fact that just about all the texts we will consider here bear an implicit reference to the inquiries of Smith and Ferguson with which my investigation begins means that idle contemplation will be consistently defined in relation to a notion of labour. As in Wordsworth's 'Gipsies', all the analyses and examples of aesthetic capability from Schiller onwards will be contending that intellectual activity can be work-like in many important ways. Beginning the investigation with Smith and Ferguson's thought gives access to this important orientation of those texts that seek to define poetic capability. It should also be remarked that the notion of idle contemplation emerging out of this investigation is one animated by a deliberate sense of paradox. Whilst Smith and Ferguson strive to delimit idleness as a simple negation of the characteristics that are responsible for the progression of the species, every other writer this study considers portrays idle thought as containing elements of several different, often antithetical faculties. Thus the attempt of the speaker of Wordsworth's 'Gipsies' to define his essential activity will be made several times in the texts that follow, often with even more clarity and precision.

Also, as is the case in the priest's speech that begins *The Brothers*, many of the accounts this investigation will study construct a hierarchy of human occupations conforming to their various agendas. Noticeably, for

Schiller and those that anticipate or follow his concerns, such a hierarchy is the opposite of the priest's, supporting the priorities followed by the text of *The Brothers* as a whole. Idle contemplation is repeatedly raised above manual labour in terms of the number of faculties it sets in play. Wheeling about in the landscape, or looking and scribbling intensely, become occupations of more importance to one's humanity as a whole than continuing with one's repetitive work. This study will explore the psychological explanations offered for this inversion of priorities, and will chart the wider consequences of such stances.

It remains to be explained, finally, why this set of texts has been selected as the matter of an investigation into the notions of idleness and contemplation in this period. Beginning with Smith and Ferguson's model of the division of labour and ending with Coleridge's direct and premeditated attempt to expose the flaws in that method of describing and administering society, this study charts the construction of the category of idle, aesthetic contemplation in this period up until the very point at which this category is put to work in opposition to the political economy that inflected, and indeed anticipated, its parameters. The study is thus bounded by a kind of circular movement of growth and confrontation. In this scheme, importantly, Schiller's *On the Aesthetic Education of Man* fulfils a dual function. In addition to offering a counterpart to Bentham's thought – insofar as both philosophers concern themselves with a society organized by the division of labour as Smith and Ferguson describe it,[7] both interpreting this situation rather differently – Schiller also serves as a more general point of comparison, one relevant to the entire British tradition this study considers. The *Aesthetic Letters* represent a handily complete model of how idle contemplation relates to a nation's political circumstances, and thus offer the opportunity of understanding the English-language attempts to map out this connection very clearly. This investigation thus uses Schiller as a point of comparison and contrast, at once in and out of synch with the circle of texts it sets out to consider, enabling it to chart the various ways in which the British thought of this period formulates the notion of idle contemplation and positions it in a scheme of human behaviours and engagements.

CHAPTER 1

The division of labour

I want to begin by offering some observations on the pictures of the division of labour and commercial society put forward by Adam Smith and Adam Ferguson. The purpose of my doing this is to explore the significances of a notion of idleness or repose to these models, with a view to demonstrating that the positions from which Smith and Ferguson write turn on a conception of what it means to be in a state of inactivity. I seek to show that the concept of idle, private contemplation as somehow a purer, more intense and necessary mode of existence is almost impossible for them to avoid, despite their various tactics for doing so. Thus these two systems of thought, propounding fundamentally different priorities for the individual to follow and activities for him or her to engage in, must be seen to have important logistical similarities. Such similarities, moreover, carry important consequences for how we position both projects in relation to the type of thought that succeeds and opposes them. As we will see, these two versions of a grand narrative in fact open up fields of thought far removed from their premises and aims.

Smith, to begin with, builds his *Inquiry into the Nature and Causes of the Wealth of Nations* of 1776 around the concept of the division of labour. He not only uses this model of specialization to explain the progress of the arts to their present state in eighteenth-century Britain, but also positions it as a vital stage in man's 'necessary' (*WN*, p. 25) emancipation from the state of nature. Unlike other races of animals, he tells us, humans obtain what they are most in need of by means of 'treaty, by barter, and by purchase' (*WN*, p. 27), by virtue of an inherent 'propensity to truck, barter, and exchange one thing for another', which 'originally gives occasion to the division of labour'. His picture of this process is interesting. Imagining a 'tribe of hunters or shepherds', Smith suggests:

a particular person makes bows and arrows, for example, with more readiness and dexterity than any other. He frequently exchanges them for cattle or for venison with his companions; and he finds at last that he can in this manner get more cattle and venison, than if he himself went to the field to catch them. From a regard to his own interest, therefore, the making of bows and arrows grows to be his chief business, and he becomes a sort of armourer. (*WN*, p. 27)

Here, a kind of model primitive community is shown to advance almost unthinkingly in the manner in which its members interact with one another. The implication is that even though the armourer in this example is acting in 'his own interest', society will advance, naturally as it were, if every one of its members behaves in this manner.[1]

I will be returning to the ideas represented in this passage shortly, but we should note for now that they create a problem for Smith. Although his armourer is endowed with more readiness and dexterity than his companions, in the next paragraph Smith is keen for this to be forgotten about. There, the difference in people's abilities is explained as the effect and not the cause of the division of labour:

The difference between the most dissimilar characters, between a philosopher and a common street porter, for example, seems to arise not so much from nature, as from habit, custom, and education … without the disposition to truck, barter, and exchange, every man must … have had the same duties to perform, and the same work to do, and there could have been no such difference of employment as could alone give occasion to any great difference of talents. (*WN*, pp. 28–9)

Smith's contention that specialization engenders difference and not the other way around is a contention primarily with Plato, but also with many of his contemporaries, including Ferguson, as we will see.[2] Here it is made with what seems to be deliberate self-reflexivity: 'a philosopher and a common street porter' are only to be understood as different insofar as their 'habit, custom, and education' have rendered them so. This passage functions in one sense as a rewriting of the armourer example Smith has just given us. He invites us to imagine the same hunter-gatherer society without their natural tendency to exchange: 'without the disposition' to 'truck' and 'barter', there would be 'no such difference of employment'.

Building on the notion of habit implied in this passage, Smith goes on to tell us that the division of labour intensifies men's habits to such an extent, by specializing their exertions, that their understandings are frequently raised to a level at which they can make improvements to the type of work they have been taught, and the method by which they have been taught to do it. The emphasis on habit in Smith's exposition needs to be understood to be a feature of many contemporary accounts of the progress of the arts as well. Francis Hutcheson, Smith's teacher, observes that a labourer will 'soon acquire skill and dexterity' if given 'a certain sort of work of one kind', just as Lord Kames suggests that both the 'fine' and the 'useful' arts are engendered by the tendency of habitual actions to require an act of will only at their commencement.[3] But Smith is taking the notion of habit significantly further than these models. In his view, the large-scale specialization of men's occupations in an advanced commercial society leads to a situation like that of contemporary Britain, in which a 'great part of the machines made use of in those manufactures in which labour is most subdivided, were originally the invention of common workmen' (*WN*, p. 20). Like the hunter-gatherer example above, Smith attempts to convey this idea by means of a kind of anecdote:

> In the first fire-engines, a boy was constantly employed to open and shut alternately the communication between the boiler and the cylinder, according as the piston either ascended or descended. One of those boys, who loved to play with his companions, observed that, by tying a string from the handle of the valve, which opened this communication, to another part of the machine, the valve would open and shut without his assistance, and leave him at liberty to divert himself with his play-fellows. One of the greatest improvements that has been made upon this machine, since it was first invented, was in this manner the discovery of a boy who wanted to save his own labour. (*WN*, pp. 20–1)

The division of labour seemingly naturally increases the productivity of manufactures by specializing the skills of a workforce in this manner. In this passage the boy's knowledge of the machine has been augmented to a state in which he is able to make amendments comparable with those of the machine's inventor. Smith's point, similar to that of the armourer example above, seems to be that the self-interest of this particular worker leads, accidentally and unthinkingly, to the technical advancement of the machine he is working with. We are invited to imagine the effect if this kind of progress was taking place in every type of manufacture at work throughout Britain.

Importantly in the scheme of the *Wealth of Nations* as a whole, the opinions we have encountered so far, all of which have come from the text's first book, are complicated by the altogether less positive account of the state of the individual under an advanced division of labour that occurs in Book v:

> In the progress of the division of labour, the employment of the far greater part of those who live by labour, that is, of the great body of the people, comes to be confined to a few very simple operations; frequently to one or two. But the understandings of the greater part of men are necessarily formed by their ordinary employments. The man whose whole life is spent in performing a few simple operations, of which the effects too are, perhaps, always the same, or very nearly

the same, has no occasion to exert his understanding, or to exercise his invention in finding out expedients for removing difficulties which never occur. He naturally loses, therefore, the habit of such exertion, and generally becomes as stupid and ignorant as it is possible for a human creature to become. (*WN*, pp. 781–2)

The same notion of habit that was used in Book I to explain the rapid advancement in manufacturing technology is now employed to question the individual effects of that process. Since people's abilities, strengths and weaknesses are formed by their habits, their constant neglect of their 'understandings' must be seen to render them 'stupid' and 'ignorant' to the world outside their limited, and in this view limiting, occupations. From the perspective he now takes up the division of labour leads to three things for Smith. Men are made incapable of 'conceiving any generous, noble, or tender sentiment'; incapacitated from performing most of the 'duties' of private, let alone those of public life; and inhibited from 'defending' their society in combat (*WN*, p. 782). Smith is discovering, or recording, the manner in which advanced specialization restricts those who work from fulfilling any of their duties as citizens. The division of labour does more than simply erode their capacities for private sentiments, it renders them utterly useless, politically and martially speaking, to the state of which they are members.

It is clearly the case that the considerations espoused by Smith in Book V of the *Wealth of Nations* undermine, to some extent at least, the positive tone of his first sentiments concerning the division of labour and its effect of radically increasing productivity in the arts.[4] Yet some commentators have found it possible to read Smith in ways that do not detract from the value of his observations in the opening sections of the work, possible to take a stance less ironic than Marx does in finding the goal of the division of labour to be precisely the suppression of the labourer's understanding and political capacities.[5] Samuel Fleischacker, as one example, points out that Smith argues that the social hierarchy that is almost inseparable from the division of labour in polished states, whereby the labouring poor are seemingly much worse off than those who do not need to labour for their maintenance, in fact benefits the worst-off in comparison to other stages or sorts of societies. Not only does Smith tell us that the condition of the meanest labourer in an advanced commercial society is better than that of a king in (egalitarian) hunter-gatherer societies, but the very inequality of polished states helps engender political stability and thereby supports the administration of justice to the poor themselves.[6]

The stance Fleischacker is taking, as extreme or tenuous as we might think it is, can be usefully extended to reconsider the kinds of judgements

Smith is making about the division of labour in Book v, as well. There, we could say that Smith is not simply going back on the hopes he entertained for specialization in Book 1, but rather continuing to offer the kind of comparative approach to understanding societies that has been a feature of his accounts throughout the work (as Fleischacker demonstrates, indeed). The comments quoted above are introduced by the following paragraph:

> In some cases the state of the society necessarily places the greater part of individuals in such situations as naturally form in them, without any attention of government, almost all the abilities and virtues which that state requires, or perhaps can admit of. In other cases the state of the society does not place the greater part of individuals in such situations, and some attention of government is necessary in order to prevent the almost entire corruption and degeneracy of the great body of the people. (*WN*, p. 781)

The sense of balance constructed by these two sentences serves to render Smith's subsequent conclusion, that states under an advanced division of labour belong to the latter group, distinctly composed and untroubled. This is owing to the fact, implied in the above paragraph, that this section, entitled 'Of the Expence of the Institutions for the Education of Youth', is designed to discuss what 'attention of government' might be requisite in polished commercial states. This passage, therefore, together with the one quoted above that seems to consider the division of labour as a kind of curse on the individual, are in fact part of a project aimed at delineating the kind of education a society built on advanced specialization might need, and speculating, indeed, how such 'attention' might be administered and implemented (see *WN*, pp. 785–6).[7]

Phrasing Smith's argument in this manner, it becomes possible to understand the level of power he sees in the division of labour as a force of progress and a generator of wealth. Although it creates problems in its advanced state, these are manageable by government intervention; and not only is the division of labour the necessary result of man's propensities, but the benefits of a society organized by it (wealth and justice, for example), in Smith's view, hugely outweigh its failings.[8] Yet the kind of positivity represented in a reading such as this, no doubt faithful to the scheme of Smith's thought itself, seems to be challenged, immanently as it were, by the resonances we have already begun to notice in the way in which Smith illustrates his contentions. Looking again at those moments in Smith's argument, paying attention to the kind of picture of human nature he is constructing, will make it clear that the *Wealth of Nations* also explores the effects of the division of labour from a slightly different perspective from the one that posits wealth and justice as its primary effects.

We have already seen how Smith changes his viewpoint slightly, in illustrating the manner in which specialization advances human progress, offering us not an account of a whole community's activities or an entire country's manufactures, but the individual case, the way in which one labourer might transform a community's prospects by simply following his self-interest. What is remarkable in his doing so is that Smith is opening up a perspective and a set of concerns that seem to challenge his primary and initial stand-point, that stance which seems to pride itself on noticing the society-wide effects of individual actions. In the case of the boy's improvement to the fire-engine, for example, it is apparent that the boy in question is characterized entirely by his desire to 'play with his companions', to 'save his own labour' so that he can do what he 'loved'. In the hunter-gatherer example, likewise, the 'armourer' is depicted as avoiding exerting himself in the field, also saving his own labour, by trading the commodity that he finds easiest to make. The effect of these human details on the points Smith is attempting to make is significant. In the case of the fire-engine, if this is increased productivity, it seems to be characterized by a boy playing with his friends rather than working. So whilst Smith tells us that the nation's productivity is being transformed in this manner, more and more work being done and more and more products being produced because of the greatly increased effectiveness of each worker, it would appear to be more accurate, if we follow this illustration, to imagine labourers being set free from the need to work by the improvements they are making.

Increased productivity, in this sense, is also characterized in the illustrations Smith offers of it by increased leisure time. The same quantity of a product seems to take less and less time to manufacture. It is noteworthy however, if this is the way Smith's observations tend, that the *Wealth of Nations* barely offers any account of the kinds of leisure activity occurring in advanced commercial societies. Where such pursuits are mentioned, they are either summarily dismissed or given a purpose so specific as to render them almost banal. In Book II, as an instance of the former, labourers such as 'players', 'musicians' and 'opera-singers' are simply categorized as 'unproductive', and thus dismissed as irrelevant to Smith's enquiry, rather than discussed as producing actual activities or amusements (*WN*, pp. 330–1). In Book V, even more curiously, where Smith very briefly considers such pursuits as actual activities, they occur among his observations on the institutions for 'religious instruction' (*WN*, p. 788), and are positioned as a useful remedy to the 'enthusiasm and superstition' of small religious 'sects' (*WN*, p. 796):

> Publick diversions have always been the objects of dread and hatred, to all the fanatical promoters of those popular frenzies. The gaiety and good humour which those diversions inspire were altogether inconsistent with that temper of mind, which was fittest for their purpose, or which they could best work upon. (*WN*, pp. 796–7)

While this manner of understanding leisure time seems coldly utilitarian, it also seems to fall short of an adequate definition of a society that appears to be reducing the amount of time each individual needs to labour for his subsistence. Indeed, the brevity with which Smith deals with leisure in these examples is especially surprising given that, unlike Mandeville before him, Smith argues for a high-wage economy throughout the *Wealth of Nations*. One is almost compelled to conclude, on this evidence, that Smith does not consider public diversions as in any way related to his account of labour practices.

In one sense, however, this omission, if that is what it is, can be explained by the fact that Smith writes, most of the time, as if the labouring classes should work constantly, as if leisure activities do not need to be considered when advanced commercial society is characterized so strongly by the amount of labour taking place within it and the quantities of goods it produces. Amidst a discussion of the superiority of urban over rural industry, for example, Smith offers the following observations:

> A country weaver, who cultivates a small farm, must lose a good deal of time in passing from his loom to the field, and from the field to his loom. When the two trades can be carried on in the same workhouse, the loss of time is no doubt much less. It is even in this case, however, very considerable. A man commonly saunters a little in turning his hand from one sort of employment to another. When he first begins the new work he is seldom very keen and hearty; his mind, as they say, does not go to it, and for some time he rather trifles than applies to good purpose. (*WN*, pp. 18–19)

In this image it is not just the case that the country workman loses time travelling between his various tasks. More exactly, any change in occupation, even within the same location, seems to bring about a lack of productivity in the form of 'sauntering'. In the scheme of the *Wealth of Nations* more generally, Smith is demonstrating the kind of unproductiveness that contemporary Britain has largely eliminated, and that its continued progress by the rules of the division of labour will further restrict. Advanced specialization, we can infer, has meant that the individual labouring in an urban manufacture never has any need to suspend his concentration from his particular task.

Another moment at which Smith hints at the style and duration of work he associates with an advanced division of labour comes amidst his discussion of the peculiar infirmities 'occasioned by excessive application' in various trades. Even though he considers particular trades as posing 'dangerous' and 'sometimes fatal' consequences to those who over-exert themselves in them, Smith concludes that 'in every sort of trade … the man who works so moderately, as to be able to work constantly, not only preserves his health the longest, but, in the course of the year, executes the greatest quantity of work' (*WN*, p. 100). The answer to the problem of too much work is to lower its intensity, so that more hours can be put in and more can be achieved. While we might find it remarkable that Smith's emphasis on productivity should be underwritten by the instruction to work 'moderately', then, we should note that such advice is framed, as is the case throughout the *Wealth of Nations*, by the reminder that it is 'constant' work that is expected.

Smith's manner of expressing himself in moments such as these gives the impression that any deviation from work is to be avoided, and that the labourer should be expected to work constantly and intensely if their task is specialized enough. We could say that there seem to be two different currents or styles of thought at work in Smith's mode of argumentation. The details of labour Smith carefully delineates, the manner in which an advanced division of labour simplifies work practices to such an extent that the labourer becomes akin to the machine itself, able to work constantly and repetitively on one simple task, is undercut, undermined from within, as it were, by the picture of human nature his illustrations of specialization construct. In this individualistic perspective, the view that sees how the labourer himself encounters highly specialized work, we could say that repose, relaxation and play are simultaneously forbidden and the goals of labour. They both inhibit work and reward it. It is for this reason that Smith's text is scattered both with hints of the constant nature of work under the division of labour, and with reminders that it is the tranquillity of rest, or of not labouring, at least, that the individual desires.[9] The tension between the two is unresolved in the *Wealth of Nations*. Smith's theoretical and practical accounts of labour do not entirely match.

Smith's thought could be described as rigidly schematic in this respect. It strives to contain human nature, which seems to desire not to work, within the rules of progress by specialization, which is constructed around man's apparently inherent tendency to work. It is for this reason that the thought of Adam Ferguson functions as a vivid counterpoint to Smith's project. While the two currents of thought in Smith's text might be understood to confront each other, or to fail to match, Ferguson's *Essay on the History of Civil Society* of 1767 seems open to the possibilities and contradictions that inhere in both the human character and in human life. Ferguson achieves this openness by considering human nature as a kind of relief, suggesting that every time a positive character trait is picked out, its opposite will also inevitably be the case for some periods of time. Ferguson foregrounds human qualities in the same way that describing a landscape as mountainous necessarily implies its abundance of valleys or ravines.[10]

This stance or tactic of Ferguson's enables him to negotiate the differences and connections between activity and indolence extremely smoothly, in comparison to Smith. Considering the desire for the former as the most important positive trait, as the impulse that engenders a whole range of useful secondary outcomes (as we will see), and the latter as its necessary shadow or compensation, the state in which we must 'recruit our limited and our wasting force' (*Essay*, p. 43), Ferguson is able to position activity as the central feature of human life, while asserting that man is often passive and indolent in the extreme. Where Smith's two models of human life appeared to clash, privileging, as they did, one of each of these alternatives, Ferguson's manner of approaching human behaviour stops them from being mutually exclusive. Man can be both characterized by his labour and inactive most of the time.

Ferguson's emphasis on activity, holding together the various strands of the *Essay*'s argument, and the various types of human societies and behaviours it considers, can be registered in just about all of his opinions and ideas. To begin to see how this emphasis informs his portrait of contemporary life, rather than of the human character more generally, one needs to look at one of the first examples of the *Essay*'s many comparisons of classical and modern societies. It is 'peculiar to modern Europe', Ferguson tells us, 'to rest so much of the human character on what may be learned in retirement, and from the information of books'. Since the sentiments contained in those books were engendered by an active exertion in life and the 'animated spirit of society', making the learning of them a solitary activity is in some sense mistaking their function and their very nature:

we endeavour to derive from imagination and thought, what is in reality matter of experience and sentiment: and we endeavour, through the grammar of dead languages, and the channel of commentators, to arrive at the beauties of thought and elocution, which sprang from the animated spirit of society, and were taken from the living impression of an active life. (*Essay*, p. 30)

Ferguson's priorities and opinions of correct behaviour are figured here in his subordination of 'imagination and thought' to 'experience and sentiment'. He considers activity as the source of every beauty of 'thought and elocution', and therefore denigrates the passivity of reading as a kind of false school of conduct.

In accordance with this privileging of activity and the active faculties, the *Essay* goes on to attack another form of recollection and retirement, seeking to refute the idea that most human feelings can be reduced to a set of passive sensations. Ferguson views the mind as being 'employed in active exertions, not in merely attending to its own feelings of pleasure and pain' for 'the greater part of its existence' (*Essay*, p. 42). Being active, for Ferguson, is not the realm of life in which we lay up a store of pleasant memories to satisfy us in moments of rest. It is synonymous with what people ordinarily term happiness:

Happiness is not that state of repose, or that imaginary freedom from care, which at a distance is so frequent an object of desire, but with its approach brings a tedium, or a languor, more unsupportable than pain itself ... it arises more from the pursuit, than from the attainment of any end whatever; and in every new situation to which we arrive, even in the course of a prosperous life, it depends more on the degree in which our minds are properly employed, than it does on the circumstances in which we are destined to act[.] (*Essay*, p. 49)

In this portrait mental activity is subsumed under the category of physical occupation: happiness is not to be found in a 'state of repose', but in one of 'pursuit'. When the 'pursuit' or the task is over, life can only be characterized by 'tedium' and 'languor'. It is for this reason that Ferguson considers life insufferable without an occupation: 'existence is a burden, and the iteration of memory is a torment' (*Essay*, p. 43).

The 'pursuit', however, the arduous part of a task itself, must be understood to offer more, in Ferguson's scheme of thought, than simply the evasion of the tedium of inertia. At other points in the *Essay* Ferguson constructs a portrait of the human abilities in which more is at stake in employment than happiness. In his exposition 'Of Intellectual Powers', for example, Ferguson offers the following observations on the manner in which man can be said to think:

Thinking and reasoning, we say, are the operations of some faculty; but in what manner the faculties of thought or reason remain, when they are not exerted, or by what difference in the frame they are unequal in different persons, are questions which we cannot resolve. Their operations alone discover them: when unapplied, they lie hid even from the person to whom they pertain; and their action is so much a part of their nature, that the faculty itself, in many cases, is scarcely to be distinguished from a habit acquired in its frequent exertion. (*Essay*, p. 26)

Not only are the faculties of thought and reason 'scarcely to be distinguished' from their use, but their continued existence, if unused, is cast into doubt. Ferguson seems to be suggesting that the correct employment of certain faculties is all that guarantees their existence, that their use is responsible for their development in the same way that their inactivity would lead to their atrophy.

The most overt expression of this conception of exertion occurs in Ferguson's *Principles of Moral and Political Science* of 1792, a thorough retrospective tour through his system of philosophy published twenty-five years after the *Essay*, and seven years after he retired from teaching. In that work, Ferguson considers employment's effect on the individual in slightly more general terms:

The human mind, in whatever manner it be employed, if its faculties are brought into exercise, ever receives some increment of power and some modification of habit: so that, without intending to operate upon itself, it nevertheless partakes of the effect that is produced, and receives an addition to the stock of personal qualities in the midst of attentions that were bestowed on a different subject. (*Principles*, Vol. 1, 240–1)

When faculties are 'brought into exercise', they are 'operate[d] upon' and improved, as if by accident. The individual's development, the 'addition to the stock' of his or her 'personal qualities', takes place as a side-effect of exertion, as a by-product of normal behaviour.[11] It is in this sense that Ferguson can write of certain employments or activities as 'correct' or 'proper', for by ensuring that one's exertions use the faculties of reason or sentiment, for example, one is advancing oneself intellectually and emotionally every time one acts. As Ferguson goes on to explain at this same point in the *Principles*, moreover, this process becomes one of the ways in which 'nations' as a whole advance: 'in the midst of labours bestowed in procuring their subsistence', people 'receive instruction and habits of civilization' (*Principles*, Vol. 1, p. 241).

Ferguson's system thus offers, and is built upon, a portrait of human nature in which several traits are characterized as positive, while others are deemed negative. The former lead, necessarily, to the augmentation of the individual's powers, while the latter are nothing but the former's shadow or compensation. Ferguson's take on the division of labour and commercial society, which we are to turn to now, emerges, in both the *Principles* and the *Essay*, as a function of what he is suggesting about human nature more generally. In the *Principles*, for instance, it is by means of a further consideration of the connection between happiness and repose that the idea of actual employment is introduced:

> The notion, that happiness consists in relief from any active engagements, is easily accounted for … in the case of those who, having a task to perform, never engage in it willingly. The task possibly confines them, and prevents their application to any thing else, while it does not supply those real exertions of mind, which never fail to make the time that is well employed pass away with delight. The person who is thus confined, without being occupied, mistakes his aversion to confinement for an aversion to business; and his longing for a change of occupation he mistakes for a dislike to exertion. (*Principles*, Vol. II, p. 88)

In this description, Ferguson's contention that it is proper employment that leads to happiness is taken to its logical extreme. The 'aversion to business', the belief that we would be happier if we could be exempted from work, is explained as an 'aversion to confinement'. What we desire when we do not want to work is now revealed to be what supplies 'real exertions of mind'. The feeling of wanting not to work is an illusion for Ferguson, a consequence of being given a task that is not difficult enough.

Applying this theory to an example, Ferguson comes up with the following:

> Thus, while the school-boy is confined on his form, his heart and his mind are in the play-field. As he does not apply to his lesson, nor even attend to it, while he reads it, he is only confined, not occupied. What we term his aversion to application, and his longing for the hour of dismission, is an ardor for employment; and, in fact, when free to chuse for himself, he betakes him to a labour, in which every muscle of the body, and every faculty of the mind, is strained or exerted to obtain the object of some hazardous or toilsome contest. (*Principles*, Vol. II, p. 88)

This illustration, replicating in one sense Smith's fire-engine example, serves to compare the types of mental and physical exertions required by the different tasks the 'school-boy' is acquainted with. In Ferguson's view the boy's 'lesson' is not taxing enough. In being stretched neither mentally nor physically, he is left yearning for 'the hour of dismission', the time at which he can employ 'every muscle' of his body and 'every faculty' of his mind to its utmost.

This identification of different levels of behaviours and satisfactions goes to the heart of Ferguson's understanding of human nature. Conceiving of man as active above all, he comprehends contest and struggle, pitting oneself against a worthy adversary, as the scene of man's complete use of his capacities, and the best school of active life. From this allegiance he can confidently defend warfare or the martial opposition of groups of people, since people brought together under a common cause simultaneously test their powers to their limits and engender the strongest strains of fellow-feeling (*Essay*, pp. 23–4). For Ferguson we could say that there are engagements that are distinctly more business-like than business itself. He considers a boy's school-work to occupy him less than amusing himself and competing with his friends, just as he finds the sport and risk of hunting, for example, to be in many important respects more fully occupying than mechanical work under an advanced division of labour (*Essay*, pp. 40, 98, 101).

The absolute centrality of activity to Ferguson's system bears important connections with his portrait of specialization. In comparison with Smith, however, it should be noted that Ferguson says much less about the division of labour, and gives it a much less prominent position in his thought than it has in the *Wealth of Nations*. His account of its genesis appears, as do many of his observations, as a consequence of his model of human psychology, rather than as a thesis for understanding the complexity of human interactions, as in Smith. Observing, in the *Essay*, that man has a set of instinctive urges that prompt his preservation in a very similar manner to all animals, Ferguson notes that what distinguishes humans in this field is the way in which they combine these considerations with 'reflection and foresight'. The desire for self-preservation thus leads to a notion of property, and creates 'that object of care which he calls his interest' (*Essay*, p. 11). This process is important for Ferguson since, although all other passions are characterized by the intermittency of their operation, what humans term their interest becomes 'the object of their ordinary cares' and therefore a pretty consistent prompt 'to the practice of mechanic and commercial arts' (*Essay*, p. 12). Indeed, later in the chronological progression he is describing, such interest is uniform enough for man to 'confine himself to a tedious task, and wait with patience for the distant returns of his labour' (*Essay*, p. 97).

Significantly in this connection, Ferguson takes up the opposite stance to Smith's when it comes to the range of talents to be found in a division of labour, understanding skills and abilities not primarily as the effects of specialization, but as one of the many factors that contribute to its natural organization. Seeing men as 'qualified by a great diversity of talents' (*Essay*, p. 63), Ferguson suggests that each naturally finds his station when men are brought together: 'The accidents which distribute the means of subsistence unequally, inclination, and favourable opportunities, assign the different occupations of men; and a sense of utility leads them, without end, to subdivide their professions' (*Essay*, p. 180). This characterization of the division of labour as occurring by random distribution seems to limit the force of specialization in comparison to how Smith understands it. Similarly Ferguson is more inclined to highlight the factors working against its extension. In his account of the progress of 'rude nations', for example, Ferguson suggests that these societies are retarded in their movement towards extending the notion of property by the 'indolence of mankind' and 'their aversion to any application in which they are not engaged by immediate instinct and passion' (*Essay*, p. 96). Ferguson holds this trait to be one of the earliest characteristics of humankind as they have been observed anywhere (*Essay*, p. 98).[12] Although Smith also sees the division of labour as advancing 'very slow[ly] and gradual[ly]' (*WN*, p. 25), it must be observed that the *Essay* is considerably more restrained in the power it bestows on specialization as a force of progress in its own right.

By the time Ferguson came to write the *Principles*, the division of labour seems to have sunk even further in his model of human life. There we are given a decidedly ironic appreciation of the practice of work under an advanced division of labour. While happiness is to be located in occupation rather than repose in both the *Essay* and this later work, in the *Principles* Ferguson takes this position to its logical and rather subversive extreme: 'Separate departments are opened for the different descriptions of men; tasks of labour for the strong, of address and sleight of hand for those who are defective in strength; tasks of skill for the inventive and knowing; laws of nature to be investigated, and obscurities to be cleared up, by the ingenious and comprehensive' (*Principles*, Vol. 1, p. 250). The division of labour has become a kind of useful service here, rather than an organizing principle of society. It is a service ideally suited to the range of human natures, personalities and talents Ferguson observes in human life more generally. This assessment goes beyond simply opposing Smith's view as to which came first out of specialization and different talents. Ferguson, writing now over a decade after the appearance of the *Wealth of Nations*, is suggesting that the concept so central to Smith's conception of human progress, as well as to his understanding of the formation of human abilities, characters and morals, is to be understood as a convenient coincidence, a useful and incidental opportunity for every type of individual to exhaust their capabilities, and thus leave themselves happy and satisfied. Such a stance seems deliberately to ignore the economic necessity of labour. Ferguson is contending, almost mockingly, at the end of his career, that man would desire to labour for a kind of sport, even if he did not need to for his subsistence.

Whether we consider this quite extreme position on the division of labour to belong to the *Principles* alone, or whether we choose to read a similar irony in the *Essay*'s assertion that contemporary man must 'confine himself to a tedious task' in order to be rewarded for his labour, it is apparent that Ferguson places himself in some sort of opposition to the realities of an advanced commercial society. The thoroughly developed psychology of human activity Ferguson places at the head of both the *Essay* and the *Principles* is one matrix of beliefs that stands behind this opposition. But there is another set of reasons for Ferguson's stance on commerce, both entwined with and independent from his conception of the value of labour, which lies in an area of his thought we have only been touching on in passing so far. The different treatments Smith and Ferguson give to the division of labour need to be understood by reference to their different opinions on the comparisons to be made between contemporary commercial societies and the classical societies they both refer to almost constantly.

For Ferguson, members of classical Greek society, for example, were 'distinguished by their personal spirit and vigour, not by the valuation of their estates, or the rank of their birth' (*Essay*, p. 197). Likewise, unlike the culture of learning in retirement we saw Ferguson condemn in contemporary Europe, the 'understanding' of an ancient Grecian 'was chiefly cultivated in the practice of affairs', since the 'most respectable personages were obliged to mix with the croud, and derived their degree of ascendancy, only from their conduct, their eloquence, and personal vigour' (*Essay*, p. 198). The tone of these comments alone, not to mention their emphasis on the kinds of activity we have seen Ferguson value so persistently, makes clear that Ferguson is writing from a perspective that understands classical society to foster types of humanity under threat, if not significantly on the wane, in contemporary commercial conditions. Hence at the very beginning of the *Essay* Ferguson can be found contrasting the moral spirit of commercial societies with that of classical ones. In comparison to the 'sanguine affection which every Greek bore to his country' and 'the devoted patriotism of an early Roman', it is in modern commercial states 'that man is sometimes found a detached and a solitary being: he has found an object which sets him in competition with his fellow-creatures, and he deals with them as he does with his cattle and his soil, for the sake of the profits they bring' (*Essay*, p. 19). By promoting interactions built upon self-interest commercial society seduces man away from employing the range of feelings his interaction with other men should inspire. Given the level to which thoughts such as these permeate the *Essay* and the *Principles*, Ferguson's writing must be understood to belong to what is now called a classical-republican tradition, the style of thought that positions the individual's virtuous, public-orientated behaviour as the perfection of his or her nature, and that therefore understands any movement away from the classical organization of society to be a kind of decline.

Such a perspective, as many commentators have noted, stands in opposition, almost by definition, to the style of thought that seeks to understand commerce as a positive force, that is open to the possibility that exchange might be a constructive force in human progress, and that is prepared to attempt organizing society by harnessing individual self-interest, rather than by appealing to each citizen's love of the public good.[13] In this respect, of course, Smith's project in the *Wealth of Nations* stands in opposition to both Ferguson's outlook and premises. In attempting to understand commerce as integral both to human nature and to society's development, in suggesting that an individual's self-interest might actually benefit a community, Smith's thought seems to contend that contemporary society represents at least an equally valid, if not a more advanced form of culture than that of the ancient Greeks.[14] We have already seen instances of the manner in which Smith makes this claim: the way in which he understands commercial society to foster the administration of justice, for example, or the manner in which contemporary Britain can rapidly augment its wealth even in times of peace. But we have not touched on his belief that classical societies declined, in part at least, because the slave who performed the manual labour from which the citizen was prohibited had no interest in the success of his labour, and hence no prompt to refine and advance it.[15] For Smith, proving that human nature is inherently commercial would demonstrate the fragility of the classical model of society. Smith's commercial man could not be expected to renounce his self-interest indefinitely. The love of the public good, in his model, would not be enough to order and control society for any significant length of time.

What Smith and Ferguson's different stances on the division of labour come down to, therefore, are two radically different conceptions of the human character. Since, for Smith, man is primarily a commercial and self-interested being, requiring him to be taught a second nature on the classical model, and requiring him to act in accordance with that nature in all his social interactions, represents a kind of unsustainable contrivance. For Ferguson, by contrast, man is first and foremost a civic being, interested above all in the public good, at least until his self-interest is exaggerated by the economic organization of society.[16] This is the reason Ferguson's *Essay* repeatedly analyses the condition of the Native American in such detail. It strives to demonstrate that man can be as refined morally, at all stages of his existence, as he is in polished states. Ferguson is attempting to demonstrate that it is not commerce that propelled man out of the state of nature, and thus rendered him virtuous, but that the civic model of virtue is part of man's very nature.[17] It is for this reason that John Pocock understands Ferguson to be describing the citizen in a manner that approaches closer and closer to the condition normally termed savagery. And it is for this reason that Ferguson references Joseph-François Lafitau whenever he describes Native Americans, for it was he who had studied these tribes in such detail as to be 'able to discover the virtues of Homeric heroes in the Huron and the Seneca'.[18] It is of central importance for Ferguson to depict man as always, and in any observation, already fully endowed with the attributes he associates with the perfection of human nature.[19]

It must already be apparent, however, that there are also ways in which Smith does not fit simply into a role of opposition to Ferguson's classical-republican perspective. We saw, for example, the impartial and balanced tone with which Smith compared how much 'attention of government' different societies require. One might also read civic priorities in the manner in which Smith noted the inability of the manual worker to function as a citizen. Equally, there are moments in the *Wealth of Nations* at which the term 'self-interest' seems to come closer to meaning interest in the category of self than strictly interest in one's own subsistence, as if an individual might be concerned for the well-being of others through the same impulse. In these ways, we must acknowledge that Smith's agenda is not entirely distinct from Ferguson's. As Pocock has observed, Smith can be understood to be arguing that commerce actually engenders virtuous autonomy in the classical sense. By giving people the opportunity to advance their station by the acquisition of wealth, a society built on commerce also gives them the opportunity to free themselves from the obligation to work, to move gradually up the ranks of society, and eventually to attain that state of disinterestedness and moral virtue epitomized by the landed gentry.[20] Smith can be read as contending that because the labourer in a polished commercial state is better off than a king in a more savage society, commerce moves the lower ranks of people in European nations towards a state of increased autonomy, increased self-sufficiency and hence, also, increased virtue in civic terms. Yet it ought also to be observed that Smith's description of commercial society in the *Wealth of Nations* is also open to the criticism that it replicates the division in classical societies between slaves and freemen. The labouring classes can be compared to the former group in terms of morality and autonomy, and commercial nations can be seen to be made prosperous by a very similar type of subservience and social separation.

The ways in which Smith can be understood to engage with or, alternatively, move beyond a classical republican agenda could be further drawn out by reference to his earlier *Theory of Moral Sentiments* of 1759, which is in many respects completely in line with Ferguson's stance on the individual and his place in society. In that work, Smith positions virtue as the key to the happiness of man and his community – 'What institution of government could tend so much to promote the happiness of mankind as the general prevalence of wisdom and virtue? All government is but an imperfect remedy for the deficiency of these' (*TMS*, p. 187) – conceives of benevolence as the pinnacle of human sentiments – 'And hence it is, that to feel much for others and little for ourselves, that to restrain our selfish, and to indulge our benevolent affections, constitutes the perfection of human nature; and can alone produce among mankind that harmony of sentiments and passions in which consists their whole grace and propriety' (*TMS*, p. 25) – and views the admiration of wealth as leading straight to corruption –

> This disposition to admire, and almost to worship, the rich and the powerful, and to despise, or, at least, to neglect persons of poor and mean condition, though necessary both to establish and to maintain the distinction of ranks and the order of society, is, at the same time, the great and most universal cause of the corruption of our moral sentiments. (*TMS*, p. 61)[21]

These examples, representative of a great number of other points at which Smith's ideas in the *Theory* could be equated with Ferguson's stance in the *Essay*, give some sort of idea of the problems commentators find themselves in when trying to align the type of analysis found in the *Wealth of Nations* with Smith's apparent opinions in this earlier work.[22] In this last quotation, for example, which almost seems to prefigure the type of perspective Smith will take up and explore in the *Wealth of Nations*, the difficulty of such a task is manifest. Smith is suggesting that the 'most universal cause of the corruption of our moral sentiments' is 'necessary' to 'maintain' the 'order of society'. He is condemning such 'corruption' in no uncertain terms at the same moment that he excuses it. Rather than becoming entwined in these notorious difficulties in rather general terms, however, I want to concentrate on an area in which *The Theory of Moral Sentiments* and the *Wealth of Nations* can definitely be seen to interact. In the valencies this earlier work gives to the ideas of activity and repose, in the manner in which it depicts human nature, and in the portrait of human desires and tendencies it thereby promotes, there is, as we will see now, a striking anticipation of one of the perspectives we saw at work in the *Wealth of Nations*.

Smith's portrait of human nature, in the *Theory*, is constructed for the most part by the investigation of sympathy with which the text begins. He takes the case of someone relating a sorrowful or painful circumstance to a group, and tells us that the sufferer in this case 'longs for that relief which nothing can afford him but the entire concord of the affections of the spectators with his own'. Hence, '[t]o see the emotions of their hearts, in every respect, beat time to his own, in the violent and disagreeable passions, constitutes his sole consolation' (*TMS*, p. 22). But this intense desire, Smith goes on, this need to be understood and consoled by the group, encounters a problem of perspective. The sufferer yearns for the others to feel his pain as keenly as he does, but he also knows that this is not possible. Although the spectators can enter into an approximation of his feelings by having the details of the wrongs inflicted on him explained to them, for example, they can never fully recreate the intensity of feeling of the original sufferer.

What takes place, Smith explains, if the group does not refuse to align their sentiments (in which case they become 'intolerable to one another' (*TMS*, p. 21)), is that the sufferer reduces the intensity of his passion 'to that pitch, in which the spectators are capable of going along with him' (*TMS*, p. 22). Just as the spectators attempt to place themselves in the sufferer's position and see things from his perspective, so the sufferer must put himself in the position of spectator to his own sorrow in order to locate that level of grief at which his interlocutors can understand and sympathize with him: 'He must flatten, if I may be allowed to say so, the sharpness of its natural tone, in order to reduce it to harmony and concord with the emotions of those who are about him' (*TMS*, pp. 21–2). This conversation as a whole, in Smith's model, takes place at the same time as, and by means of, a search for the middle ground on which all participants can feel a connection of their sentiments.

What is striking in this set-piece is that in attempting to share his emotions with others Smith's sufferer must subdue the very passions he wants legitimated. He must quell his emotions in order to have them understood at all. The pattern of this process, moreover, leads Smith to identify one of the principal purposes of an exchange like this to be the calming of the sufferer:

> The mind, therefore, is rarely so disturbed, but that the company of a friend will restore it to some degree of tranquillity and sedateness. The breast is, in some measure, calmed and composed the moment we come into his presence. We are immediately put in mind of the light in which he will view our station, and we begin to view it ourselves in the same light; for the effect of sympathy is instantaneous. (*TMS*, pp. 22–3)

The power of company in subduing someone who suffers, we are now told, does not even require a conversation to take place. The concord of sympathy begins to take effect as soon as one is not alone, as soon as we have a different perspective to imagine. More importantly, however, it seems that a state of tranquillity, one of mental and physical repose here, is both natural and desirable to an individual, while one of agitation and strong passion must be calmed and subdued. It is as if the excitement of passion were nothing but a temporary interval in a life characterized by composure and peace, an interval, furthermore, the individual almost unthinkingly desires to keep as brief as possible.[23]

Later in the *Theory*, when Smith has identified the standard group perspective as the view of the 'impartial spectator', he is even more direct in his assertions of the differences between a state of repose and one of agitation:

> When we are about to act, the eagerness of passion will seldom allow us to consider what we are doing, with the candour of an indifferent person. The violent emotions which at that time agitate us, discolour our views of things; even when we are endeavouring to place ourselves in the situation of another, and to regard the objects that interest us in the light in which they will naturally appear to him, the fury of our own passions constantly calls us back to our own place, where every thing appears magnified and misrepresented by self-love. Of the manner in which those objects would appear to another, of the view which he would take of them, we can obtain, if I may say so, but instantaneous glimpses, which vanish in a moment, and which, even while they last, are not altogether just. (*TMS*, p. 157)

The mind, for Smith now, is deluded by passion in the midst of certain kinds of action. The two perspectives he has already shown us are now figured as irreconcilable opposites when 'we are about to act'. Our 'passions constantly call us back' to ourselves, even if we attempt to consider the 'situation of another'. It is in accordance with this view that Smith suggests (somewhat quaintly) that we consult our internal 'impartial spectator' every evening, as if days made up of several kinds of activity must be monitored and reconsidered in a period of repose that gives space for contemplation, and access to a style of thought unattainable at the moment one acts (*TMS*, p. 262). If a state of mental and physical repose seems natural and desirable to the individual in Smith's model of sympathy, we can now add that the state of mind such inactivity promotes, one of internal questioning and reprioritizing, is also understood as a more reliable and truthful mode of thinking or being. Not only does activity need to be complemented and monitored by contemplation, but the former is treated with a kind of suspicion in this analysis. It is a state in which the individual seems to be self-involved to an almost delusional extent.

The Theory of Moral Sentiments, consequently, seems to bear striking affinities with the perspective we saw held in the individualistic illustrations Smith used in the *Wealth of Nations*. Both figure repose or the absence of exertion as the natural state of the individual, the condition man seems to want to return himself to when under the influence of any passion or activity whatsoever. Further, the fact that the *Theory* begins by describing how the operations of sympathy pertain to every individual, to even 'the most hardened violator of the laws of society' (*TMS*, p. 9) for example, renders the accounts that follow distinctly inclusive. Smith is describing a constant and ever-present feature of human mental life, rather than the operations of any sort of elite social group. Whether we choose to see the kind of ideas and schemes of thought found in *The Theory of Moral Sentiments* as relevant to a consideration of the *Wealth of Nations* or not, therefore, whether we understand the earlier work's moral priorities to influence the later text in any way, both construct a model of human nature characterized by repose rather than exertion. Although in the later work this model seems to be deployed almost accidentally, and although the alternative to repose in the *Theory* is mental agitation and strong passion, while it is physical exertion or labour in the *Wealth of Nations*, the reader of either work must be left with the impression that human nature for Smith is most naturally understood in a state of 'sedateness' and 'tranquillity'. We could say that Smith's attempt, in the *Wealth of Nations*, to align human activities and desires with the model of the division of labour, encounters the problem of human nature as he had already expressed it in the *Theory*. Smith struggles, in this view, to assimilate ideas of tranquillity and happiness into his portrait of a society characterized so strongly by mechanical labour.

Whilst Smith and Ferguson can be seen as having antithetical and incompatible positions when it comes to understanding how activity, exertion and labour fit with human nature, it must also be observed that, if we were to take the case of the project of the *Wealth of Nations* alone, their models of human life would also be in one sense logistically similar. Just as Ferguson attempts to eliminate the category of idleness as an aversion to work, Smith, in the primary and largely predominant perspective of that work, seeks to characterize human life by its labours to such an extent that any period of repose or rest can only be understood by what it lacks, by its absence of work and its temporary suspension of those powers that cause the species to progress so rapidly. For both, human life is to be understood by its activities, occupations and exertions. Indolence and idleness are but temporary states, brief departures from normal behaviour, that are largely insignificant in any portrait of the attributes of the species.

In this comparison, Ferguson's relationship between activity and repose stands out as a radical extension of his thought, but at the same time one of its most attractive attributes. By defining labour as its own objective, he rejects any identification of idleness as an aversion to work. Yet in lieu of this category he erects a more positive and therefore more compelling portrait of human nature. In his thought, man seems to desire to fulfil his capacities almost constantly, and hence, because of activity's indirect effect on his powers, move directly towards the perfection of his nature. Human nature is conceived, in Ferguson's writing, as a relentlessly self-fulfilling mechanism. Both the species and the individual will grow and advance by simply following their inherent tendencies and using their natural abilities.[24]

While the human character is depicted in radically positive terms by Ferguson, however, the conditions of commercial society, as he understands and describes them, seem to fall short of providing the means for such human fulfilment. Where man desires to exert himself, commercial life will confine him only. When he wants to give rein to his benevolence, he will be forced to interact with his fellow men on the maxims of self-interest and profit. In this connection it is to be observed that Smith's project, in the *Wealth of Nations*, aims at depicting human life and the human character as essentially in accord. Man is characterized by his tendencies to labour and to exchange, and commercial society is the ideal consummation of such activities. There, for Smith, man will do what has come naturally to him for his whole existence. By acting in accordance with his self-interest, he, his family and his society will all be better off.

That we observed the manner in which this sense of harmony was undermined and disrupted in the *Wealth of Nations*, however, signals that for Smith, ultimately, as for Ferguson, commercial society and human nature do not entirely match. The individualistic illustrations that punctuate the text open up the same idea of human tranquillity expressed at greater length in *The Theory of Moral Sentiments*. The constant labour advocated by the primary perspective of the *Wealth of Nations* becomes an unsustainable fiction. A state of advanced specialization must make scarce the conditions of contentment Smith imagines, even when one of the main contentions of the work is that a society made up of competitive markets based on the division of labour will place the labouring poor in a much happier condition than they would otherwise be able to maintain.[25] Idleness and repose are simultaneously central to Smith's conception of happiness and forbidden in an advanced division of labour.

Just as the two expositions of the division of labour we have been considering can be aligned by the incongruity they discover between man and commercial life, the reader of both works will be left with a similar impression of the relationship between their authors and the societies they describe. Smith and Ferguson both consider the philosopher to be as much implicated in the division of labour as the maker of pins or the steam-engine operator. Ferguson observes that 'reason itself becomes a profession' in commercial nations (*Essay*, p. 189) in much the same way that Smith describes 'philosophy or speculation' as, 'like every other employment, the principal or sole trade and occupation of a particular class of citizens'. Smith goes on to suggest that this 'subdivision of employment ... as well as in every other business, improves dexterity, and saves time' (*WN*, pp. 21–2). This supposition stems from the idea, again common to both thinkers, that while specialization contracts the mental capacities of some workers, the understandings of those who oversee their operations, or arrange them into a larger pattern, are actually enlarged by the variety of occupations they must consider. Variety is the key idea in this context:

In a civilized state ... though there is little variety in the occupations of the greater part of individuals, there is an almost infinite variety in those of the whole society. These varied occupations present an almost infinite variety of objects to the contemplation of those few, who, being attached to no particular occupation themselves, have leisure and inclination to examine the occupations of other people. The contemplation of so great a variety of objects necessarily exercises their minds in endless comparisons and combinations, and renders their understandings, in an extraordinary degree, both acute and comprehensive. (*WN*, p. 783)[26]

This perspective, occurring as another facet of Smith's reconsideration of the stultifying effects of specialization on the majority of labourers, must be seen to be problematic. Firstly, whereas Smith understood the philosopher to be as much a part of the division of labour as any other worker in my previous quotation, in this passage Smith equates the speculative enterprise with being attached to no particular occupation. Secondly, as John Barrell has remarked, if the philosopher is as much a part of the division of labour as every other specialized worker, then he is also motivated by the same tendency to truck and barter, and importantly is also blinded from the real interests of society by the same self-interest that guides every mechanic. These problems lead Barrell to conclude that Smith has to invent a fictitious social spectator in order to imagine an individual who could be situated somewhere that would let him view the whole scene of man's occupations in a state of advanced specialization, since for someone implicated in such division, there is no access to any general view.[27]

It is possible to understand this problem slightly differently of course, since for Smith it is not exactly a general view but a multiplicity of particular views that leads to the possibility of some sort of wider understanding. It is the variety available to be sought out in an advanced commercial state that he thinks could enlarge the understanding of a thinker well beyond that of a specialized mechanic, who has but one object constantly in his view. So it is possible to imagine Smith striving to visit as many different manufactures and sites of industry as possible in order to begin to comprehend just some of the endless comparisons he is in a position to make. It is for this reason that he describes the philosopher as needing both leisure and inclination. Yet, even if we consider the speculative task facing Smith as philosopher in this manner, as a multiplicity of the particular perspectives to be comprehended instead of a single, immensely broad view, it is still evident that in order to present his findings, he must imagine himself as having grasped or understood the general view, at least more than any other man.

This problem of perspective seems to be behind the fact that the *Wealth of Nations* is written in a subjunctive tone that pervades the entire work. Phrases such as 'may be said to be', or 'some notion may be formed', or 'it may be laid down as a maxim', do more than just pepper the text, they qualify just about all its beliefs and conclusions. It is as if the imaginary nature of Smith's viewpoint can be traced in the conditional nature of the language he uses. Moreover, it seems as though many of these phrases become more subjunctive as the editions of the *Wealth of Nations* progress. Several occurrences of the phrase 'may be said to be', for example, read 'must be' in the text's first edition (see, for instance, *WN*, p. 50), and there are countless more examples like this. Smith must imagine himself as occupying a position from which the entirety of the interrelations of a modern commercial society can be viewed and comprehended in order to write a work as comprehensive as the *Wealth of Nations*. The work enacts the difficulty or impossibility of attaining such a panoramic viewpoint in its use of the subjunctive mode, and this unease seems to augment in Smith's mind after the publication of its first edition.[28]

In many respects something very similar can be said for Ferguson's *Essay*. Barrell has noted a similar use of 'may' and 'perhaps' that creates an impression of Ferguson as necessarily distanced and ironic in that work.[29] Likewise, the inclusive stance we have seen Ferguson write from seems to render the *Essay* somehow disinterested or reserved. The *Essay* proceeds as if the position from which it considers human nature and commercial society were just one of several possible takes on such subject matter. The content of Ferguson's deliberations, however, means that a consideration of his position in relation to the division of labour must be slightly more complex than it is for Smith. Ferguson's stance on action and activity, which informs so much of what he says about a range of topics, impacts upon how we can understand the philosopher's tasks of understanding and writing. We should remember that he finds the emphasis placed on book-learning in modern Europe to be problematic. He takes the case of books that teach us about ancient, classical cultures and finds that, since the spirit that engendered those books and the lessons they attempt to teach us are concerned with active life, heroic action and, in all cases, the individual's active engagement with his society, a culture that learns of these things in retirement, in a contemplative mode, and in withdrawal from his or her society, mistakes their teaching and their very nature. Ferguson is concerned that active political engagement and interest are being subsumed under a culture of contemplation that imagines idle thinking as an appropriate way to learn the lessons that should be learnt first-hand from doing and being. It is for this reason that he sees the task of the human mind in its proper condition as to seek out the interesting situations of life that will cultivate the individual by the range of skills and sentiments he must use and master. But it is clear that these beliefs, so central to the kind of advice Ferguson gives and the scheme of his thought as a whole, are at odds with the intellectual enterprise of writing a book such as the *Essay*, and wanting it to be read. Are we to imagine Ferguson wanting the *Essay* to be the last philosophical book his readers read, since in doing so they are enlightened as to where real knowledge should come from? Or, are we to see a problem in the fact that the intellectual enterprise for Ferguson, marked so strongly by the distanced and therefore contemplative tones of his comments, signifies a kind of intellectual work that seems like idle reflection? If his examples of full occupation are various sports and risks, is there such a thing as intellectual work that engages the mind fully and is therefore in no way idly contemplative?

To some extent these questions can be answered by paying careful attention to the roles the contemplative abilities play in Ferguson's thought. In his exposition of the genesis of self-interest and specialization, for example, the urge for self-preservation must be combined with the very frequent use of reflection and foresight (ruminative, idle abilities) in order for interest to become the object of our ordinary and constant care. It would seem, from this example, that if the active faculties are the protagonists in Ferguson's portrait of intellectual and physical life, the contemplative abilities hold more hidden roles of intensifying feelings, urges and powers. But we can go further than this. The intellectual contemplative exercise that is the conceiving and writing of the *Essay* itself (not to mention the process of reading it) is an instance of the power of the contemplative abilities to achieve things the active parts of the individual cannot. We could say that Ferguson implicitly discovers what Friedrich Nietzsche does a century later, that if forgetting is essential to acting, remembering must at some times be more potent and, moreover, can be harnessed for specific and often important purposes.[30] Importantly and conspicuously, therefore, two instances of the unique powers of reflection are the thorough accounts of commercial society presented by Smith and Ferguson.

Identifying these two expositions of the division of labour as products of the contemplative powers of the individual in this manner is isolating something about the logic by which Smith and Ferguson's accounts operate. It is as if, by striving to delineate labour so thoroughly, and by aiming thereby to delimit idleness as that suspension of our habits in which we gather our wasting force, both thinkers focus attention on the space between these two poles, and foreground the types of activity that fail to match their definitions. While the most obvious products of the activities that lie between physical exertion and passive repose are

Smith and Ferguson's accounts themselves, it is also possible to imagine a whole range of outcomes of employments such as these that, while not physically tradeable, are nevertheless useful in another manner. When Smith identifies the kind of accidental utility of public diversions, for example, we could say that he is very briefly working in the same grain as the logic we have identified. After categorizing these activities as 'unproductive', and after telling us at such length how productivity must be understood, Smith is then in a position to see the intermediate space left by these definitions. While it is unsurprising, therefore, that his account of leisure pursuits, undeveloped as it is, occurs at the very end of the *Wealth of Nations*, we should also note that the moments at which Smith's secondary, individualistic perspective of specialization emerges are also moments in which this logic shows itself, briefly and almost incidentally. At the moments Smith aims to illustrate his contentions most graphically, what is not labour but still significant human activity is most clearly visible.

In the process of identifying moments in the *Wealth of Nations* at which such logic shows itself, as it were, it becomes clear that Smith's 'philosophic eye', the eye of the discipline invoked in the text in order to consider an endlessly specialized society in one view, and which is figured in the subjunctive tones of the text, is a kind of fictional, pure manifestation of the contemplative, creative possibilities of the mind. Not a moment in the text but an all-encompassing fiction of a kind of ideal state of knowledge, Smith's philosophic eye has been erected by the contemplative abilities of the mind and allows the manifold and various labours of a community or nation to be related to each other. In the same way that Ferguson's 'reflection and foresight' motivate labour, the philosophic eye is the essential but unseen intellectual component in the act of understanding specialization on a national scale. In this sense such a presence in the *Wealth of Nations* seems to bear affinities with the 'impartial spectator' in *The Theory of Moral Sentiments*. In that work, this ideal perspective was the direct product of contemplation, that act conceived of as more reliable and natural than the passion engendered by activity. The 'impartial spectator' was the ideal state of moral knowledge raised up by the mind in moments of intellectual activity but physical idleness, without which man would be adrift in a moral world of merely partial, subjective opinions. We might say that both of Smith's texts are over-arched and structured by the contemplative abilities of the mind. His thought not only relies on such fictions, but positions them as ideal presences in the worlds he describes.

The creative possibilities of the idle mind are thus tacitly, or somehow accidentally, opened up by the projects of Smith and Ferguson. We should also recognize that these two accounts of the division of labour uncover the very territory that will be explored in the poetic thought and German-influenced philosophy of the generations to follow. Friedrich Schiller's enquiry into the aesthetic education of man will take the gulf between physical activity and passive repose as its sole object, positioning this territory as the realm in which man must be understood to be most intensely alive and closest to the perfection of his nature. Similarly, many British thinkers in the succeeding decades, in many different disciplines, will focus on the manner in which idle thought can be conceived as particularly potent and valuable. The thought of the decades following this debate over the division of labour will attest to this gap between activity and repose being the most perplexing and powerful area of intellectual life. Consequently, the type of thought that is understood both to succeed and to oppose these political economic texts – the aesthetic inquiries of the last decades of the eighteenth century – could be said to follow on from the logic of their analyses. Since, as we will see, such aesthetic thought takes up the private, individualistic perspective that is most naturally opposed to the schematic concerns of the *Wealth of Nations*, its impetus to do so must be understood to have been anticipated and prefigured within that text itself.

Finally, using the terms of Smith and Ferguson themselves, we could say that this tacit widening of the realm of contemplation owes its existence to the division of labour itself. For both philosophers it is not until specialization creates such a plethora of objects of study in one nation that speculative thinking can reach the heights from which such variety can be (or can be attempted to be) comprehended and assessed. Thus, in these terms, the contemplative abilities of the mind have also only been rendered so 'acute and comprehensive' by the variety available to them. This process, furthermore, enables us to say something more about the philosopher's niche in the division of labour. The subjunctive modes of Smith and Ferguson signify the impossibility of their position without the society they see as separate from and beneath them. Their contemplation, at once passive and concretely constructive, is predicated upon, and only made possible by, the intense activity of the rest of their society.

CHAPTER 2

Utilitarian education and aesthetic education

One of the themes sharpened by Smith and Ferguson's debate over the division of labour that we have not considered in much detail so far is the role to be played by education in addressing the problems attendant on commercial progress. If highly specialized labour contracts the worker's understanding, as both philosophers agree, then some sort of recuperative or preventative education would seem to be required in order to maintain the political and martial health of the nation. In turning to this theme now, however, rather than remaining within the limits of political economy's interest in education, which as we saw was concerned with attaining and demonstrating the equivalence of a community's mental capacities to various classical models, it will be beneficial to take a somewhat wider view of the types of education germane to late-eighteenth- and early-nineteenth-century thought. That a need was both felt and acted upon in these decades, and in all sectors of society, for a systematized and comprehensive method of education, is apparent from even a cursory glance at printed titles containing the term. Systems of education emerged specifically for daughters, for sons, for children of either sex, for young ladies, for young gentlemen, for the poor, for 'exposed and deserted young children', for deaf and dumb children, for religious instruction, for a life of industry, and for many other specific groups and reasons. Rather than attempt to offer an entirely representative sample of this cross-section, something it would seem hard to do given the comprehensiveness of this list, I want to concentrate on the two strands of educational thinking that might be said to be most influential on all these areas, and which also appear to be most opposed to each other, at a first glance at least. These strands are the scheme for utilitarian education, as it is figured in the educational and penal thought of Jeremy Bentham, and that of aesthetic education, specifically as it receives its fullest and most pronounced articulation in the thought of Friedrich Schiller.[1]

Utilitarian education and aesthetic education

Bentham's project of utilitarian education is by no means confined to his *Chrestomathia* of 1815–17, his most overt educational treatise. Just as the Chrestomathic School was to be housed in the Panopticon structure designed by Bentham's brother, Sir Samuel Bentham, the *Panopticon Letters* of 1791 are also the occasion for Bentham's first significant foray into educational thinking. Amongst his thoughts on 'Pauper Management' likewise, another scheme projected to use the Panopticon structure which appeared in Arthur Young's *Annals of Agriculture* for 1797, the reader is presented with a 'résumé' of an unpublished chapter on the 'education of pauper children'.[2] As these instances and their connection to the Panopticon building imply, Bentham's ideas on education are dispersed into his penal and poor-law thought to a considerable degree. In order to begin examining utilitarian education, we must begin where the Panopticon begins, with the *Panopticon Letters*.

The *Inspection House* or *Elaboratory* (*Writings*, p. 33), as Bentham first denominates the Panopticon, was to be a circular building, organized so that the 'apartments of the prisoners occupy the circumference'. These apartments, or *cells*, as Bentham calls them in the case of the building being a penitentiary, were to be

> divided from one another, and the prisoners by that means secluded from all communication with each other, by *partitions* in the form of *radii* issuing from the circumference towards the centre, and extending as many feet as shall be thought necessary to form the largest dimension of the cell … The apartment of the inspector occupies the centre; you may call it if you please the *inspector's lodge*. (*Writings*, p. 35)

As Bentham's rather teasing tone implies – 'as many feet as shall be thought necessary', 'you may call it if you please' – the Panopticon was not at this point a reality. The *Letters*, which were written in 1787 but not printed until 1791, begin with the assertion that his brother is 'about erecting' it 'here' (in White Russia), but tell us, in a footnote to this same sentence, that the 'sudden breaking out of the war between the Turks and Russians, in consequence of an unexpected attack made by the former on the latter, concurred with some other incidents in putting a stop to the design' (*Writings*, p. 33). Thanks to their overt aim of applying the principles of the building to the needs of a penitentiary, the *Letters* function as a manifesto for the building's construction and use in more general terms. In line with this purpose, drawings of the structure were included with the *Letters* in both 1787 and 1791.

The Panopticon design can seem wildly idiosyncratic or startlingly modern in comparison with the architecture we associate with this period. Yet the architectural innovations inspired by the prison reform debates of the last decades of the eighteenth century make clear that this is not the case. John Howard's *The State of the Prisons in England and Wales*, of 1777, one of two main impetuses to penal reform in this period, offered an incredibly thorough account of the practices of every prison in those two countries. Giving both statistical evidence and moral arguments for reform, Howard found that the many malpractices he had first observed at Bedford Gaol were as prevalent elsewhere.[3] It is in its proposals for reform, however, that *The State of the Prisons* was most influential. Following Howard's European travels – his accounts of 'Foreign Prisons' are presented at length and organized by country – he proposed a regime built around 'as much regularity, as any other house where the family is equally numerous': 'The hours of rising, of reading a chapter in the bible, or prayers, of meals, of work, &c. should all be fixed by the magistrates, and notice of them given by a bell.'[4] In addition, as Michael Ignatieff summarizes, Howard planned to make use of 'uniforms, cellular confinement, and constant inspection'.[5]

The second and perhaps somewhat larger impetus to penitentiary reform was the American Declaration of Independence of 1776. By inhibiting the transportation of British criminals, and thus restricting the options for the punishment of felons, this event significantly raised native prison populations over a short period of time. In the wake of 1776, Howard, William Eden and William Blackstone put together the Penitentiary Act of 1779, which altered the punishment for many crimes from death or transportation to a fixed period of incarceration, and which proposed the building of a national penitentiary specifically for this purpose. Such an emphasis on confinement is not only to be understood pragmatically, however, for the Penitentiary Act, and Howard's work itself indeed, are also manifestations of a significant shift in the conception of the relationship between punishment and the human character. This shift originates in David Hartley's materialist psychology, which, according to Ignatieff, was influential in reformist circles in the 1770s and 1780s. Hartley's system was founded on the notion that external sensations engender all human ideas, including, importantly, moral ones. It followed, for those men interested in the idea of criminal behaviour, that to control those sensations – the subject's external environment – was to control his or her intellectual development, and thus, crucially in this context, his or her moral principles. Ignatieff phrases this belief succinctly: 'a regimen applied to the body by the external force of authority would first become a habit and then gradually be transformed into a moral preference'.[6]

In line with this set of beliefs, which were implicitly written into the 1779 Penitentiary Act, prison design underwent significant changes throughout the 1780s. The most notable new structures in this decade were by architect William Blackburn, whose designs, in John Bender's description, 'bristled with innovations, ranging from geometric radial plans that allowed guards full view of all exterior yards and apertures, to ingenious details of construction that supported architecturally contradictory aims of ventilation, cleanliness, and isolation'.[7] In the context of these very much realized developments – Blackburn's Gloucester penitentiary, for example, under the management of George Onesiphorus Paul, became the paradigm for all British prison reform – Bentham's Panopticon does not stand out as more radically innovative, or more starkly conceptual, than the designs being put into practice all over the country. Where Bentham's Panopticon project stands apart from the designs and plans of his contemporaries is in the characteristic thoroughness and depth with which he analyses the principles and details of inspection and confinement, ideas that the Penitentiary Act had made central to the idea of an inmate's character-reformation.

In general terms the proposals built around routine suggested by Howard in *The State of the Prisons* also characterize life in the Panopticon as envisaged by Bentham. This 'new mode of obtaining power of mind over mind' (*Writings*, p. 31) would be characterized chiefly by cellular confinement and constant inspection. Since, according to Bentham, 'the trouble of inspection is diminished in no less proportion than the strictness of inspection is increased' (*Writings*, p. 45), the inspector's family would occupy the *lodge* at the centre of the structure with the inspector:

> Secluded oftentimes, by their situation, from every other object, they will naturally, and in a manner unavoidably, give their eyes a direction conformable to that purpose [inspection], in every momentary interval of their ordinary occupations. It will supply in their instance the place of that great and constant fund of entertainment to the sedentary and vacant in towns – the looking out of the window. The scene, though a confined, would be a very various, and therefore, perhaps, not altogether an unamusing one. (*Writings*, pp. 44–5)

If this suggestion seems at all absurd, or coldly utilitarian, it is worth bearing in mind that Howard's 'first question' at each foreign prison he visited was 'Whether the Gaoler or Keeper resided in the House', a question to which the answer was, apparently, 'always in the affirmative'.[8] In the case of Bentham, this consideration is nevertheless justified by means of a distinctly macabre logic. Bentham is suggesting that every minute human tendency might be put to some purpose, and aligned, in this case, to provide perfect inspection.[9]

Another area of the Panopticon's make-up that carries overtones of the macabre is its emphasis on the labour of its inmates. The centrality of work to the Panopticon's regime is implied in Bentham's observation that 'If a man won't work, nothing has he to do, from morning to night, but to eat his bad bread and drink his water, without a soul to speak to' (*Writings*, p. 66). Apart from Sundays, indeed, every day in the Panopticon was to be spent working, if one was an inmate. Labour was not simply to be a casual occupation in this project, for Bentham, therefore. The Panopticon was to be managed in this respect by 'contractors': 'I would farm out the profits, the no-profits, or if you please the losses, to him who, being in other respects unexceptionable, offered the best terms' (*Writings*, p. 51). Thanks to this crucial detail, Bentham was of the opinion that his Panopticon held the promise of significant success, since the plans for a national penitentiary, which the 1779 act was designed to enable, were rejected in 1784 for being too expensive.[10] On this front however, Bentham was distinctly mistaken. His suggestion that a penitentiary could be profitable by this means actually represented a significant discrepancy between his thought and that of the other, more official reformers, Howard, Eden and Blackstone.

Whilst all the reformers were united in the belief that the criminal must be reformed by discipline rather than simply restrained, for all except Bentham this was to be achieved by means of hard labour.[11] Bentham, on the contrary, clearly had something different in mind: 'I neither see the great danger nor the great harm of a man's liking his work too well; and how well soever he might have liked it *elsewhere*, I should still less apprehend his liking the thought of having it to do *there*' (*Writings*, p. 57). Even though at this point in his reasoning Bentham casts doubt on the actual likelihood of the inmate liking his work '*there*', in the Panopticon, slightly further on in the *Letters*, the picture is different. Following his assertion that the prisoner who refuses to work will have absolutely nothing to do 'from morning to night', Bentham presents the alternative picture of the prisoner who works exactly as he is told to:

If he will work, his time is occupied, and he has his meat and his beer, or whatever else his earnings may afford him, and not a stroke does he strike but he gets something, which he would not have got otherwise. This encouragement is necessary to his doing his utmost: but more than this is not necessary. It is necessary every exertion he makes should be sure of its reward; but it is not necessary that such reward be so great, or any thing near so great, as he might have had, had he worked elsewhere. (*Writings*, pp. 66–7)

In this passage, even if the 'rewards' of an inmate's labour are nowhere near 'so great, as he might have had, had he worked elsewhere', the portrait Bentham offers of the prisoner who works is distinctly cheery. He will be 'occupied' (the condition of happiness in Ferguson's thought), he will have 'meat' and 'beer', as well as anything else he may 'afford'.

Clearly the provision of 'reward' for the prisoner who works, especially as Bentham describes it, stands at some distance from the desire or the necessity of inflicting misery, and the thinking behind hard labour. Bentham is alone among the reformers of the 1770s and 1780s in his desire to let the inmate earn from the work he or she does inside the penitentiary. Rather than just being a specific anomaly in Bentham's thought, however, this consideration is a manifestation of the Panopticon's specific ideology. This ideology revolves around what Bentham terms elsewhere the 'junction of duty and interest'.[12] By attempting to align the inmates' satisfaction or pleasure with what they are required to do, Bentham aims to alter the inmates' characters in a direction mutually advantageous to themselves and to the society of which they are a part. Whilst this goal had been given its most concise description by Blackstone, who described it as the aim to 'inure them to habits of industry', the phrase seems more apt for Bentham's significantly positive approach than it does for those schemes built around hard labour as a kind of punishment.[13]

The latent positivity of Bentham's plan can also be registered in his conception of physical punishment as a kind of evil or 'mischief'. As he observes in *An Introduction to the Principles of Morals and Legislation*:

It is the idea only of the punishment (or, in other words, the *apparent* punishment) that really acts upon the mind; the punishment itself (the *real* punishment) acts not any farther than as giving rise to that idea. It is the apparent punishment, therefore, that does all the service, I mean in the way of example, which is the principal object. It is the real punishment that does all the mischief.[14]

In accordance with this conception of punishment as a kind of potentially needless damage, where Bentham suggests that '*real* punishment' is to take place in the Panopticon, he does so by rethinking the objective of such an act: 'If you must torment them, do it in a way in which somebody may be a gainer by it. Sooner than rob them of all society, I would pinch them at their meals.'[15] By rendering any punishment useful inside the Panopticon, Bentham is striving to align all aspects of penitentiary life with the reformation of its inmates.

We should note, in this last quotation, that solitude, robbing the inmate 'of all society', is conceived of as a punishment too severe to be inflicted even on the criminal who 'must' be tormented. That this quotation comes from the 'Postscripts' to the *Panopticon Letters*, and that this material was added to the *Letters* for their 1791 publication, points to the fact that Bentham's ideas on solitude develop and alter after 1787. To understand why this is, one must return to Howard. The regimen of solitude implemented across the country in the 1780s came directly from Howard's proposals for reform in 1777 and the Penitentiary Act they led to. Yet following the changes of the 1780s, Howard denounced what he saw as the over-zealous application of his ideas by Paul and other county prison reformers. Continuing his researches, he found, at Nottingham County Gaol, for example, that one man had been 'sentenced to two years [*sic*] solitary confinement', and that at 'Sherborn' prisoners were allowed out of their cells 'for only *one* hour in a day' (Howard's emphasis). Howard's account of these continued problems was published in 1789 and included an account of the potential uses and abuses of solitary confinement. In his now more nuanced view, solitude was a kind of tool available to be used by gaolers, but one that must be used with caution:

> The intention of this [solitary confinement], I mean by day as well as by night, is either to reclaim the most atrocious and daring criminals; to punish the refractory for crimes committed in prison; or to make a strong impression, in a short time, upon thoughtless and irregular young persons, as faulty apprentices, and the like ... The beneficial effects on the mind, of such a punishment, are speedy, proceeding from the horror of a vicious person left entirely to his own reflections. This may wear off by long continuance, and a sullen insensibility may succeed.[16]

Solitude, in this view, should not be a sentence in itself, but is to be used for the punishment of 'crimes committed in prison'. Its effects are 'speedy', but will lead, if continued, to 'a sullen insensibility'.

This account had a direct impact on Bentham, and its influence is distinct in the Panopticon 'Postscripts'. In addition to quoting Howard at greater length than I have done, Bentham also reuses Howard's terminology in his own analysis, suggesting that solitude is 'productive of a gloomy despondency, or sullen insensibility', and asking 'What better can be the result, when a vacant mind, is left for months, or years, to prey upon itself?'[17] In the wake of Howard's 1789 analysis the Panopticon scheme was revised so that between two and four prisoners could be placed in each cell. This 'somewhat mawkish' plan, as Janet Semple describes it, is designed to restrict the inmate's mind from having any opportunity to 'prey upon itself', at the same time as avoiding the evils of 'promiscuous association'. The inmates sharing a cell would be carefully selected, and could be 'varied every moment' on any suspicion of plotting to escape, for example.[18]

That Bentham's aims in the Panopticon could still be accomplished, or could still be conceived of as accomplishable, with up to four inmates in each cell, is a consequence of the particular process that was to take place inside the structure. For Howard, a Quaker, the process of change taking place inside the penitentiary was comparable to a kind of spiritual awakening. In Ignatieff's terms, Howardian penitentiary life was like a Quaker meeting: 'From out of the silence of an ascetic vigil, the convict and believer alike would begin to hear the inner voice of conscience and feel the transforming power of God's love.'[19] Bentham, on the other hand, had no such religious ambitions for his Panopticon.[20] In that structure, as we have already begun to see, the inmate was to be reformed by the alignment of his interests and his obligations. By being taught that life could be characterized by the satisfaction of reward as long as he made labour the main occupation of his time, Bentham's inmate would be 'inured' to industry. Pleasure and utility would become one in those leaving the Panopticon after successful reformation. They would labour happily and effectively, and, since it is 'idleness' that engenders 'crime' in Bentham's view, would have little cause to reoffend.[21] It is for this reason indeed that Bentham 'confesses' to 'know of no test of reformation so plain or so sure as the improved quantity and value of [the inmate's] work' (*Writings*, p. 57). Labour is central both to the Panopticon's operation and to its long-term effects.

The trajectory of Bentham's thought in this respect was conceived of by the other reformers as a significant departure from their official consensus, however. For Paul, whose tenet of 'reformation by seclusion' was entirely representative of national penal practices, Bentham was too interested in the commercial possibilities of his inmates' activities. In addition to restricting the punishment that hard labour was designed to inflict, Paul was appalled that Bentham was prepared to sacrifice inmates' solitary confinement to what he saw as the dictates of profitability and specialization. More crucially to the Panopticon scheme as a whole, when Bentham's proposals came under the scrutiny of an 1810 Commons committee, the committee replicated Paul's opinion, rejecting the project on the basis of its contract management.[22] This event is significant both for Bentham and for penal thought more generally. Just as Bentham's two decades of campaigning to get the Panopticon penitentiary built came to an end with this decision, it also marked the definitive rejection of the idea to align the inmate's duty and interest. Rather than positive reform along the lines of the rewards of labour, the 1810 committee chose concrete punishment and the hope of a spiritual awakening brought on by hardship.

While we might be tempted to align Bentham's emphasis on labour as the activity that should characterize the inmate's life, and as what would lead, ultimately, to happiness and satisfaction, with Smith and Ferguson's positioning of work as the central feature of human behaviour, we should note that idleness, as the opposite of labour, has undergone a significant shift in Bentham's penal thought. In Smith and Ferguson's expositions of commercial society, idleness functioned as a kind of relative term of motion, as a shorthand for the cessation of activity or for the suspension of those engagements that cause the species to progress so rapidly. In what we have just seen of Bentham's thought, idleness has become a psychological category. In proposing labour as the means to effect moral reform, Bentham is not simply attempting to harness the power of reward to motivate good behaviour. He is also, as we have seen, attempting to sidestep the tendency of the mind to 'prey upon itself' if left alone and unoccupied. That this is no accidental or incidental consideration in Bentham's thought, moreover, that this shift from relative motion to internal, mental well-being is a significant one, becomes apparent if we turn to Bentham's *Chrestomathia*, his most overt piece of educational thinking.

First published in 1815, just half a decade after the Panopticon's official rejection, Bentham's *Chrestomathia* is both a thorough application of the theme of utility to education, and an extension of the Panopticon project insofar as it applies the 'inspection principle' to schools. Like the Panopticon penitentiary, the Chrestomathic School is not as wildly idiosyncratic as it can appear. For the most part it is comparable to other educational schemes contemporary with its conception. The school was to follow the 'monitorial' system associated with the names of Andrew Bell and Joseph Lancaster, in which the master taught the senior pupils, who in turn taught the rest. Since, by this means, one teacher was reckoned to be able to teach as many as a thousand pupils, the monitorial system offered the prospect of educating large groups extremely efficiently.[23] Bentham's version of this system was superior to it, in his mind, thanks not only to its employment of the Panopticon structure and the perfect inspection it provided, but also to the vast array of 'principles' of instruction he provided for its operation, and which make up the bulk of the text of the *Chrestomathia*.

Somewhat surprisingly, given its apparent objective of detailing a superior plan for monitorial education, Bentham begins the *Chrestomathia* by offering an in-depth account of the terms 'ennui', 'désœuvrement' and 'avocation'. These definitions make up Bentham's second *'Advantage'* 'DERIVABLE FROM LEARNING OR INTELLECTUAL INSTRUCTION', the 'Security against ennui', but take up significantly more space than any of the 'advantages' around them (*Chrestomathia*, p. 19). Bentham begins with 'ennui' itself: 'Ennui is the state of uneasiness, felt by him whose mind unoccupied, but without reproach, is on the look out for pleasure; pleasure in some one or more of all shapes; and beholds at the time no source which promises to afford it.' This is followed immediately by 'désœuvrement': 'désœuvrement is the state in which the mind, seeing before it nothing to be done, nothing in the shape of business or amusement which promises either security against pain or possession of pleasure, is left a prey to the sort of uneasiness just designated' (*Chrestomathia*, p. 20). In expanding on the 'securities' listed in the first 'Chrestomathic Table', these definitions begin to sketch out Bentham's conception of 'pain' in this context. The pain under consideration is not physical, but entirely psychological. It seems to exist only in a state of absence, when the mind has neither anything to do nor anything to amuse it, and is thus more akin to a 'sort of uneasiness' than a physical injury. 'Ennui', in this portrait, is thus a species of pain. It is a 'state of uneasiness' brought on by a lack of occupation and the mental inactivity such a physical state engenders.

The third term in Bentham's account of 'ennui' is 'avocation'. In order to fit this concept into his scheme, Bentham has to counter what he sees as its recent mutation in meaning:

> The word avocation, a most incompetent and equivocal term, has of late years been vulgarly, and we may almost say commonly, obtruded upon the words calling, vocation, employment. A vocation is a *calling*; an avocation is a *calling off*. Engaged in an avocation, a man is engaged in that, whereby being called off from everything, he is not left free to apply himself to anything.

In the context of the two preceding definitions, an 'avocation' is a state of occupation par excellence. In the state of 'avocation', a man is 'called off' from every other task so that he 'is not left free to apply himself to anything', so that all his attention is on one object exclusively. As one might expect, furthermore, if one has been following the preceding definitions closely, for Bentham this state represents a powerful and desirable condition: 'In this same case, in which so efficient a security is afforded against pain in all its shapes, as well as against the extinction of all pleasures, may be seen an equally efficient and much more extensively necessary security against the pain of mental vacuity or ennui' (*Chrestomathia*, p. 20). The power of the state of 'avocation' is twofold. Not only does it 'efficiently' resist all 'shapes' of pain, it also offers the 'security' of continued 'pleasures'. Bentham makes clear here, however, that he is particularly interested in its resistance to the state of absence he has already defined – 'the pain of mental vacuity or ennui'. An 'avocation' is not only the opposite mental state from 'ennui' by virtue of the one's complete employment and the other's total vacancy, but also inhibits the latter from forming or arising. It is a 'security' that is also an amusement, both defending against and attacking 'ennui' at the same time.

The seemingly boundless 'efficiency' and power of an 'avocation' is only tempered by one consideration in Bentham's account. This is recorded in the paragraph immediately following the definition we have just seen:

> It is true, to a mind engaged in the toil of business, a state of repose is in the intervals of business a state of pleasure. For a time, yes; but, especially when the nature of the business includes not in it anything peculiarly toilsome, that time must be short, otherwise the pain of ennui soon succeeds to the pleasure of repose. (*Chrestomathia*, p. 20)

Although in one sense its opposite, an 'avocation', a calling off from business, we are now told, runs the risk of sliding into the pain of 'ennui' if extended too long. Further, this danger varies according to the nature of the occupation from which one is 'called off'. As was the case in Ferguson's thought, Bentham here categorizes various employments by their relative levels of toil. An 'avocation' would seem to be most effective if it is a calling off from something 'peculiarly toilsome'.

That Bentham's account of these interrelated terms functions as some kind of psychological framework for understanding the aims, benefits and failings of a system of education is made explicit by the remaining advantages of this system of instruction. Reading on, none of the 'pains' the Chrestomathic School is designed to offer 'security' against are ever entirely separable from 'ennui'. In the case of the third advantage, for example, the 'Security against inordinate sensuality, and its mischievous consequences', Bentham sketches out a portrait of the 'pleasures of the sense' and the mental effects they are likely to have in rather familiar terms:

Not in any degree to diminish, but to increase to the utmost, the sum of innoxious enjoyment, is the object of this system. But, to secure that increase, it is necessary to render men duly sensible of the value, and to engage them in the steady pursuit of those perennial springs of enjoyment which are the more productive the more copiously they are drawn upon, in preference to those which, in proportion as they are drawn upon to excess, yield in the shape of ennui, at the least, if not in still more afflicting shapes, pain and grief instead of the expected pleasure. (*Chrestomathia*, p. 23)

In this description, just as ennui was defined as that feeling engendered by the unoccupied mind failing to find pleasures, and just as an avocation would slide into a state of vacancy if continued too long, 'inordinate sensuality' will lead to ennui the 'more copiously' it is 'drawn upon'. Additionally, ennui is now positioned as a kind of first step or gateway to 'still more afflicting shapes' of 'pain and grief'. We might say that Bentham is constructing a portrait of human activity in which all occupations slide into pain and vacancy, a portrait in which man must be constantly wary of his level of activity and the duration for which he has been engaged in it, if he is to avoid a mixture of misery and inertia.

Glancing at the fourth advantage, likewise – the 'Security against idleness and consequent mischievousness' – we find Bentham seeking to describe and classify the effects of mental vacancy rather similarly. Without even mentioning, let alone demonstrating, the connection between 'idleness' and 'mental vacuity', Bentham tells us that 'A mind completely vacant, if any such there be, is a mind in which there exists neither pleasure nor pain, nor any expectation of either. But, scarcely has such a state of mind time to take place, when it is succeeded by ennui' (*Chrestomathia*, p. 23). In this scenario, the vacant mind is classified as problematic by virtue of its susceptibility to a kind of exterior threat. The mind must not be left vacant, for Bentham, in case negative forces rush into it, or upon it, as if from elsewhere. In this instance again Chrestomathic instruction is represented as offering security against something ultimately reducible to the threat of ennui. The pupils of the Chrestomathic school will be taught in such a way that, because their minds are never 'completely vacant', they are never to be led to ennui by this path. Moreover, that there are eleven more comprehensively detailed and thoroughly reasoned advantages in this first section of the *Chrestomathia* alone, serves to suggest that the Chrestomathic student will learn to evade ennui by every path of which Bentham is aware.

Turning our attention to the actual means that will effect these securities, many of the facets of Chrestomathic education also bear a direct connection to the definitions with which Bentham began his exposition. The *Short Lesson principle*, for example, attempts to restrict the possibility of any mental vacuity in the Chrestomathic pupils. The principle follows the logic that, as 'in a *fleet*, the pace of the slowest *vessel*, so in a class the pace of the dullest *scholar* is necessarily the pace of the *whole*'. Since the 'longer the *lesson* is, the longer must be the *time* allowed – allowed to all – for *getting* it', Bentham suggests that Chrestomathic lessons will be restricted to 'no more than *ten minutes*'. By this means, the '*maximum* of *idleness*' that any pupil is forced to endure is significantly restricted, in comparison to the hour-long lessons Bentham rejects (*Chrestomathia*, pp. 114–15).

Going hand in hand with the idea of short lessons is the *Employment varying principle*. Under this head Bentham suggests that 'In proportion as exercises are varied, each affords relief, and operates as a sort of recreation or play, with relation to every other' (*Chrestomathia*, p. 116). Hence, in addition to lessons lasting no longer than ten minutes, the Chrestomathic School will also ensure that each lesson is varied enough from that preceding it to ensure that it functions as a kind of pleasant change of occupation for the pupils. Whether we find this plan for education to be rather light and mercurial, or whether we consider it simply to answer the needs of a youthful concentration, it is apparent that, in the terms in which Bentham has framed his account, the Chrestomathic School seems to be attempting to harness the power of avocation in its formal make-up. By 'calling' pupils 'off' from their employment every ten minutes, they are not left free to apply themselves to anything else, and are thereby shielded from the dangers of mental vacuity and its attendant ennui. By being placed in a literally continual state of avocation, that state offering not just protection from pain but continued pleasures, every 'task', in the Chrestomathic School, will be, as Bentham says, 'converted into play' (*Chrestomathia*, p. 27).

The formal constitution of Bentham's plan for education must be understood to be customized, as it were, to suit the portrait of the mind's tendencies with which the *Chrestomathia* begins. We should also note that the types of knowledge to be taught in this system also seem to be put together with ennui, avocation and désœuvrement in mind. Back in the 'Advantages' section, for instance, the variety of subjects to be taught in the Chrestomathic School is expressed as a function of the mind's means of avoiding the pains we have already encountered:

> the greater the variety of the shapes in which pleasures of an intellectual nature are made to present themselves to view, and consequently the greater the degree of success and perfection with which the mind is prepared for the reception of intellectual pleasures, the greater the chance afforded of security from the pains by which sensual pleasures are encompassed, and the more advantageous the terms on which the purchase of that security is effected. (*Chrestomathia*, p. 23)

In this consideration education has become a task built around preparing the mind for the 'reception' of a great 'variety' of 'intellectual pleasures'. The pupil experienced in the enjoyment of all different types of mental occupations and experiences, it seems, will be well prepared to evade merely 'sensual pleasures' as well as the ennui to which we have already been told they lead.

In the same vein as this passage, and at the same early stage in the *Chrestomathia*, Bentham also depicts the dangers threatening the mind by means of the metaphor of a patch of ground or a flower-bed:

weeds of all sorts, even the most poisonous, are the natural produce of the vacant mind. For the exclusion of these weeds, no species of husbandry is so effectual, as the filling the soil with flowers, such as the particular nature of the soil is best adapted to produce. What those flowers are can only be known from experiment; and the greater the variety that can be introduced, the greater the chance that the experiment will be attended with success. (*Chrestomathia*, pp. 24–5)

In this image, a great variety of subjects of instruction is necessary because of the impossibility of knowing in advance which types of knowledge will interest each particular mind, which 'flowers' will best suit the 'soil' in question. Chrestomathic instruction will thus be to some extent hit-and-miss. The mind must be filled with intellectual objects and areas of interest, because a superfluity of tuition is needed in order to ensure complete coverage.

In expressing the aims and rationale of Chrestomathic education in this manner, Bentham must be understood to be expressing the same interest in the power of avocation and the threat of ennui we have already seen to inform the physical parameters of the lessons to take place in his school. By filling the mind with a variety of shapes of intellectual pleasure, Chrestomathic education, in Bentham's description, will enable the mind to engage in a kind of self-avocation. The Chrestomathic student will be able to call him- or herself off from any mental employment but still remain intellectually active. He or she will be able, continually and cannily, to evade the risk of vacancy, désœuvrement and their attendant, ever-present ennui.

Just as the mind was understood to prey upon itself in the Panopticon project – a consideration causing Bentham to radically restructure his plans, and that led in some part to the project's rejection in 1810 – the Chrestomathic School is orientated around the threats attendant on the vacant, idle and unemployed mind. In the former instance, the danger to the mind came from within, insofar as it would render itself 'insensible' if left alone and unoccupied. In the latter, Bentham's exposition figures the mind as being threatened somehow, nebulously, from without, by something that will rush upon it and fill any slight pause in its activity, or vacuum in its thought. In both cases the inactive mind is treated as deeply problematic. Idleness has become a psychological category in this manner of thinking that poses significant problems not only to the mind's stability, but, considering Smith and Ferguson's assessment of human life, to what happens to the individual when he or she ceases physical occupation. We might say that Bentham's thought offers an in-depth account of the failings and shortfalls that lead to political and martial problems in a society made up of labourers uneducated beyond their manual occupations.

It is also to be borne in mind that for Bentham such an agenda is motivated entirely by its utility. The interest held by the Chrestomathic School in the mind's potential ennui, like the Panopticon's interest in avoiding the insensibility of its inmates, lies distinctly in the realm of efficaciousness, rather than compassion. Inmates and pupils must be rendered healthy enough, psychologically speaking, so as simply not to inhibit them from being useful to their society. In this sense both the Panopticon penitentiary and the Chrestomathic School orientate themselves around labour. The Panopticon strives to turn out reformed characters, secure in the knowledge that a life of labour would be a life of satisfaction. The *Chrestomathia* similarly asserts that the 'more things' the pupil is 'more or less acquainted with, the more things' he or she 'is fit for' and the 'better chance' he or she has of 'meeting with some *occupation*' (*Chrestomathia*, p. 36; Bentham's emphasis). Despite the aspects of Chrestomathic instruction we have been focusing on, in other words, labour is as much the goal of Bentham's institutional plans in 1815 as it is in 1787.

Characterizing Bentham's ambitions in this way (an assessment, it seems, of which Bentham would have approved) marks his project out as diametrically opposed to the philosophy of Friedrich Schiller. Schiller's *Über die ästhetische Erziehung des Menschen, in einer Reihe von Briefen* (*On the Aesthetic Education of Man, in a Series of Letters*), of 1795, sets out to rethink the rationale of 'Utility' itself, and, as we will see, comes up with something significantly opposed to a life of labour.[24] Schiller characterizes 'Utility' as 'the great idol of our age, to which all powers are in thrall and to which all talent must pay homage'. 'Art', for example, can barely 'tip the scale' in comparison to this 'tyrannical yoke' (*Aesthetic*, 8).[25] Equally for Schiller, the needs and priorities of the individual are almost invisible in comparison to such a dominant and totalitarian manner of thought. They are as 'geistig', as immaterial and ghostlike,[26] as 'Kunst', Art.

Looking at this question of relative worth the other way round, from the perspective of the individual, Schiller tells us slightly later in his argument that contemporary man must be understood to be empty, as a receptacle of knowledge and feeling, except for the ability to carry out his occupation:

> Ewig nur an ein einzelnes kleines Bruchstück des Ganzen gefesselt, bildet sich der Mensch selbst nur als Bruchstück aus; ewig nur das eintönige Geräusch des Rades, das er umtreibt, im Ohre, entwickelt er nie die Harmonie seines Wesens, und anstatt die Menschheit in seiner Natur auszuprägen, wird er bloss zu einem Abdruck seines Geschäfts, seiner Wissenschaft. (*Aesthetic*, p. 34)

> Everlastingly chained to a single little fragment of the Whole, man himself develops into nothing but a fragment; everlastingly in his ear the monotonous sound of the wheel that he turns, he never develops the harmony of his being, and instead of putting the stamp of humanity upon his own nature, he becomes nothing more than the imprint of his occupation or of his specialized knowledge. (*Aesthetic*, p. 35)

This is the same complaint against advanced specialization that Smith acknowledged in Book v of the *Wealth of Nations*. If a man's occupation is limited in terms of its scope and responsibility, then it is also limiting, as the bulk of his faculties and abilities are not given any chance to develop themselves. For Schiller this is a result of society's emphasis on its 'great idol' at the same time as it is a 'curse' on the individual (*Aesthetic*, p. 43): 'little by little the concrete life of the Individual is destroyed in order that the abstract idea of the Whole may drag out its sorry existence' (*Aesthetic*, p. 37).

Schiller is proceeding, in these moments, by making a set of distinctions that he considers to have been obscured in contemporary thought, between the individual and the whole, for instance, or between one man's powers and the accomplishments of a community at large. It is by extrapolating from these distinctions that his argument develops. In the same way that the worker has become merely the mould or impression of his part in advanced material production, Schiller tells us that it was the 'increase in empirical knowledge' that also reconstituted man in its image:

> Sobald auf der einen Seite die erweiterte Erfahrung und das bestimmtere Denken eine schärfere Scheidung der Wissenschaften, auf der andern das verwickeltere Uhrwerk der Staaten eine strengere Absonderung der Stände und Geschäfte notwendig machte, so zerriss auch der innere Bund der menschlichen Natur,

und ein verderblicher Streit entzweite ihre harmonischen Kräfte. (*Aesthetic*, p. 32)

Once the increase of empirical knowledge, and more exact modes of thought, made sharper divisions between the sciences inevitable, and once the increasingly complex machinery of State necessitated a more rigorous separation of ranks and occupations, then the inner unity of human nature was severed too, and a disastrous conflict set its harmonious powers at variance. (*Aesthetic*, p. 33)

This assertion is crucial to the argument of the *Aesthetic Letters*. By employing the Rousseauvian idea of the pre-societal harmony of man's faculties, Schiller is characterizing contemporary human life as fragmented at the same time as he is paving the way for his solution to the problems of commercial society.[27] In terms of the distinctions with which he began, Schiller characterizes the mental state of the over-specialized labourer as the predominance of one mode of thought over another, as one part of the mind operating discordantly in relation to the others. Specialized work, for Schiller, is an instance and a product, of 'Vernünftelei' (*Aesthetic*, p. 30), the over-use of or over-dependence on 'die Vernunft' (the faculty of reason), a kind of sophistry or over-thinking.[28] This term, moreover – Elizabeth Wilkinson and Leonard Willoughby translate it as 'the abuse of reason' – is one manifestation of a pair of symptoms central to the project of the *Aesthetic Letters* as a whole.[29]

To understand these symptoms and their place in Schiller's educational ambitions, one must turn forward a few pages in the *Aesthetic Letters*, to the eleventh letter. There, just as society was separated into collective and individual priorities, man himself is characterized as being made up of both his 'Person' and his 'Condition'. That Schiller's lust for binary pairings is given full rein at this moment in his thought, and that he is keen to demonstrate the pertinence of this division in a variety of areas of intellectual and physical life, means that the task of understanding or of describing these terms can appear difficult. Broadly speaking, since man's 'Person' is his 'persistence' or changelessness, and since his 'Condition' is 'that which changes', the former could be characterized as man's intellectual existence, and the latter as his material or physical existence (*Aesthetic*, p. 73). The one is the sense of continuity by which one might describe mental life, the other the incessant mutability and changefulness of the physical parameters of that life and the body in which it is lived. Michael John Kooy phrases this opposition as follows: 'as creatures of sense, we are clearly part of the world and subject to some degree at least to the same necessity that governs nature; and yet as creatures of reason we seem hardly at home here, possessed rather of an awareness of our own freedom from all natural determination'.³⁰

The fact that these two functions or elements of human life are in one sense opposites and alternatives means that, although Schiller is not saying that either tendency can in reality be entirely eliminated, their operations can be expressed as 'contrary challenges to man'. Man's 'sensuous nature ... insists upon absolute reality: [it] is to turn everything which is mere form into world, and make all his potentialities fully manifest'. One's 'rational nature' on the other hand 'insists upon absolute formality: [it] is to destroy everything in himself which is mere world, and bring harmony into all his changes' (*Aesthetic*, p. 77). Since these challenges or tendencies might appear too abstract or conceptual to bear much of a relation to actual life, Schiller restrains them rather, or holds them in check, in his twelfth letter. There, each challenge is allotted a 'drive':

Der erste dieser Triebe, den ich den sinnlichen nennen will, geht aus von dem physischen Dasein des Menschen oder von seiner sinnlichen Natur und ist beschäftigt, ihn in die Schranken der Zeit zu setzen und zur Materie zu machen ... Der zweite ... den man den Formtrieb nennen kann, geht aus von dem absoluten Dasein des Menschen oder von seiner vernünftigen Natur und ist bestrebt, ihn in Freiheit zu setzen, Harmonie in die Verschiedenheit seines Erscheinens zu bringen und bei allem Wechsel des Zustands seine Person zu behaupten. (*Aesthetic*, pp. 78–80)

The first of these, which I will call the sensuous drive, proceeds from the physical existence of man, or his sensuous nature. Its business is to set him within the limits of time, and to turn him into matter ... The second ... which we may call the formal drive, proceeds from the absolute existence of man, or from his rational nature, and is intent on giving him the freedom to bring harmony into the diversity of his manifestations, and to affirm his Person among all his changes of Condition. (*Aesthetic*, pp. 79–81)

Human life, for Schiller in this portrait, is simultaneously sensual and rational. These impulses coexist within man, both challenging and complementing each other, both in one sense seeking to eliminate the other, but also both potentially balanced by their counterpart. It is for this reason that Schiller characterizes their alternating and complementary interaction as containing the seeds of man's 'accomplished destiny':

Gäbe es ... Fälle, wo er dieser doppelte Erfahrung zugleich machte, wo er sich zugleich seiner Freiheit bewusst würde und sein Dasein empfände, wo er sich zugleich als Materie fühlte und als Geist kennen lernte, so hätte er in diesen Fällen, und schlechterdings nur in diesen, eine vollständige Anschauung seiner

Menschheit, und der Gegenstand, der diese Anschauung ihm verschaffte, würde ihm zu einem Symbol seiner ausgeführten Bestimmung[.] (*Aesthetic*, p. 94)

Should there ... be cases in which he were to have this twofold experience simultaneously, in which he were to be at once conscious of his freedom and sensible of his existence, were, at one and the same time, to feel himself matter and come to know himself as mind, then he would in such cases, and in such cases only, have a complete intuition of his human nature, and the object which afforded him this vision would become for him a symbol of his accomplished destiny[.] (*Aesthetic*, p. 95)

In this vision Schiller positions the 'complete intuition of ... human nature' as lying in the simultaneous operation of what is 'Materie' and what is 'Geist' in each individual, of what is concrete or substantial and what is spiritual or intellectual.[31]

We are now in a position to understand the significance of 'Vernünftelei' in Schiller's analysis of contemporary life. It is the interaction of man's impulse to matter and his impulse to form, which lead to the fulfilment of his nature. Thus 'Vernünftelei', the over-use of the rational or intellectual in one's constitution, represents a kind of deformity or imbalance of man's capabilities. In the portrait of contemporary life under the idol of Utility presented to the reader at the *Aesthetic Letter*'s commencement, therefore, Schiller is characterizing modern life as made up predominantly of imbalanced characters, of one type or another, rather than of harmonious and balanced individuals. The specialized worker's fragmentary existence has been engendered by an over-dominant reason's impulse to specialization. Schiller also characterizes most aspects of lower-class life as representing an over-active sensuous impulse: 'Among the lower and more numerous classes we are confronted with crude, lawless instincts, unleashed with the loosening of the bonds of civil order, and hastening with ungovernable fury to their animal satisfactions.' Contemporary life, for Schiller, has departed so far from its pre-societal harmony that 'two extremes of human depravity' have been 'united in a single epoch' (*Aesthetic*, p. 25).

Quite clearly, Schiller's exposition of the drives coexistent within man tends towards the notion of harmony and the reconciliation of opposite tendencies. We should note, in this connection, that Schiller's figuring of the 'reciprocal action' (*Aesthetic*, p. 95) of the sense-drive and form-drive as the act that might bring about a sense of consummation or destiny, occurs, in his account, by means of a concrete 'object'. Schiller is suggesting that the harmonious development of man's faculties will not necessarily be brought about naturally in contemporary life, but must be re-instigated, or re-prompted, by an external source of some kind.

As one continues to follow Schiller's argument, what this object is becomes more and more apparent. 'Assuming' that complete intuitions of human nature 'could actually occur in experience' (*Aesthetic*, pp. 95–7), Schiller tells us that 'they would awaken in [man] a new drive which, precisely because the other two drives co-operate within it, would be opposed to each of them considered separately and could justifiably count as a new drive' (*Aesthetic*, p. 97). Schiller denominates this third drive the 'play-drive', and describes its activity as follows:

In demselben Masse, als er den Empfindungen und Affekten ihren dynamischen Einfluss nimmt, wird er sie mit Ideen der Vernunft in Übereinstimmung bringen, und in demselben Masse, als er den Gesetzen der Vernunft ihre moralische Nötigung benimmt, wird er sie mit dem Interesse der Sinne versöhnen. (*Aesthetic*, p. 98)

To the extent that it deprives feelings and passions of their dynamic power, it will bring them into harmony with the ideas of reason; and to the extent that it deprives the laws of reason of their moral compulsion, it will reconcile them with the interests of the senses. (*Aesthetic*, p. 99)

The play-drive, by rendering the passions less sensual, and by making the laws of reason less intellectual, will function as a kind of fulfilment of the two impulses by which Schiller initially characterized human life. More precisely, given Schiller's description of its action as taking away powers and characteristics,[32] the operation of the play-drive is at once the annulment and the consummation of what is contradictory in human nature. By exercising the 'Spieltrieb', one is letting both of one's primary tendencies get their way, as it were, at the same time as one is restricting both impulses from becoming over-dominant.

Because we have already seen Schiller's description of this act as the 'accomplished destiny' of human nature, in one sense all that remains in his exposition is to name the object that can set man at play, and that will bring about this more physical intellectualism and more reasoned sensuality. He does this in the fifteenth letter. There, as Schiller summarizes, since the sense-drive concerns itself with life in its widest meaning, and since the form-drive's object is physical matter and its form, the play-drive, as the simultaneous consummation and annulment of these two drives, is directed towards 'living form', or what Schiller immediately explains as beauty (*Aesthetic*, p. 101). The beautiful, the attention to which is the 'consummation' of one's 'humanity' (*Aesthetic*, p. 103), operates as a kind of emancipatory tool for the mind:

Da sich das Gemüt bei Anschauung des Schönen in einer glücklichen Mitte zwischen dem Gesetz und Bedürfnis befindet, so ist es eben darum, weil es sich zwischen beiden teilt, dem Zwange sowohl des einen als des andern entzogen. (*Aesthetic*, p. 104)

Since, in contemplation of the beautiful, the psyche finds itself in a happy medium between the realm of law and the sphere of physical exigency, it is, precisely because it is divided between the two, removed from the constraint of the one as of the other. (*Aesthetic*, p. 105)

By means of the physical and extended sight of what is beautiful, man is 'removed' from his two governing 'constraints' and led to a sort of negative freedom, a temporary deliverance from restraint. That freedom is a suitable classification for the sensation or experience Schiller is describing is made even more apparent as this fifteenth letter progresses. In addition to defending his choice of the term 'play' by categorizing its effect as one of 'expansion' rather than 'limitation' (*Aesthetic*, p. 105), he also asserts that 'man only plays when he is in the fullest sense of the word a human being, and he is only fully a human being when he plays' (*Aesthetic*, p. 107).

Although the 'contemplation of the beautiful' brings about a sensation of 'sensuo-rational ... expansion' (*Aesthetic*, p. 77) for the individual, it should be observed that such an experience is by no means to be enjoyed gratuitously, or idly, in Schiller's scheme. On the contrary, whilst the detail with which Schiller analyses the categories and states we have been examining might lead one to assume that his interest in human life is strictly theoretical, as one reads on from this rhetorical centre of the text, it becomes apparent that the *Aesthetic Letters* are animated by a significant pragmatic edge to their concerns, an interest in real life that connects the precise effects of aesthetic contemplation to the portrait of society with which Schiller began his investigation. By the time one reaches the end of the *Aesthetic Letters*, the aesthetic can only be understood as a sort of politically motivated detour, a recourse to the psychological effects of beauty almost specifically designed to foster development in the material world.[33] Turning to the twenty-third letter, for example, such latent pragmatism is expressed by reference to the theme of education itself, albeit without using the term 'Erziehung', which figures in the text's title:

Es gehört also zu den wichtigsten Aufgaben der Kultur, den Menschen auch schon in seinem bloss physischen Leben der Form zu unterwerfen und ihn, so weit das Reich der Schönheit nur immer reichen kann, ästhetisch zu machen, weil nur aus dem ästhetischen, nicht aber aus dem physischen Zustande der moralische sich entwickeln kann ... Soll er fähig und fertig sein, aus dem engen Kreis der Naturzwecke sich zu Vernunftzwecken zu erheben, so muss er sich schon innerhalb der erstern für die letztern geübt und schon seine physische

Bestimmung mit einer gewissen Freiheit der Geister, d. i. nach Gesetzen der Schönheit, ausgeführt haben. (*Aesthetic*, p. 164)

It is, therefore, one of the most important tasks of education to subject man to form even in his purely physical life, and to make him aesthetic in every domain over which beauty is capable of extending her sway; since it is only out of the aesthetic, not out of the physical, state that the moral can develop ... If he is to be fit and ready to raise himself out of the restricted cycle of natural ends towards rational purposes, then he must already have prepared himself for the latter within the limits of the former, and have realized his physical destiny with a certain freedom of the spirit, that is, in accordance with the laws of beauty. (*Aesthetic*, p. 165)

The experience of freedom aesthetic contemplation engenders in the mind is now equated with moral freedom in everyday life. '[F]reedom of the spirit' renders one 'fit and ready', for freedom in the political sphere. Additionally, since the 'step from the aesthetic to the logical and moral state' is effortless (in comparison to that from the 'physical' to the aesthetic; *Aesthetic*, p. 163), aesthetic contemplation, in Schiller's view, will deliver contemporary man from his deformed condition, emancipating him from his over-dependence on the monotonous sound of the wheel with which he works.

To describe aesthetic freedom as functioning as a kind of moral freedom by example, or by intuition, as Schiller is doing here, must be understood to be a crucial element of his thought not only because it brings his text and its argument full circle, back once again to the concerns and problems with which it began, but also because this feature of Schiller's thought departs significantly from the model that is in many respects the impetus behind the *Aesthetic Letters*, Immanuel Kant's third Critique. The *Kritik der Urtheilskraft* of 1790, or the *Critique of Judgement*, as it is most often translated, goes about exploring the parameters of the aesthetic realm after associating it with 'Urtheilskraft', the power of judgement, which Kant positions between understanding and reason. Since his interest in the aesthetic is a consequence of his investigation into the occurrence of judgements without categories of the understanding as their basis, Kant describes the aesthetic, like Schiller, as a realm of freedom, as a sphere of experience at once free from the concepts of the understanding and from the constraints of reason. Importantly, however, in Kant's thought this idea of freedom is not attached to an idea of morality to anywhere near the same degree as it is in the *Aesthetic Letters*. That a judgement of beauty is pleasurable by virtue of the manner in which it sets our faculties at play (Kant also uses the term 'Spiel' in this context[34]), that it is disinterested, and that it contains no cognitive element, mean that, for Kant, aesthetic judgements are autonomous in relation to the sphere of ethics as well. Whilst it has been demonstrated that the *Critique of Judgement* allows for a development of the connection between the aesthetic and the moral, or that it at least does not explicitly inhibit such a connection, the relationship of these two ideas or areas of intellectual life is by no means a feature of the third Critique in comparison to what we have already seen of Schiller's thought.[35]

It is as a consequence of this significant departure from Kant, as well as of the centrality of moral consciousness to the scheme of the *Aesthetic Letters*, that Schiller's thought might quite plausibly be characterized by this trajectory from the contemplation of aesthetic objects to a kind of psychologically engendered moral awareness, from a specific style of intellectual cultivation to fully realized political and social responsibility. Whereas for Kant the aesthetic realm set man at play and offered the experience of freedom, for Schiller this activity is not only central to all human experience by virtue of the harmony, and thus perfection, it throws over the individual in question, but is also positioned as the remedy to the very problems attendant on highly advanced civilizations that frame his analysis. Moreover, since these were the very same problems that haunted Smith and Ferguson's appreciations of the division of labour, we must also recognize that, in comparison to Kant, Schiller's analysis and priorities represent a significantly more focused investigation of the importance and relevance of the intellectual, contemplative abilities to contemporary life and to the dangers attendant on advanced specialization.[36] Even if we find it in one sense absurd that the concrete problems pertaining to highly specialized societies that Smith and Ferguson identified might be solved by the contemplation of fine art, it is nevertheless the case that Schiller's *Aesthetic Letters* function as a precisely targeted and thoroughly developed argument for the place of the contemplative abilities in contemporary life.[37]

Describing the trajectory and concerns of the *Aesthetic Letters* in this manner, as confronting the priorities and realities of advanced specialization with a portrait of complete humanity conceived in contemplative, intellectual terms, Schiller could not stand further from Bentham, preoccupied as he was with finding means to make labour the mainspring of individual life. For Schiller, a life of manual labour is both a product and an instance of deformed, lopsided humanity. For him, from what we have seen so far at least, fully realized human life would be made up of intellectual exertion, moral decision-making and, almost consequently and inevitably in Schiller's scheme of things, political freedom.

It would be possible, of course, to develop this fundamental opposition or antagonism between the projects of utilitarian education and aesthetic education further, and to point to a whole host of sources and assessments that consider the schools of thought associated with the names of Bentham and Schiller to be absolute opposites, as much in terms of aims as premises. One such example might be the experiences and subsequent thought of John Stuart Mill. Educated along the lines of a strictly utilitarian system thanks to his father's meeting with Bentham in 1808 and their ensuing close acquaintance, Mill was, as Alan Ryan summarizes, 'taught Greek at three, read the Roman historians before he was ten, embarked on logic at twelve and in his early teens learned economics by assisting his father in the composition of his *Elements of Political Economy*'.[38] The well-known result of Mill's adherence to this incredible schedule, as detailed in his *Autobiography* of 1873, was the 'important change' in his 'opinions', accompanied by what is now termed his 'breakdown', which took place in 1826. That Mill describes this experience as being brought about by the intense cultivation of his 'active capacities' at the expense of his 'passive susceptibilities', that it is 'poetry and art' that rescue him from the adverse effects of his upbringing, and that he goes on to apply his experiences to English education in more general terms, describing national educational practices as developing individuals with severely 'limited' 'spiritual' lives, mean that Mill's thought seems to replicate almost exactly the opposition we have been constructing. What was geared entirely towards the labours of 'action' and 'speculation', the intense course of accomplishments suggested by Bentham's thought, needed to be complemented, in Mill's mind after 1826, with the cultivation of more contemplative, ruminative and aesthetic accomplishments, with the kind of attention to fine art we have seen Schiller advocating at such length.[39]

In his *Autobiography* Mill eventually suggests the coexistence of these two strands of instruction in any educational programme. In his 'Inaugural Address' on becoming Rector of the University of St Andrews in 1867, similarly, Mill supplements his account of 'intellectual' and 'moral' education with a 'third division' of what is 'needful' in man, the 'culture' of the 'aesthetic'.[40] Thus an opposition between Bentham and Schiller would seem to be well-founded. For Mill at least, what is aesthetic and what is utilitarian represent two fundamentally different understandings of human nature and of human need, two strands of thought in need of juxtaposition, if not combination, in order to provide adequately for the complete life of any individual. Glancing at Mill's thought would seem to confirm the antagonism of Schiller's emphasis on the contemplative abilities and Bentham's interest in enabling his pupils and inmates to labour effectively and consistently.

Importantly however, to describe Schiller as envisaging what would happen if society were reordered in accordance with his conception of the centrality of the contemplative abilities to human life is to misrepresent, to some extent at least, the development of the *Aesthetic Letters*. Whilst in one sense Schiller's interest in the effects of aesthetic contemplation lies in his hostility towards advanced specialization and its effects on the individual labourer, when one reaches the final stages of his exposition, the portrait of a fully realized 'Aesthetic State' he offers to the reader there is in fact one devoid of any concrete markers of actual change, in comparison to the portrait with which the *Letters* began:

In dem ästhetischen Staate ist alles – auch das dienende Werkzeug ein freier Bürger, der mit dem edelsten gleiche Rechte hat, und der Verstand, der die duldende Masse unter seine Zwecke gewälttätig beugt, muss sie hier um ihre Beistimmung fragen. Hier also, in dem Reiche des ästhetischen Scheins, wird das Ideal der Gleichheit erfüllt, welches der Schwärmer so gern auch dem Wesen nach realisiert sehen möchte[.] (*Aesthetic*, p. 218)

In the Aesthetic State everything – even the tool which serves – is a free citizen, having equal rights with the noblest; and the mind, which would force the patient mass beneath the yoke of its purposes, must here first obtain its assent. Here, therefore, in the realm of Aesthetic Semblance, we find that ideal of equality fulfilled which the Enthusiast would fain see realized in substance. (*Aesthetic*, p. 219)

In this penultimate paragraph of the *Letters*, as Kooy observes, what seems to be being described is a new or different 'attitude to the object at hand', rather than a different style of life or set of occupations of any sort.[41] The 'tool which serves', endowed with rights akin to those of the noblest citizen is, even in this case, still a 'tool' of society. Likewise, whether we choose to read irony in the fact that even if the mind of society needs the 'assent' of the 'mass' to force it 'beneath the yoke of its purposes' in the 'Aesthetic State', it sounds very much as if it will be given; or whether we consider the irony to lie in the fact that such 'assent' will never be given, Schiller's plans for aesthetic education appear to go significantly less against the grain than they did at the beginning of his investigation. The apparently intense antagonism to 'the great idol of our age' with which the *Letters* began seems to have decayed into a pedestrian addition of the idea of 'rights' to ordinary contemporary life.

Utilitarian education and aesthetic education

The *Letters*' final statement will not be of much comfort to the reader who observes this discrepancy either. There, Schiller turns to the question of where 'such a State of Aesthetic Semblance' might be found:

> Dem Bedürfnis nach existiert er in jeder feingestimmten Seele; der Tat nach möchte man ihn wohl nur, wie die reine Kirche und die reine Republik, in einigen wenigen auserlesenen Zirkeln finden, wo nicht die geistlose Nachahmung fremder Sitten, sondern eigne schöne Natur das Betragen lenkt, wo der Mensch durch die verwickeltsten Verhältnisse mit kühner Einfalt und ruhiger Unschuld geht und weder nötig hat, fremde Freiheit zu kränken, um die seinige zu behaupten, noch seine Würde wegzuwerfen, um Anmut zu zeigen. (*Aesthetic*, p. 218)

> As a need, it exists in every finely attuned soul; as a realized fact, we are likely to find it, like the pure Church and the pure Republic, only in some few chosen circles, where conduct is governed, not by some soulless imitation of the manners and morals of others, but by the aesthetic nature we have made our own; where men make their way, with undismayed simplicity and tranquil innocence, through even the most involved and complex situations, free alike of the compulsion to infringe the freedom of others in order to assert their own, as of the necessity to shed their Dignity in order to manifest Grace. (*Aesthetic*, p. 219)

While this expansive and rather tantalizing sentence might be said to develop the idea of 'rights' Schiller has just given us – in the Aesthetic State, we are now told, man will be 'free' from 'the compulsion to infringe the freedom of others in order to assert' his 'own' – it is manifest from the sentence's very first clause that 'every finely attuned soul' and a 'few chosen circles' are not the answers one has been led to expect to the question of where such a State might exist. One cannot ignore the fact that the *Letters*' ambition to educate by the means of fine art, which was expressed as being the answer to the widespread hardships of the lower classes, has decayed to the simple hope that the example of a few will lead a whole community to the realization of its political, moral and intellectual potential. Schiller may be telling us that by working on ourselves, by fostering our own aesthetic capabilities, we are thereby implicitly working for the good of our community at large, as Wilkinson and Willoughby suggest.[42] Yet, by the time one reaches their conclusion, the *Aesthetic Letters* function not so much as a plan for education in the way that Bentham's *Chrestomathia* does, for example, but as a kind of manifesto for the importance of certain contemplative abilities to contemporary life. We might say that the term 'aesthetische Erziehung' should be classified as misleading, when one has read the text in its entirety. The *Aesthetic Letters* may be aimed at engendering the same effects that a system of education founded on the appreciation of the beautiful would, presumably, produce, but they propose the realization of such an aim by means of an infrastructure so sparse, that one can only imagine that the majority of a community would not even be aware of its existence.[43]

Schiller's apparent ambitions, in his final letter, cause the project of the *Aesthetic Letters* to appear in a rather different light than it did previously, when Schiller seemed to be seeking to transform life into the exercising of man's intellectual abilities and attempting, thereby, to bring about political freedom par excellence. What seemed to be a plan for a comprehensive system of education constructed around the state of mind aesthetic objects engender might be said to have become, by the time one reaches the end of the twenty-seventh letter, a plan for ensuring that those who are already interested in art objects realize their power and precise effects. That this is an important transformation, furthermore, that the orientation of Schiller's project in relation to the world he describes at such length is significant, is made absolutely apparent when we consider the relationship the *Aesthetic Letters* hold in both cases to Bentham's thought.

Formerly, Schiller's project could be described as seeking to confer upon the contemplative abilities more prominence and value than they have in contemporary life, as aiming to reorder a life of purely manual or intellectual operations into one of more balanced tendencies and more harmonious developments. In the latter case, after having completed the *Aesthetic Letters*, aesthetic education is to be described as seeking to leave life entirely unchanged except for the addition of a different attitude to what is being done, a different intellectual state in which all the same manual operations are carried out. In this second case, moreover, Bentham's *Chrestomathia*, concerned with turning out young men and women capable of working consistently and effectively thanks to the state of mind they have been taught to value and maintain, might be said to function rather similarly to Schiller's thought. Schiller's project propounds an attitude or a style of contemplation that renders manual labour no longer harmful, or that provides the opposite mental state to physical work so that the individual's exertions are balanced and harmonized. Bentham's educational programme seeks to habituate its pupils to intellectual pleasures, to a world of flowers and beauties, in order to protect them against the dangers of entirely un-intellectual, un-contemplative, manual work. Both might be said to be proposing a specifically tutored species of contemplation in order to disarm manual labour of its threat. Both seem to consider the intellectual, contemplative abilities to be a necessary supplement to a certain kind of work.

Importantly, therefore, in comparison to the debate over the details of man's primary nature we witnessed taking place between Smith and Ferguson, both Bentham and Schiller can be understood to be proposing essentially similar models of a 'second nature' by which commercial society, for all its attendant problems, might continue to function. Although Ferguson's contention with Smith was over the inclusion of commercialism and self-interest in man's primary nature, and although Schiller begins the *Aesthetic Letters* by contending for the primacy of contemplation in human life – that activity ignored by political economy – by the end of Schiller's treatise, such contention has been reduced to a more pragmatic compromise. No longer challenging Smith's model of humanity, Schiller rather ends the *Aesthetic Letters* with the modest assertion that the *Wealth of Nations*' model of human behaviour might be modified so as not to clash with any consideration of intellectual well-being. The decay of Schiller's ambitions in the *Aesthetic Letters* move that work, in other words, into the same vein of writing as that to be found in Book v of the *Wealth of Nations*. Both accept the priorities of commercial society as the ultimate testing ground to any theory of human capability, and both seek subtly to modify capitalist social relations in order to cause the smallest number of problems to the individuals making up that system. That the *Aesthetic Letters* did not commence in that fashion, and that Schiller's project entails a rewriting of Utilitarianism's model of human capability in fundamentally psychological terms, signals that the work is marked by a tension between working within, and working against, the assumptions of political economy.

The opposition between the projects of aesthetic education and utilitarian education can be undermined, therefore, by a consideration of both systems' relationship with political economy, as well as by a consideration of the position and importance they both allot to the contemplative abilities of the mind. For both Bentham and Schiller, the untutored mind, the mind left to its own devices while the body works, is significantly problematic. For Schiller, such a state leads to the lopsided development, or the stunted nature, of one's personality and capabilities, man becoming nothing more than the wheel that he turns. For Bentham, the idle mind is liable either to prey upon itself, bringing about a complete insensibility to the world around it, or to be attacked from without, left to the ravages of an ever-present and multifaceted ennui. Idleness has not only become a psychological category in these two systems of thought: it is a category positioned by both systems as the most central and harmful intellectual state pertaining to contemporary life. To be intellectually inactive, from both the utilitarian and the aesthetic stand-point, is to risk ceasing to be fully human, to risk collapsing into a state more akin to bestiality and incapacity than humanity as these thinkers conceive of it.

Such a comparison could be taken slightly further. We saw Schiller classify being at play as a kind of paradoxical state, a reconciliation of opposite tendencies that is also their consummation, an engagement in which man is at once active and passive, reposing yet more fully alive than when he labours. Bentham's avocation, the state around which the Chrestomathic School was constructed, is a similarly contradictory condition. By harnessing the power of avocation to evade vacancy and ennui, by calling pupils off from their employment every ten minutes, the Chrestomathic programme aims to put its pupils in a state that is work insofar as it is made up of intellectual tasks, and repose to the extent that it is a calling off from business. Such a state is an enjoyable vacation from employment but also toil, a state of repose that is at the same time concretely productive. It is for this reason that Bentham tells us that every activity can be converted into play, if the master is well-acquainted with his task. Chrestomathic education, like Schillerian aesthetic contemplation, will unlock and utilize the terrain of human activity we saw arising from Smith and Ferguson's analyses, therefore – the space between physical activity and passive repose. Both educational projects take this paradoxical middle ground, this state in which man can be described as both active and passive, as the means to solve the problem of the stultifying effects of advanced specialization. In this sense, we might want to describe the internal logic we saw operating in those speculative analyses of the division of labour as being somehow realized, or carried to its next stage, in these two projects. Here, an occupation that is neither physical activity nor passive repose, neither work as Smith describes it nor idleness as Ferguson defines that term, is explored in some detail. Here, the consequences of ignoring this terrain of human experience are fleshed out in both specific and general cases, in the inmate left to prey upon himself for want of any activity to practice, for example, or in the society led to produce stunted manifestations of complete humanity by virtue of its over-reliance on one side of human capability.

We should note, finally, that the fact that one of the developments of the analyses of Smith and Ferguson we have been exploring takes place in Germany does not mean that its discoveries and trajectory become irrelevant to English thought of the succeeding decades. Schiller's thought, on the contrary, which reacts directly to Ferguson's, and which is given its particular stamp by the idealist philosophy out of which it emerges, will, as we shall see, re-enter the English tradition through the writing of the mature Samuel Taylor Coleridge. Yet the relevance of Schiller's inquiry for the style of thought we are exploring here is far from confined to Coleridge's ruminations on the relevance of aesthetic contemplation to British society. As we turn away from Bentham now, we will find that Schiller must always be kept in mind in what follows, since his thought (especially in the opening pages of the *Aesthetic Letters*) will serve as a paradigm for a fully realized appreciation of the importance of aesthetic contemplation, and of idle thought more generally, to human life. By offering a thoroughly reasoned and transcendentally deduced account of the individual's ruminative intellectual abilities, and by connecting these powers succinctly and directly with man's moral life and the political stability of his communities – the theme that preoccupied Smith and Ferguson – Schiller hovers over the English-language thought of this period as a kind of high-water mark of valuing man's contemplative, passive abilities. Further, as we will see now, even though it is not until the second and third decades of the nineteenth century that the *Aesthetic Letters* will have a direct impact on English thought, this does not mean that the parameters of Schiller's reasoning will not be foreshadowed and recreated in the last decades of the eighteenth century.

CHAPTER 3

Cowper, Coleridge and Wollstonecraft

The space between physical activity and passive repose, that terrain of human activity tacitly and internally opened up by the thought of Smith and Ferguson, should not be understood simply to lie unnoticed or unexplored until the philosophical and educational projects of Bentham and Schiller. In a different set of registers and genres, a series of interrelated accounts of human experience and capability, beginning in the early 1780s, probe this territory repeatedly and carefully. Strikingly, this string of accounts of the potency and importance of idle thought seems to be set in motion by a recurrence of the very same logic that operated immanently in Ferguson's writing. In William Cowper's *The Task* of 1784, the most apparent result of the poet's almost unceasing examination of the ideas of employment – tasks – and retirement is the identification of types of occupation or attention that fit neither category. By setting out to consider the boundaries and connotations of labour and idleness, in line with Smith and Ferguson, Cowper must discover the manner in which these terms fail to map on to the range of human engagements his work records. Yet what stands out in Cowper, above and beyond the schematic (and hence in this respect limited) nature of those accounts of the division of labour, is his subsequent exploration of and engagement with the space that is left between employment and retirement. What were necessarily latent in Smith and Ferguson – the logic itself as well as its results – become, at several moments in Cowper, both explicit and manifest.

It was from the moments at which Smith and Ferguson moved closest to positions of self-reflexivity, the moments in which they tried to align their own enterprise with a scheme of national specialization, that the areas outside the realms of labour or rest became most clear. *The Task* can be seen to function in a similar manner. In that work, it is by means of a series of moments of direct self-reflection that the world of non-physical but yet intense activity begins to be revealed to the reader. Such moments of overt self-consciousness, spaced as if at random amid the meandering six-book poem, seem to serve as testing grounds for the poet's knowledge of the parameters and uses of idle contemplation. Indeed, it can seem as if Cowper's confidence and awareness of what happens when one is unengaged by an employment augment during and following each attempt to define the kinds of attention and enjoyment these moments give rise to. The first such moment in the poem, occurring in Book II, 'The Time-Piece', functions by considering the types of tasks pertaining to poetic composition, that activity that one might assume is to be classified as a type of leisure, taking place as it does in Cowper's carefully advertised rural retirement. In turning his mind to the nature of his activity up to this point in the poem, however, Cowper constructs a portrait of poetic labour that is both intricate and protracted, a portrait in which it would not be difficult to identify Ferguson's notion of human satisfaction:

> There is a pleasure in poetic pains
> Which only poets know. The shifts and turns,
> Th' expedients and inventions multiform
> To which the mind resorts, in chase of terms
> Though apt, yet coy, and difficult to win –
> T' arrest the fleeting images that fill
> The mirror of the mind, and hold them fast,
> And force them sit 'till he has pencil'd off
> A faithful likeness of the forms he views;
> Then to dispose his copies with such art
> That each may find its most propitious light,
> And shine by situation, hardly less
> Than by the labor and the skill it cost,
> Are occupations of the poet's mind
> So pleasing, and that steal away the thought
> With such address from themes of sad import,
> That lost in his own musings, happy man!
> He feels th' anxieties of life, denied
> Their wonted entertainment, all retire[.]
> (*Task*, II, 285–303)

By means of the extended, meandering and elaborate second sentence of this quotation, poetic composition, made up of what seem to be individual 'pains' but 'a pleasure' when considered as a whole, is depicted as a task capable of producing a specific effect on the individual who practises it. It is precisely the number and intricacy of tasks needing to be completed in the act of writing poetry (those tasks taking up thirteen almost breathless lines before the reader is delivered from their intricacy by the phrase 'So pleasing') that cause the poet to get 'lost in his own musings' to such an extent that his thought is inhibited from considering 'themes of sad import'. In this state of intense and prolonged concentration and employment, the poet is both protected from 'the anxieties of life' and cast into a state of almost serene self-reflection.

Although Cowper depicts poetic activity as being characterized by an involved and extended manner of employment or concentration at this moment, it should also be observed that he contrasts this portrait, immediately, in his exposition, with the case of the reader of or listener to such poetry:

> Such joy has he that sings. But ah! not such,
> Or seldom such, the hearers of his song.
> Fastidious, or else listless, or perhaps
> Aware of nothing arduous in a task
> They never undertook, they little note
> His dangers or escapes, and haply find
> There least amusement where he found the most.
> (*Task*, II, 304–10)

The tasks Cowper depicted so dramatically are now classified as almost completely invisible to the reader. The 'hearers of his song' are in no position to 'note' the poet's 'dangers or escapes', for example. The intense and complete enjoyment experienced by the poet in the act of composition cannot be said to be transferred to his readers either. They, perhaps, 'find / There least amusement where he found the most'. While this first prominent moment of self-reflexivity in the poem serves to unpack the kinds of intense, arduous and yet pleasing types of mental activity that Cowper practises in rural retirement, it does so at the same time as rendering these processes problematic by virtue of their absolute exclusivity. At this stage in the poem, mental activity is to be understood as potentially taxing and pleasurable, as made up of all kinds of exertions and enjoyments, but as only combining these facets in the case of one, very specific activity.

Turning to the final moment of overt self-consciousness in the poem, one finds the parameters of Cowper's delineation of poetic composition emancipated, as it were, from their reliance on this single type of activity. Book VI's 'Winter Walk at Noon', proceeding by means of a vividly simple account of the landscape surrounding the poet and an equally concise account of the particular condition of his thoughts in this environment, positions intense, productive and satisfying mental activity as being engendered by the landscape itself, rather than being induced by the employment in which the poet is engaged:

> Stillness accompanied with sounds so soft
> Charms more than silence. Meditation here
> May think down hours to moments. Here the heart
> May give an useful lesson to the head,
> And learning wiser grow without his books.
> Knowledge and wisdom, far from being one,
> Have oft times no connexion. Knowledge dwells
> In heads replete with thoughts of other men,
> Wisdom in minds attentive to their own.
> (*Task*, VI, 83–91)

This passage, picked out from the verse surrounding it by its arrestingly ruminative pace, figures the state of mind stimulated by the landscape's intense stillness as one of measured yet potent self-reflection. More precisely, there is a sense, created primarily by the gentle pushing apart and probing of binary terms that is taking place, that the intense experience of nature has somehow reordered the human world here. The heart is now the domain of the useful, tutoring the head, while knowledge and wisdom are spaced so far apart as temporarily to lose all connection. In this inverted existence, likewise, hours are to be experienced as moments.

Whilst the mind experiences a world essentially reconfigured and reprioritized here, it is nevertheless one in which it can still learn, albeit not in the form of discrete items of knowledge. Learning, in this context (and this is stressed for the reader at some length) is to be understood as distinct from, and more reliable than, what is to be gleaned from books, which can deceive, seduce with rhetoric or even bore a reader into acquiescence (*Task*, VI, 98–108). It is nature itself that stands in opposition to the inconsistency and potential deception of book-learning for Cowper. The multiform objects and appearances of the natural world '[d]eceive no student' (*Task*, VI, 114):

> Wisdom there, and truth,
> Not shy as in the world, and to be won
> By slow solicitation, seize at once
> The roving thought, and fix it on themselves.
> (*Task*, VI, 114–17)

The language of reordering and inverting is importantly extended in these lines. Not only is it asserted that what was hard-won from books now actively seizes thought itself, all agency thereby being transferred from the mind to nature, but it must also be registered that such a relationship with the environment represents some sort of withdrawal or displacement from ordinary life, wisdom and truth no longer being shy as they are 'in the world'. This shift, together with its set of reconfigured relationships, seems to be behind the manner in which learning has departed from its connection to books. What can be learnt in this kind of presence of nature is no longer a set of discrete items of knowledge, analogous to the contents of a series of books, but is made up rather of transcendent and universal wholes – wisdom and truth – coming on the mind at once rather than being attained incrementally.

The fact that the end-point of this meditative encounter with the woodland is to be understood as a transcendent sense of self-knowledge or truth, means that it is an end-point, in function as much as genesis, akin to that of Schiller's mode of aesthetic contemplation. For both Cowper and Schiller there is a state in which the individual can be apparently passive, yet engaged in a kind of attention that fully occupies the mind. Further, for both this state is brought about by the pleasurable activity and attention of the subject's senses (here, sight and hearing), but then transports his or her attention to a different sort of knowledge (for Cowper, wisdom and truth). Whilst we will see ways in which other writers in this series of accounts move closer to the exact parameters of Schiller's model of human capability, what we see here in Cowper, in one sense appearing to be the terminus of his investigation of the potency of idle contemplation, should be understood as an important instance of a very similar trajectory of thought. Both figure a certain style of contemplation, engendered almost unconsciously from outside the individual, as giving access to cognitive realms unavailable to ordinary experience.

To consider this woodland meditation scene as the high-water mark of Cowper's ruminations on this potent state of repose, however, is to ignore the influence that another scene of the poem has enjoyed, as well as its resonance within the text itself. The 'brown study' passage, from Book IV, 'The Winter Evening', standing out from the poem as a moment of particularly vivid and perplexing insight, will serve at once as paradigm and starting point for several subsequent explorations of the potency of repose.[1] Importantly, much like the woodland meditation passage, this period of extra-ordinary thought, again in some respects reconfigured as inverted or un-worldly, is instigated more by the particular physical characteristics of the scene encompassing the poet than by his initial state of mind. It is the 'glowing hearth' that sets the scene, 'multiplied / By many a mirrour' (*Task*, IV, 274, 269): 'With faint illumination that uplifts / The shadow to the ceiling, there by fits / Dancing uncouthly to the quiv'ring flame' (*Task*, IV, 274–6). The 'gloom' (*Task*, IV, 278) of this fitful dumb show, marvellously strange but at the same time perhaps disturbingly alien (the meanings most strongly invoked by the adverb 'uncouthly'), matches and 'suits' (*Task*, IV, 279) the poet's mind, ebbing and flowing with the fantastical and the unfamiliar:

> Me oft has fancy ludicrous and wild
> Sooth'd with a waking dream of houses, tow'rs,
> Trees, churches, and strange visages express'd
> In the red cinders, while with poring eye
> I gaz'd, myself creating what I saw.
> (*Task*, IV, 286–90)

That this state of mind is experienced as a form of pleasure for the poet is asserted at the scene's commencement, and reasserted in the clause immediately following this quotation (see *Task*, IV, 272–3, 291). Yet what is perhaps most striking here is the mixture of quite extreme emotional language. A cumulatively powerful effect of agitation, thrown into relief for the reader by terms such as 'ludicrous' and 'wild', and then perplexingly implied by the poet's 'poring eye', is set against the soothing effect of a 'waking dream'. What seems to be taking place here, or in the first three-and-a-half lines of this last quotation at least, is a confrontation between the fancy and the more worldly elements of the scene, which belong to the 'waking' world. And if this confrontation were to be followed up on, it might be said to be taking place between something that soothes and something that enlivens, between agitation and repose. Yet the last line-and-a-half of this quotation has a different effect. There, it is as if we are reassured. Both sides of the preceding opposition are to be understood as part of the same process. The poet is himself 'creating' all that he sees. Significantly then, what was at odds is now defined as being contained within one operation. It is the free play of the fancy we are witnessing, toying with the visual and mental stimuli on offer to it, at once agitating and soothing, pleasurable and disturbing.

It is in reference to the intense and free activity of the fancy that Cowper subsequently classifies this process as entirely unaffected by the 'understanding', the normal cognitive faculty of the individual:

> 'Tis thus the understanding takes repose
> In indolent vacuity of thought,
> And sleeps and is refresh'd. Meanwhile the face
> Conceals the mood lethargic with a mask
> Of deep deliberation, as the man
> Were task'd to his full strength, absorb'd and lost.
> (*Task*, IV, 296–301)

These lines, important in that they have been used as a starting point for critical readings of the poem that treat its idleness more like torpor or inertia (more of which shortly), are also significant for their slightly wider perspective on the kind of activity we have just witnessed. The fancy had been set in motion in the previous quotation, and it can now be added that the understanding was entirely dormant or 'indolent' during this time. Further, such activity, taking place beneath and concealed by the face acting as a 'mask', appeared (to an imagined spectator) to be 'deep deliberation', complete employment by, and engagement with, a task. These lines, therefore, operating in one sense ironically, playfully pull apart the manner in which this fireside state could be characterized as passivity or indolence. If this is lethargy, is it not a lethargy characterized by an intensity of activity, and a vividness of imagery, almost unparalleled in the rest of the poem? Similarly, whilst this may not be a task in the formal sense of the word, is it not an engagement that appears to be at least creative, if not concretely constructive? It is certainly not to be denied, at the very least, that the understanding has been 'refresh'd' by its temporary suspension, but it is apparent that the precise nature of this suspension is still open to question. How is it that the cognitive faculty can be put to sleep, when other parts of the individual remain fully conscious and even intensely at work?

Some sort of answer to this last question is given as this brown study scene comes to a close:

> Thus oft reclin'd at ease, I lose an hour
> At evening, till at length the freezing blast
> That sweeps the bolted shutter, summons home
> The recollected powers, and snapping short
> The glassy threads with which the fancy weaves
> Her brittle toys, restores me to myself.
> (*Task*, IV, 302–7)

Further exploiting the imagery of the homely and the strange, these lines figure what has taken place in this scene as a period of vacation or alienation from the self. The understanding's 'sleep' now appears as a euphemism for its absence, and it is one that stands in for the greater part of the poet himself. Those objects, images and emotional responses that took on such energy and life when animated by the fancy are now put into a new perspective as fragile or insubstantial. They were but 'glassy threads' and 'brittle toys' to be snapped immediately and involuntarily when the concreteness of the world – 'the freezing blast' – reaches the poet. These lines serve not only to define the processes of concentration and suspension at work when the fancy takes over, but to bring out those elements in the original description that were foreign, alien and inhuman. Importantly, they recast this episode in a troubling light. Where Schiller will find man to be moving very close to the perfection of his nature, Cowper considers him disturbingly unlike himself, temporarily absent from his faculties, which, almost uncannily, idly play in his absence.

The opposing currents at work in this episode, this mixture of the creative, the disturbing and the ironic, cannot be said to find their parallel in the responses this section of *The Task* has received in critical writing. Recent responses to the poem most often highlight the irony at work in Cowper's verse. Dustin Griffin, as one example, picks up on the ironic or the playful in the poem to characterize Cowper as proceeding defensively in his assertion that domestic and rural pleasures are made up of all kinds of real activity. He highlights the self-mocking flavour of a phrase like 'studious of laborious ease, / Not slothful' (*Task*, III, 361–2), and observes the ornamental and trivial cast of Cowper's rural tasks – 'weaving nets for bird-alluring fruit' and 'twining silken threads round iv'ry reels' (*Task*, IV, 263–4; note that these tasks occur just two lines before the brown study episode begins). Martin Priestman, in a very similar vein, considers the brown study episode as operating in the main ironically or self-mockingly, finding Cowper to be punning on the appearance of being 'task'd' to 'full strength' and the poem's significantly more serious exploration of a Christian task.[2]

Were one to expect another strand of criticism that foregrounded the creative aspects of the brown study episode, and of *The Task* more generally, one would have a hard time locating it. Yet it would be possible, at least, to imagine a position that might stress what is creative and in earnest in the brown study with no more bias than Priestman and Griffin give to its ironic elements. This positive stance would argue, presumably, that although Cowper erects a kind of defensive coda over the meditative centre of the episode, this secondary perspective, in many ways appearing as an afterthought, should be understood more as modesty or reticence than disavowal. Hence it would attempt to clear the path for the task of picking out those creative and vivid consequences of the fancy's free play. It might then be possible to suggest that Cowper is uncovering something essential, never-before-seen and significantly potent in the field of idle thought.

Despite this conspicuous absence, it is significant that Kevis Goodman does move towards this latter position in her recent *Georgic Modernity and British Romanticism*, illustrating the manner in which Cowper 'tilts' two contemporary discourses – post-Lockean philosophy and the psychology of newspaper reading – towards the new direction of 'creative', proto-aesthetic 'repose' in the brown study. By drawing out the resonances of these two discourses, Goodman also reads the fancy's workings in the brown study as containing a kind of double-edged sociability. Following on from *The Task*'s portraits of 'crazy Kate' and Omai (in Book 1, 'The Sofa'), as well as from the newspaper passage that introduces the brown study, 'indolent vacuity of thought' is, for Goodman, a defence against the strangeness in the 'apprehension of historicity', but a defence that also 'admits the threat it parries'. The 'strange visages expressed / In the red cinders' thus represent the 'world's strangeness' entering through the 'aperture' of normal understanding that Cowper's episode explores. What this means, in Goodman's analysis, is not only that the retirement of the brown study is one allowing for considered reflections on 'history-on-the-move', but also that such distancing is another way in which Cowper's model of idle contemplation generates types of knowledge unavailable elsewhere. Rather than being a style of insight tied to solipsism, however, Goodman opens up the manner in which such contemplation might also be socially, and thus politically, implicated.[3]

These two critical stances on the import of the brown study, then – the one prevalent, the other still largely imagined despite the flexibility of Goodman's reading – are significant for two reasons in this context. First, they replicate the very difference I noted earlier between Ferguson and Cowper: a difference, it will be remembered, between latent and explicit logic, between schematic and more open-minded thought. Hence these positions function as stances on the validity of the logic common to both thinkers. So when Griffin, for example, stresses the ironic elements of the poem, he is putting himself in a position very much like Ferguson's, denying that the terms retirement and employment in any way fall short of an adequate definition of human activity. The imagined positive stance, by contrast, or the version of it that occurs in Goodman, could be seen as emphasizing the gap between employment and repose in its judgement that the state between the two might have unique characteristics and consequences. The first position negates the potential creativity, and the intensity of activity, of the idle mind. The second not only gives access to this intensity – hence Goodman's identification of proto-aesthetic repose – but begins to unfold the ways in which its operations could be explored even more directly. The second position, consequently, would seem to have the potential to distil what was potent, perplexing and disturbing, from the ironic and the defensive, which are nevertheless quite correctly observed by the likes of Priestman and Griffin.

Yet here we reach the second significance of these critical positions. Even if we take the ironic elements of the brown study episode to be opposed to those elements that are more earnest about the creativity of idle thought, it is remarkable that, in the case of 'Frost at Midnight', for example, in many respects the most sympathetic reaction to Cowper's trajectory and style of thought, we encounter a distinct persistence of irony and defensiveness alongside its considerable sincerity. That this persistence lasts over three decades, through several rewritings of one key section of the text, indicates that the apparently separable currents represented by these two positions in fact represent something much more closely linked. The reason it is hard to find positive accounts of the creative elements of the brown study episode, therefore, is that those potent elements, although concretely present, are never entirely separable from the ironic. As we are about to see in Coleridge, the two are bound together for important reasons.

'Frost at Midnight' replicates Cowper's brown study episode in its use of a first person protagonist engaged in a consideration of his 'low burnt fire', the 'sole unquiet thing' in the scene ('FM', and all other versions, 14, 16[4]). This is the context from which the succeeding memories and meditations that make up the last fifty lines of the poem emerge. They rise up from the fire almost physically, as Cowper's 'sooty films' figure 'some stranger's near approach' (*Task*, IV, 292–5). It is Coleridge's delineation of how this fire might reflect and refract the poet-protagonist's thoughts that will need to be rewritten several times, however. In 1798, in the first published version of the poem in quarto pamphlet form, these lines run as follows:

> Methinks, its motion in this hush of nature
> Gives it dim sympathies with me who live,
> Making it a companionable form,
> With which I can hold commune. Idle thought!
> But still the living spirit in our frame,
> That loves not to behold a lifeless thing,
> Transfuses into all its own delights,
> Its own volition, sometimes with deep faith
> And sometimes with fantastic playfulness.
> ('FM', 17–25)

The companionable nature of the fire, the sense (already fleshed out by Cowper's version of this relationship) that its motion amidst such 'extreme silentness' ('FM', and all other versions, 10) makes it analogous with the poet himself, is significantly questioned by the anthropomorphism of the last lines of this quotation. At that moment, such a connection is almost explained away as 'idle' – as if the mind had constructed the relationship for sheer want of anything else to do. This posture of uncertainty on the poet's part functions in a similar manner to the ironic postscript of Cowper's account. It begins playfully to deconstruct the association between poet and fire that is the foundation of the scene's action and argument. Yet in this version of the sentence that makes up these lines, irony does not reign unchallenged. The anthropomorphic logic that acts against the companionship of the poet's mind and the fire is further classified as either operating 'with fantastic playfulness', or, alternatively, as being engendered as if subconsciously by a 'deep faith'. The connection was either constructed in play or with profound, if un-willed, sincerity.

In 1798, then, the problem of whether it is faith or playfulness that brings about the association of the mind and the fire is left unsolved. Irony persists as somehow undermining the thrust of the poem or defending the possibility that the poet is not entirely serious, in this first verse paragraph at least. In Coleridge's next two rewritings of these lines, published in 1808 and 1817, this sense is not significantly counteracted. While the 1808 version that appeared in the *Poetical Register* expands on the manner in which playfulness could have brought about the connection (by 'stealing pardon from our common sense',[5] for example), in 1817 playfulness and accidental profundity seem to coexist more simply, as necessary companions whose alternating action barely merits observation:

> Making it a companionable form,
> To which the living spirit in our frame,
> That loves not to behold a lifeless thing,
> Transfuses its own pleasures, its own will.[6]

It is not until 1829, and the second edition of Coleridge's *Poetical Works*, that the sense and implications of these lines are significantly altered in this respect. The final version of this sentence that appears there runs as follows:

> Methinks, its motion in this hush of nature
> Gives it dim sympathies with me who live,
> Making it a companionable form,
> Whose puny flaps and freaks the idling Spirit
> By its own moods interprets, every where
> Echo or mirror seeking of itself,
> And makes a toy of Thought.[7]

This version of the sentence elides the poles of 'playfulness' and 'faith' into an interpretive act that takes place through the 'idling' Spirit's 'own moods'. Thus irony and faith are no longer set against each other. Indeed, the possibility has now arisen that the two could be experienced simultaneously or in compound form, for interpretation seems to be taking place through more than one mood at once. So if the irony of previous renderings can be traced in the clause 'every where / Echo or mirror of itself', it must be observed that this phrase also serves to carry the identification of the fire and the Spirit into the language of the sentence itself. The clause, attached definitively to neither the 'idling Spirit' nor the 'film' that 'flutters' on the 'grate' ('FM', and all other versions, 15–16), describes rather their shared physicality. More obviously, 1798's 'idle thought' has been reclassified as 'the idling Spirit', 'Thought' now being just a 'toy'. Thus in recalling Cowper's distinction between the fancy and the understanding the 1829 text draws closer affinities between the movement of the fire and the state of the poet's mind. The two are not just companionable, they seem to be connected directly and physically.

The effect of these last changes is that the 1829 text posits a greater level of affinity between the poet's mind and the physical movement of the fire. It is an effect achieved by the suppression of those ironic and playful elements that seemed to broach the possibility that such a connection was all an illusion, that the poet was not entirely in earnest. That this possibility was no accidental occurrence, however, that it was in some way an important element of what was being depicted for the first three decades of the poem's life, is supported by one of Coleridge's slightly earlier depictions of the potency of idle contemplation, the first published version of what was to become 'The Eolian Harp': 'Effusion xxxv'.[8] Composed in 1795 and first published the following year, this poem bears similarities with 'Frost at Midnight' in its setting of a 'world *so* hush'd' except for the 'stilly murmur of the distant Sea', which 'Tells ... of Silence', and the 'soft floating witchery of sound' of the harp itself ('Effusion', 10–12, 20). In this environment of sensual presentness, for the reader is also told of the 'exquisite ... scents / Snatch'd from yon bean-field' ('Effusion', 9–10), the poet conjures an image of himself (at 'noon' rather than during the 'eve' ('Effusion', 7) at which the poem commences[9]) simultaneously in repose and in a state of exalted agitation:

> And thus, my Love! as on the midway slope
> Of yonder hill I stretch my limbs at noon
> Whilst thro' my half-clos'd eyelids I behold
> The sunbeams dance, like diamonds, on the main,

> And tranquil muse upon tranquillity;
> Full many a thought uncall'd and undetain'd,
> And many idle flitting phantasies,
> Traverse my indolent and passive brain
> As wild and various, as the random gales
> That swell or flutter on this subject Lute!
>   ('Effusion', 26–35)

In this passage, as in the brown study, ideas of indolence and passivity are confronted by an imagery of intense, dancing movement. Insofar as the poet's mind is being stimulated into movement by spontaneous, 'uncall'd' thoughts, in turn allowed to pass over the mind, this portrait also functions in a similar manner to Cowper's fireside scene. It is as if the mind is set at play when the poet ceases to control it consciously.

Yet whereas the scenes that took place in the brown study and Coleridge's version of that space in 'Frost at Midnight' were characterized by the poet's aloneness, (the sleeping state of the poet's son in the latter not impinging on the sense of solitariness in the poem's first verse paragraph), this passage from 'Effusion xxxv' is marked, in the re-telling of it we are witness to at least, by the presence of Coleridge's 'Love', Sara. It is not just this paragraph that is directly addressed to her, for the poem itself begins 'My pensive SARA!' and goes on to describe her physical presence alongside the poet, reclining on his arm and watching the clouds with him ('Effusion', 1–9). Sara's presence in the text goes beyond the roles of just watching, sharing and listening, however. Importantly, she lives up to her initial characterization as 'pensive', as she is revealed to have been 'thinking' during the poem's action (and re-telling of its action) in a manner very different from the poet. As Coleridge draws out the implications of his experience of 'idle flitting phantasies' on his 'passive brain', Sara is shown to have reached a different conclusion:

> And what if all of animated nature
> Be but organic Harps diversly fram'd,
> That tremble into thought, as o'er them sweeps,
> Plastic and vast, one intellectual Breeze,
> At once the Soul of each, and God of all?
> But thy more serious eye a mild reproof
> Darts, O beloved Woman! nor such thoughts
> Dim and unhallow'd dost thou not reject,
> And biddest me walk humbly with my God.
>   ('Effusion', 36–44)

The notion that the particular type of mental activity experienced by the poet might be representative of a more universal relationship with the world, that it might be a key to understanding the spiritual bonds pertaining to all of 'animated nature' and reveal a 'plastic' and 'vast' God-like force, is challenged in these lines by means of an unspoken but immediate 'reproof' from Sara. And if one was to think that the relative force of the assertion and the reproach might be rather unbalanced, that the poet's tentative 'And what if' were in any way over-reacted to by the darting reproof, 'mild' as it is, one would have this sense supported in the next verse paragraph. There the 'flitting phantasies' that seemed so full of possibility and life are viewed in a different light: they are the 'shapings of the unregenerate mind, / Bubbles that glitter as they rise and break / On vain Philosophy's aye-babbling spring' ('Effusion', 47–9). This final paragraph of the poem recasts the experience that seemed central to the poem's scheme and existence as flimsy and vain in no uncertain terms, therefore. Just as the state that shared the vividness of 'sunbeams' and 'diamonds' has become 'Dim and unhallow'd', the poem's engagement with the potency of idle contemplation has decayed into an almost miserable apology for presuming to go beyond praising 'him' who let the poet 'possess / PEACE, and this COT, and THEE, heart-honour'd Maid!' ('Effusion', 55–6). It is as if the only effusion allowed by this second perspective were one of thanks to God, 'who with his saving mercies healed' the 'sinful and most miserable' poet ('Effusion', 53–4).

That this is not the way in which the poet-figure is characterized until this point in the poem, that the final verse paragraph jars in its agenda and perspective with the rest of the text, is evidence that, much like the brown study and 'Frost at Midnight', this 'Effusion' is marked by two conflicting currents or opinions of its own subject matter. The earnest, engaged and positive first two-and-a-half verse paragraphs are opposed by the defensive and apologetic final paragraph and a half. It is as if Coleridge were backing down, pointing out that he did not entirely mean it, or that even if he did, he was wrong: that even if such a state of contemplation exists, it does not have the power and implications it appeared to have at the time. Moreover, unlike the case of 'Frost at Midnight', this current in the 'Effusion', associated strongly with Sara in the poem as it is, remains almost entirely unaltered in all subsequent editions.[10]

Cowper's brown study was marked by its almost simultaneous assertions and denials of the power of idle thought. These two examples of Coleridge's verse also tread the same fault-line between the earnest and the defensive. It is as if there were a danger attached to the complete engagement with the creativity of the idle mind, as if, for example, the fluidity and anarchic movement of the poets' fires threatened to undermine the solidity of their identities, or somehow to reconstitute them in its own shifting image. One such possible danger is foregrounded most effectively by recent new historical readings of 'Frost at Midnight' that seek to reconsider the received idea of the poem as entirely detached from contemporary political debates and divisions. Paul Magnuson and Judith Thompson both read politics back into the poem by reference to a host of contemporary sources that might seem unconnected to it at first glance. Thompson, most successfully, considers 'Frost at Midnight' to be part of Coleridge's ongoing conversation with John Thelwall about the various means to effect political reform. In this scheme, the 'dead calm' ('FM', 50) of the poem's third verse paragraph has troubling overtones, implying as it does that the speaker has wilfully withdrawn from the politics and interests of active life and become not just dangerously passive and introverted, but somehow 'dead' to the world.[11] In terms of the poem's first paragraph, this sense could also be registered in the '[i]naudible' nature of the 'goings on of life' ('FM', and all other versions, 12–13) and in the phrase 'Abstruser musings' ('FM', and all other versions, 6), implying, perhaps, a style of thought abstracted from the concerns of the world beyond the poet's rural retirement.[12]

But the dangers that seem to dog the speaker's complete valuing of the power of idle thought seem to be of another kind as well. Returning to Cowper's brown study, what is perhaps most notable is the disturbing or perplexingly strange flavour of events there. The fire 'dancing uncouthly' and 'by fits', the 'Pendulous and foreboding' 'films that play upon the bars' (*Task*, IV, 292–3), the manner in which the duration of the fancy's free play is considered as a temporary alienation or absence from the self: these considerations cast the scene in a dangerous, perplexing and almost supernatural light, as if what was being accessed here was not simply the powers of the idle mind, but another unworldly and shadowy existence unconditioned by the solidity of the waking world.

In Coleridge, it is apparent that the undercurrent of what disturbs or troubles is of a similarly almost sensually perplexing kind. In 'Frost at Midnight', the poet's 'solitude' does not seem to be understood as a comfort or a blessing, for example. Just as the other 'inmates' of his 'cottage' have 'left' him to his 'solitude' ('FM', and all other versions, 4–5), implying that it was not necessarily requested, the peace itself cannot be said to function in an entirely positive manner for the poet either: ''Tis calm indeed! so calm, that it disturbs / And vexes meditation with its strange / And extreme silentness' ('FM', and all other versions, 8–10). Further, as Cowper's experience in the brown study is considered as somehow an excursion out of, and alienation from, the self, the thoughts that emerge from Coleridge's fire and make up the poem's second paragraph also seem to function as a kind of escaping from, or overstepping of, his identity. Cowper's connection between the 'films' of the fire and 'some stranger's near approach' (*Task*, IV, 293–6) becomes, in 'Frost at Midnight', the memory of an eager longing to see 'the stranger's face'.[13] In the memories that constitute this verse paragraph, the 'fluttering' film seems to invoke the idea of the other, of what is not the self but somehow 'companionable' to it, and thus casts the speaker outside himself, leaving him searching for a figure to attach on to, a solid identity to return to: 'For still I hoped to see the stranger's face, / Townsman, or aunt, or sister more beloved'.[14] In this instance, of course, the terrain between self and other, or self and elsewhere, is made even more treacherous by the identity of the last figure in this list of possible objects of identification for the self – the poet's sister and 'play-mate when we both were clothed alike'.[15] The second verse paragraph ends as the self is confronted with the possibility of identification with the figure most similar to it (in appearance and blood) but also necessarily (and perhaps most precisely) distinct from it. Where Cowper eventually returned to himself, albeit by a perhaps violent process of snapping 'threads', Coleridge's speaker seems to be on the verge of settling elsewhere, of being cast out of himself never fully to return. Yet this transmigration is never fully realized. The speaker's longing for the self that is at once himself and not himself is not satisfied. As the next paragraph's change of perspective makes clear, this quandary or temptation, if that is what it was, was only ever taking place in a dream-like past tense, unable to impact upon the present of the poem.[16]

The dangers present in 'Effusion XXXV' could be said to carry similarly troubling overtones. The poet's 'idle flitting phantasies', for instance, seem to be characterized, at a second glance, by something other than creativity. They are 'wild', 'various' and 'random', they 'swell or flutter' and act on the mind to make it 'tremble into thought', and consequently their categorization as 'uncall'd and undetain'd' seems to draw out their dangerous unpredictability. They seem to bring with them the possibility of the mind being blown away, rapidly reshaped or somehow physically altered. The poet's mind does not seem capable of detaining something this frighteningly unstable that causes it to 'tremble' between this world and an undefined elsewhere.[17]

From the perspective of these troubling, dangerous and barely defined elements, it is possible to characterize the ironic elements of Cowper and Coleridge's scenes as some sort of defence against the possibilities this type of idle thought seems to contain. Detaching the ironic from the earnest would seem to risk releasing the poet into a world of anarchic and fitful movement unconnected with everyday concreteness, a world in which the self would stand no chance of containing itself or maintaining its stability as an independent entity. The processes of idle thought are dangerous not only by virtue of their separation from the political sphere; they are also so because of the intense types of physicality they offer. In Cowper's terms, if such a style of thought was more than a temporary absence from the self, the self might cease to hold its cognitive solidity – 'a soul that does not always think' (*Task*, IV, 285) might become a soul that never did.

We should also note, in this connection, that there is another dimension to the reticence Cowper and Coleridge display about engaging with the exact parameters of idle thought that is not a feature of the physical dangers attendant on that process. Taking the case of the 'Effusion', Coleridge's eventual disavowal of the importance of his 'flitting phantasies' can also be explained by the notion of guilt. The 'Effusion' describes how Coleridge lies in complete repose, stretching his limbs 'at noon', not even caring to control his mind consciously. The poet then offers a brief, tentative extrapolation from this state, connecting 'all of animated nature' to the sensations he is experiencing in such a state of inertia. The fact that this model of animated life provokes Sara's scorn might be said to characterize leisure itself as problematic. The poet is not to base a universal theory of life on sensations engendered by leisure and relaxation because such a lack of activity is not a moral, positive activity in its own right. It is as if the poet's very lack of control over his physical and mental states, his complete repose, renders him unworthy of judging the world. Much like Ferguson's characterization of repose as a temporary suspension of human powers, Sara Coleridge's reminder of the blasphemy of the poet's suggestions defines leisure as an amoral state unworthy of being the basis for any wider understanding. Following Coleridge's observation would seem to lead to a life of inactivity that would be as amoral as it would be unproductive.

In addition to depicting the physical dangers of idle contemplation, the 'Effusion' thus enacts a set of fears about the value of repose in its dramatization of Sara's response to the poet's suggestions. Leisure, ceasing to control one's mind consciously, would appear to be both amoral and the object of guilt. 'Frost at Midnight' can be read in a similar way. In the poem's second verse paragraph, the poet's 'Idle thought' becomes the memory of the young Coleridge's 'schoolboy days' ('FM', 28). Familiarly, the poet depicts his younger self gazing upon a fire's 'bars' ('FM', 30) and becoming lost in the ruminations such movement stimulates. This experience continues the morning after the 'hot fair-day': 'And so I brooded all the following morn, / Awed by the stern preceptor's face, mine eye / Fixed with mock study on my swimming book'.[18] Here again the state of mind the young poet describes seems to be one lacking conscious control. The 'book' on which he should be concentrating 'swim[s]' in and out of focus as his mind broods on other matters. Here again also this style of repose becomes an object of guilt. The 'stern preceptor's face' forces the young poet to resume the appearance at least of attention and study.

Following this pattern in Coleridge, it is possible to identify something similar in *The Task*. In the brown study Cowper begins his account of the relative operations of his various faculties with the following observation:

> Laugh ye, who boast your more mercurial pow'rs,
> That never felt a stupor, know no pause
> Nor need one. I am conscious, and confess
> Fearless, a soul that does not always think.
> (*Task*, IV, 282–5)

The rhetoric of this statement is intriguing. On the surface of things Cowper is modestly noting his inferiority to those whose 'powers' are matched to their abilities, who 'know no pause, / Nor need one'. Yet the fact that this 'confession' leads into the intensely creative centre of the brown study episode (line 286 continues 'Me oft has fancy ludicrous and wild …') means that Cowper is also undermining those who have 'never felt a stupor'. Having 'a soul that does not always think', after all, opens up the kind of aesthetic, creative and transcendent capabilities we have already witnessed, for both Cowper and Coleridge. This 'confession' is thus to be understood as double-edged. Cowper's idle contemplation is both an object of guilt and the cause of a certain distinction.

The subtlety of Cowper's treatment of this notion of guilt allows us to identify something particular about the way it operates in these texts. The guilt associated with idle thought, and the type of leisure that is ceasing to control one's mind consciously, seem to force the protagonists of these moments to assert some use, or some justification, for these experiences. Coleridge's extrapolations concerning 'all of animated nature' strive to fulfil this function, as does the level of creativity implied in the brown study. For both poets the guilt of the pervasive repose attendant on idle thought is to be balanced by some consequence, or product, otherwise unavailable. We have already seen one aspect of this justification and we will have occasion to see another presently.

The influence of Cowper's brown study is not confined to the kind of meditative poetry that deals with the world in a very similar manner, and from an almost identical perspective, to *The Task*. Indeed, neither is such influence confined to those figures broadly in sympathy with Cowper's project in the brown study. When Anna Letitia Barbauld wrote her poem 'To Mr. S. T. Coleridge' (*c.* 1797), for instance, which warns Coleridge of what she saw as the false attractions of 'mystic visions' and 'deep philosophy' ('Coleridge', 8, 21), she did so by way of enough reference to Cowper to render her poem partly a re-reading of the brown study at Coleridge's expense. For Barbauld, the Coleridge of the late 1790s lies benighted and entranced, 'Midway the hill of science', where a gothic grove of 'tangled mazes' boasts 'strange enchantment' ('Coleridge', 1, 3, 4). And importantly, for Barbauld, the paradoxically productive category of idle contemplation, which Coleridge had already explored in 'Effusion xxxv', was as much a mirage as this grove's 'huge shadows'.[19] The latter –

> stretch
> And seem realities; while things of life,
> Obvious to sight and touch, all glowing round,
> Fade to the hue of shadows.
> ('Coleridge', 10–13)

These lines, and the imagery of Barbauld's poem as a whole, function by similar means to those of Cowper's 'Winter Walk' and brown study. Barbauld's grove is a site at which everyday hierarchies are inverted, where what is 'obvious' becomes shadowy and what is shadowy seems reality, in the same way that Cowper inverted knowledge and wisdom in the 'Winter Walk', and productivity and idleness in the brown study. Here, however, such inversion serves to characterize the Coleridgean grove as significantly deceptive. For Barbauld frames this description as the observation of the poet's 'cheated sense' ('Coleridge', 9). Thus, in these lines, what 'seems' stands at an important distance from what's 'obvious'. The stretching of 'huge shadows' is a trick of light and location, a function of this 'strange' grove, rather than an insight into the secret hierarchy of objects.

In addition to parodying *The Task*'s motif of the inversion of binary terms, Barbauld's poem must also be understood to allude to the brown study directly and verbally. The poem's portrait of 'Indolence', for example, which is personified into a central figure in Barbauld's narrative, is the occasion for more sustained engagement with Cowper's verse:

> Nor seldom Indolence these lawns among
> Fixes her turf-built seat, and wears the garb
> Of deep philosophy, and museful sits
> In dreamy twilight of the vacant mind,
> Soothed by the whispering shade
> ('Coleridge', 19–23)

The brown study is clearly in Barbauld's mind, here. The 'dreamy twilight of the vacant mind', for example, might serve as a description of the setting of Cowper's scene in general terms, but it is also one that seems to refer to that poet's 'waking dream' and 'unthinking mind', albeit in slightly modified terminology. Indolence's posture similarly recalls that of the poet in the brown study, again in subtly altered terminology. Where Cowper wore a 'mask / Of deep deliberation', Indolence 'wears the garb / Of deep philosophy', both appearances functioning to deceive any spectator as to the import of such inactivity. And this pattern of replicating Cowper's phraseology and line breaks extends to the last line of this quotation. As Cowper was 'Soothed with a waking dream', Barbauld's Indolence is 'Soothed by the whispering shade' – the word 'Soothed', like the phrase 'Of deep', placed in its Cowperian position.

The effect of these subtle allusions is to parody the valorization of idleness that takes place in the brown study. Indolence, here, cheats the sense in the same way that this grove's shadows are rendered more substantial than its 'things of life'. Here, in other words, a mask of deep deliberation is indeed only a mask, for the idle individual is one who has been seduced by the 'dubious shapes' ('Coleridge', 4) and false appearances of the grove. It is important to observe, however, despite Barbauld's significant negativity concerning the priorities and possibilities of idle contemplation, that her address 'To Mr S. T. Coleridge' nevertheless renders engagement with the seeming possibilities of idle thought, that which characterized Cowper's 'Winter Walk' and Coleridge's 'Effusion', as a necessary stage in the path to useful and correct knowledge. It is in this grove, namely, that 'each mind / Of finer mould', 'In its progress to eternal truth / Rests for a space in fairy bowers entranced' ('Coleridge', 25–6, 27–8). And it is here that each mind, when 'entranced' –

> loves the softened light and tender gloom,
> And, pampered with most unsubstantial food,
> Looks down indignant on the grosser world
> And matter's cumbrous shapings.
> ('Coleridge', 29–32)

From Barbauld's perspective, then, Coleridge's tentative effusion 'And what if all of animated nature ...' was the 'indignant' product of 'unsubstantial food'. The term 'cumbrous shapings', here, recalls, in this connection, Sara Coleridge's 'shapings of the unregenerate mind'. And the connection is an important one. Fusing the features of the brown study and the 'Effusion', the 'tender gloom' and the repose 'on the midway slope / Of yonder hill', Barbauld's poem might be described as an extension of the position Sara holds in Coleridge's poem. For both figures, the seductions of idle thought lead to the misidentification of priorities and to false conclusions (shadows seeming realities; man's relationship with God being akin to a harp's with the breeze). And thus it is that for both, the possibilities implied by idle thought are to be discarded. For Sara, Coleridge must instead 'praise' him 'Who with his saving mercies healed' the poet; for Barbauld, Coleridge must move through this grove and to the next resting place of intellectual development, where 'Active scenes' will 'with healthful spirit brace' his 'mind' ('Coleridge', 38–9).

Barbauld's 'To Mr S. T. Coleridge' thus offers a very different reading of Cowper's brown study than the one Coleridge would produce in 'Frost at Midnight', as well as a reading of the 'Effusion' opposed to the role Coleridge himself occupies in that poem. The effect of Barbauld's stance is to render idleness a problematic category, a kind of morbid indulgence in a shadowy world of mysteries. Yet it is noticeable that we have already observed the manner in which 'Frost at Midnight', the 'Effusion' and the brown study all pay significant attention to Barbauld's style of contention in their own terms. That this was the role of irony, of Sara or of reticence in those texts already signalled the way in which depictions of idle thought were open to inversion in the manner of 'To Mr S. T. Coleridge'. What is perhaps most striking about Barbauld's poem, therefore, is the influence exerted by the brown study even on a figure disinclined to follow its tentative positivism. In much the same way that the brown study sets down the terms of Coleridge's investigations into idle thought, at this stage in his career, it also seems to set down the terms of that category's rejection. Those terms revolve around exploring, and enhancing, what was macabre, uncouth and uncanny in the brown study.

The influence of the brown study can also be registered further afield than a series of poetic responses to Cowper's poem, however. Mary Wollstonecraft's travel memoir, for example, *Letters Written during a Short Residence in Sweden, Norway and Denmark* (hereafter *Short Residence*), published in 1796, is in many ways the most important example of Cowper's wider influence. It is a work in which the landscapes encountered and described by the narrator seem to engender thoughts with strikingly similar tendencies, and with intriguingly comparable results, to Cowper's. Just as Cowper's fireside scene raised the possibility of being most intensely alive when one is most detached from the world, for Wollstonecraft, as we will see now, the Scandinavian landscape conjures an intensity of thought, and a clarity of emotion that is similarly precarious.

Wollstonecraft's *Short Residence*, part of a long tradition of female travel writing in the eighteenth century,[20] also contains a kind of implicit reference to Rousseau's *Les Rêveries du promeneur solitaire* (*The Reveries of the Solitary Walker*), first published, posthumously, in 1782. Rousseau's 'walks', in one sense functioning like *The Task*, depict idle contemplation as operating in a sphere removed from the physical constraints of the world. Considering his 'body' as nothing but 'a trouble' or 'an obstacle' from which he must 'disengage' himself in order to let his thoughts flourish and prosper,[21] Rousseau also casts his reflections in the language of leisure and employment. The idle contemplation he is free to practice in exile from society figures, in his reveries, as a kind of synthesis of the two.[22] For Wollstonecraft, the position of Rousseau's narrator is both liberating and problematic, however. His withdrawal from society, and the reveries such a position gives access to, seem to offer a unique perspective from which human priorities and schemes of happiness can be thoroughly questioned and explored (as indeed they are in *Short Residence*), and yet Rousseau also represents a style of thought troublingly solipsistic. The narrator of the *Reveries* seems to consider his solitude as more than simply a tool with which to consider society and the practice of human life within and outside it. Solitude is also a divine blessing in Rousseau's mind, raising the narrator above and beyond his former community, so that he is a world unto himself, untouchable by those beneath him, and in no way in need of their good opinion or civil behaviour towards him. In this respect it is important to note, as Mary Favret has done, the manner in which Wollstonecraft both 'echoes, then corrects' the egotism of the *Reveries*. Personal, inviolate contemplations are contained within, and opened up by, their framework as letters to a friend.[23]

Wollstonecraft's *Short Residence*, in one sense representing an odd juxtaposition of quotidian detail and high-flung flights of fancy, figures (by means of this jarring contrast) the grand, sublime and picturesque landscapes that inspire such moments as a window onto a world of concerns distinctly removed, but not thereby detached, from the everyday.[24] In one of the first of these moments that punctuate the text, the 'rapture' the narrator feels on encountering the 'rude beauties' of a bay serve to emancipate her from the emotional effects she is still experiencing after witnessing the 'horrors' taking place in France.[25] The scene, in which 'the sublime often gave place imperceptibly to the beautiful', has the effect of 'dilating the emotions which were so painfully concentrated', and renewing the type of emotional responses it was formerly natural for the narrator to make:

> How silent and peaceful was the scene. I gazed around with rapture, and felt more of that spontaneous pleasure which gives credibility to our expectation of happiness, than I had for a long, long time before. I forgot the horrors I had witnessed in France, which had cast a gloom over all nature, and suffering the enthusiasm of my character, too often, gracious God! damped by the tears of disappointed affection, to be lighted up afresh, care took wing while simple fellow feeling expanded my heart. (*Short Residence*, p. 247)

The manner in which 'care' departs on the wing figures what is taking place in this moment as a kind of evacuation of everyday realities. Wollstonecraft's emotional world is reordered by the visual experience on offer to her. While this scene depicts the landscape as in some sense bringing thought and emotion home, however, causing the narrator to sever her thoughts from France and enjoy the simplicity and peace of the bay itself, it should be observed that Wollstonecraft's moments of landscape-inspired contemplation do not always have this exact effect.

A little further on in this first letter, indeed, the reader is presented with an account of the Scandinavian twilight that seems to have the opposite tendency:

> Nothing, in fact, can equal the beauty of the northern summer's evening and night; if night it may be called that only wants the glare of day, the full light, which frequently seems so impertinent; for I could write at midnight very well without a candle. I contemplated all nature at rest; the rocks, even grown darker in their appearance, looked as if they partook of the general repose, and reclined more heavily on their foundation. – What, I exclaimed, is this active principle which keeps me still awake? – Why fly my thoughts abroad when every thing around me appears at home? My child was sleeping with equal calmness – innocent and sweet as the closing flowers. – Some recollections, attached to the idea of home, mingled with reflections respecting the state of society I had been contemplating that evening, made a tear drop on the rosy cheek I had just kissed; and emotions that trembled on the brink of extacy and agony gave a poignancy to my sensations, which made me feel more alive than usual. (*Short Residence*, p. 248)

This paragraph, by building on the idea of the type of thought that is homely and the type that departs elsewhere, presents this style of idle contemplation as troubling or perplexing in a manner reminiscent of the ideas we have already encountered. That Wollstonecraft's thoughts 'fly abroad' from a scene that seems so at home, that her emotions tremble between 'extacy and agony', that these effects result in her feeling 'more alive than usual': these are the parameters of idle thought wavering between creativity and sensual anarchy delineated by Cowper and Coleridge. Such a comparison indeed picks out the calmly sleeping child common to both Wollstonecraft and Coleridge, a figure that serves to incarnate what is quintessentially homely in this context. Yet whilst 'Frost at Midnight' would not appear in print for another two years, in Wollstonecraft's succeeding paragraph it becomes apparent that she has Cowper very much in mind at this point.[26]

It is as a kind of commentary on, or explanation of, the emotional responses of this first paragraph that Wollstonecraft proceeds:

What are these imperious sympathies? How frequently has melancholy and even mysanthropy taken possession of me, when the world has disgusted me, and friends have proved unkind. I have then considered myself as a particle broken off from the grand mass of mankind; – I was alone, till some involuntary sympathetic emotion, like the attraction of adhesion, made me feel that I was still a part of a mighty whole, from which I could not sever myself – not, perhaps, for the reflection has been carried very far, by snapping the thread of an existence which loses its charm in proportion as the cruel experience of life stops or poisons the current of the heart. (*Short Residence*, pp. 248–9)

The phrase 'snapping the thread' brings Cowper's excursion out of himself in the brown study strongly to mind here. Although Wollstonecraft's meaning is different – Cowper's vacation from the self was ended by the snapping of fancy's threads, while Wollstonecraft's thread ties her to life and hence will not be snapped here – the effect of the allusion is to cast a similar light over Wollstonecraft's reverie. Thus one of the ways in which this second paragraph explains the first is by defining the mental state of the narrator there as somehow outside herself, flying abroad in a fit of trembling emotion. The second paragraph's commentary, 'I was alone ...' characterizes this movement as one away from the ties of fellow-feeling, the bonds between mother and child, and the sense of repose shared by both the animate and inanimate objects in the scene, towards an undefined world of anarchic emotion.[27]

The notion that this paragraph functions by allusion to Cowper's brown study is supported by a slightly later passage in *Short Residence* that also uses the idea of 'snapping' a train of thought, and that also seems to function within the parameters and terminology of that fireside scene. In 'Letter XVIII', as the narrator arrives in Copenhagen in the aftermath of the city's fire of 1795, her reaction to the devastation takes the form of a kind of failed reverie:

The depredations of time have always something in them to employ the fancy, or lead to musing on subjects which, withdrawing the mind from objects of sense, seem to give it new dignity: but here I was treading on live ashes. The sufferers were still under the pressure of the misery occasioned by this dreadful conflagration. I could not take refuge in the thought; *they suffered – but they are no more!* a reflection I frequently summon to calm my mind, when sympathy rises to anguish: I therefore desired the driver to hasten to the hotel recommended to me, that I might avert my eyes, and snap the train of thinking which had sent me into all the corners of the city, in search of houseless heads. (*Short Residence*, pp. 319–20)

In these lines again, whilst Cowper's scheme of thought cannot be superimposed directly onto Wollstonecraft's to reveal an exact match, the terminology in use here is reminiscent of the brown study. For Wollstonecraft, the operations of the 'fancy', instigated by the physical characteristics of the scene, would normally lead one away from the concreteness of the world and withdraw 'the mind from objects of sense', even though they are prevented from doing so here. Likewise, it is as if the description of that process summons its corollary action in the narrator's mind. Although she has not experienced an excursion out of herself on this occasion, she must 'snap the train of thinking' in order to put an end to the episode even in its unfulfilled form.[28]

Considering another of the more successful flights of fancy engendered by the physical landscape in the *Letters*, we will see that the motif of an excursion out of the body and away from the world of sense is not particular to these moments alone. In 'Letter XV' Wollstonecraft relates her experience of a waterfall near Fredericstadt with remarkably similar effects:

Reaching the cascade, or rather cataract, the roaring of which had a long time announced its vicinity, my soul was hurried by the falls into a new train of reflections. The impetuous dashing of the rebounding torrent from the dark cavities which mocked the exploring eye, produced an equal activity in my mind: my thoughts darted from earth to heaven, and I asked myself why I was chained to life and its misery? Still the tumultuous emotions this sublime object excited, were pleasurable; and, viewing it, my soul rose, with renewed dignity, above its cares – grasping at immortality – it seemed as impossible to stop the current of my thoughts, as of the always varying, still the same, torrent before me – I stretched out my hand to eternity, bounding over the dark speck of life to come. (*Short Residence*, p. 311)

In this moment, one of the letters' last examples of this style of thought, the idea of the mind's movement outside itself, or vacation from itself, is given its most vivid portrayal by virtue of the image of the 'cataract'. With the same intense consistency of the waterfall, 'always varying, still the same', the narrator's 'thoughts' dart 'from earth to heaven', while her 'soul' rises 'above its cares', towards 'immortality' and 'eternity'. Here again this process carries perplexing or dangerous overtones. The narrator's reaction is both 'tumultuous' and 'pleasurable' (the latter not fully cancelling out the troubling nature of the former). It is also the case that the soul's movement is defined as feeling as unstoppable as the waterfall itself. In this respect it is striking that the paragraph ends inconclusively – 'I stretched out my hand to eternity, bounding over the dark speck of life to come' – while the succeeding one returns immediately to the quotidian details of the journey. In this instance the unworldly elements of the narrator's mental reaction to the scene cannot be contained. The possibility that such a style of thought might never cease, that Wollstonecraft might never fully return to herself, seems to be left open.[29]

If one takes this problem as significant however, it needs to be remarked that in this instance it is anticipated before the passage in question even begins. The narrator's account of the 'cascade' is introduced by the following reflection, instigated by a general account of pine forests: 'I cannot tell why – but death, under every form, appears to me like something getting free – to expand in I know not what element; nay I feel that this conscious being must be as unfettered, have the wings of thought, before it can be happy' (*Short Residence*, p. 311). The waterfall of the subsequent paragraph clearly functions in one respect as a reworking of this idea with more particularity. The soul's even temporary movement away from the body is to be understood as a movement towards freedom and happiness. But such an explanation does not remove the aspect of the uncanny or the unnerving in Wollstonecraft's description of her own reaction. It is as if, in this case, the lack of an ironic postscript, of a playful backing down telling us that the soul cannot escape the body in this manner, is what troubles her account. Wollstonecraft shows how the soul is to be taken out of the body towards an undefined elsewhere (into 'I know not what element'), but does not show or conjecture what might happen when the thread that connects the two is snapped. Perhaps most perilously, she does not seem concerned by this omission and the undefined space it leaves.

The passages of Wollstonecraft's letters that deal with her encounters with the Scandinavian landscape, therefore, are to be understood as functioning in line with, and by reference to, the dangerous emotional and sensual anarchy Cowper discovers at the site of idle contemplation. While Wollstonecraft is less reserved about the power of these moments than either Cowper or Coleridge, her accounts of them do not evade the impression that what is being flirted with has the potential to reform the individual in its own barely defined image. It is Wollstonecraft's embracing of this possibility that carries the danger in her account. It is as if she were travelling solely in order to find the most suitable site to evaporate into this ethereal, anarchic world untouched by the problems of life.

This sense is important in the scheme of the letters more generally. As Harriet Guest observes, there are moments towards the end of the narrative at which Wollstonecraft offers a sort of recontextualization of her flights of fancy from the more urban, and hence more worldly, locales of Denmark and Germany. In these moments Wollstonecraft attempts to rewrite or reinterpret what was taking place earlier in the narrative as a kind of fantasy of identification with the landscape, motivated (implicitly as it were) by disaffection with the commercial nature of everyday life.[30] This latter perspective of the letters posits that even where the narrator's accounts seem most detached from the worldly realities that surround them, they contain a constant embedded reference to the problems of commercial progress and, perhaps even more importantly, the ongoing course of the French Revolution.

It is noticeable, however, that in one sense this secondary, revisionary perspective is superfluous or tautologous. Looking again at those moments of identification with the landscape we have already encountered one notices that, simultaneous to their occurrence, inside the bubble of their experience, is the very type of consideration this secondary perspective attempts to add on. In the case of the northern twilight, it is at the rhetorical climax of the passage that we encounter the following: 'Some recollections, attached to the idea of home, mingled with reflections respecting the state of society I had been contemplating that evening, made a tear drop on the rosy cheek I had just kissed.' In the case of the narrator's encounter with the waterfall, similarly, we find the climax of the scene, again expressed in the form of a rhetorical question, to be inseparable from the 'misery' of life: 'I asked myself why I was chained to life and its misery?' Whilst Wollstonecraft eventually suggests that she had, in these early letters, 'retired from man and wretchedness' and 'left behind' all her cares 'when lost in sublime emotions' (*Short Residence*, p. 343[31]), it seems more true to characterize these concerns and considerations as central to those 'sublime' experiences themselves. In the case of the waterfall, for instance, the emotional intensity of the moment could be said to offer a clearer insight into the nature of being chained to such 'misery'.

If we were to consider this relationship between escapism and worldly concern in the light of Schiller's thought, of course, it might be possible to offer an explanation for their connection. For Schiller, aesthetic experience, by providing a realm of unbounded freedom for the mind to enjoy, sets the mind at play so that the individual in question, being now balanced and in harmony, is ready to turn to any type of activity or decision-making with equal success. It is by means of this argument that Schiller posits the moral and politically constructive effects of aesthetic contemplation, the aesthetic realm functioning as a kind of detour from political reality that serves to effect moral awareness. In terms of Wollstonecraft, therefore, the intense experience of nature, akin to aesthetic contemplation in the same way that Cowper's woodland meditations were, could be seen to bring about a type of knowledge unconnected to the natural world itself. When, in the northern twilight scene, the narrator's 'reflections respecting the state of society' emerge at the scene's epiphanic centre, it is as if they have been conjured by the particular state of mind the landscape has cast over Wollstonecraft. We should note that the narrator is, at this moment, like Cowper and Coleridge above, in one sense in a state of pervasive repose, but in another intensely alive with trembling emotions. By replicating the parameters of Schiller's aesthetic contemplation, these scenes also seem to replicate the production of a type of knowledge unconnected to the sensual stimuli that characterize them. Wollstonecraft's experience of nature could be said to bring about types of knowledge about commercial society and the individual's connection to it, involuntarily and almost unconsciously.

What stand out particularly in an attempt to describe this process however, are the general terms in which Wollstonecraft leaves these insights. Just as she barely goes beyond the vagueness of the phrase 'Some recollections' in the first example, in the second, the conditions or vexations of life appear only as 'life and its misery'. Her intense encounters with the Scandinavian landscape may serve to stimulate knowledge of her relationship with the world, 'the idea of home' or 'the state of society', but the reader is not privileged with the content of these pieces of knowledge, at the moment of their conception at least. So while the possibility remains that all the observations on commercial society found in the letters come from this source, it is more likely that Wollstonecraft is simply loath to dilute the rhetorical effect of her flights of fancy with the details of the reflections they prompt.

Yet we should remember, in this connection, that Coleridge seems able to draw out the implications of his idle contemplations and the types of reflections they inspire in him, even in the midst of the texts we have been considering. While in 'Effusion xxxv', for example, lines 36–40 ('And what if all of animated nature …') expand on the type of knowledge the speaker's contemplation has stimulated, positioning this material as central to the poem's development, the case of 'Frost at Midnight' is slightly more complicated. There, in one sense, the memories and reflections that constitute the poem's last three paragraphs are all prompted by the poet's contemplation of the flames of his fire. After making the visual connection of the grate's bars at the beginning of the second paragraph, the poem moves from theme to theme as if by association. In another sense, however, Coleridge's various descriptions of the 'idling Spirit' offer an image of the poet's mental state that brings one part of his subsequent thoughts most strongly to mind. In the 1829 text, for example, the phrase 'every where / Echo or mirror seeking of itself' seems to anticipate, by its imagery of endless reflection and refraction, the argument of the poem's penultimate paragraph, where Coleridge returns to the consideration of his sleeping son. In that passage, the poet contrasts his own upbringing with the one he anticipates his child will receive:

> For I was reared
> In the great city, pent 'mid cloisters dim,
> And saw nought lovely but the sky and stars.
> But thou, my babe! shalt wander like a breeze
> By lakes and sandy shores, beneath the crags
> Of ancient mountain, and beneath the clouds,
> Which image in their bulk both lakes and shores
> And mountain crags[.][32]

In these lines, just as the 'idling Spirit' was understood as somehow its own mirror, reproducing and replicating its own image everywhere around itself, the world that will teach the young Hartley Coleridge will constantly reflect parts of itself in every one of its constitutive objects. More precisely, there is a sense in these lines that by reflecting those parts, the 'lakes' and 'shores' and 'crags' imaged in the 'clouds', something greater will be implied, that Hartley will need to abstract something more general from these particular elements.

This sense is followed up upon in the passage's next clause:

> so shalt thou see and hear
> The lovely shapes and sounds intelligible
> Of that eternal language, which thy God
> Utters, who from eternity doth teach
> Himself in all, and all things in himself.[33]

The individual elements being reflected in each natural object are to be understood as particular 'shapes and sounds' of an 'eternal language', therefore. The endless refraction of the 'idling Spirit' is figured in these lines as an entire world or system made up of its own ceaseless reflections. Importantly, however, this language of objects and sounds is only given meaning, as it were, by the ongoing operations of 'God'. What is being communicated by each element is a moral code, delineating both how each object relates to every other ('all things in himself'), and how each object implicitly refers to a higher purpose or reality ('Himself in all').[34] Educated by the presence and attributes of objects such as these, the poet's son will receive a moral education above all else.

The similarities between this section of the text and the description of the idle mind's operations privilege this theme within the poem. The shared physicality of the fire and the poet's mind seems to engender these reflections on the physicality of the natural world as it is ordered by God. In this sense it should be recognized that 'Frost at Midnight' functions very much in line with 'Effusion xxxv'. For Coleridge, the operations of the idle mind necessarily stimulate thoughts concerning the place of the individual in a world ordered by God. In the 'Effusion' those thoughts appeared too unorthodox for Sara to leave unchallenged, but the addressee of the penultimate paragraph of 'Frost at Midnight' is not yet able to object. This outcome of idle contemplation is also related to the notion of guilt we picked out in the poems. Positioning an awareness of God's relationship with the objects and inhabitants of the world as being stimulated by the process of idle contemplation serves to define that operation as purposive and useful. 'Frost at Midnight' is thus to be seen as balancing the guilt associated with the repose of idle thought with the moral insight such a state gives access to.

This connection between idle contemplation and the moral order of the world has another important resonance. Wollstonecraft's flights of fancy functioned in a manner reminiscent of Schiller's aesthetic contemplation, and Cowper's woodland meditations invoked types of knowledge unavailable elsewhere. We can now say that Coleridge's association of idle thought and moral awareness seems to stand even closer to Schiller's exact trajectory of thought than either of these two models. Where Schiller found the free play of the individual's faculties to be the key to unlocking his or her potential as a moral (and hence a political) being, Coleridge too finds the image of moral consciousness in the workings of the idle mind. The model of the mind as an 'organic Harp' swept by God's intellectual breeze to be found in the 'Effusion', the ceaseless operations of the 'idling Spirit', everywhere its own mirror: these models function most insistently as patterns of the individual's moral sense, as physical, internal intuitions of the connections to be made between men, and between men and objects. In Coleridge's scheme, therefore, when the individual ceases to control his or her mind consciously, he or she is given access to an exact likeness of the world's moral order, an image that corresponds unerringly to the relationships between all objects, animate and inanimate. Just as Schiller found a model of, and a training for, moral freedom in the state of mind the individual enters when encountering fine art, Coleridge uncovers our moral condition in the manner in which we react to the sensual presentness of the world. For both, idle contemplation and its intense, uncontrolled mental activity serve to engender a distinct and purposive moral consciousness.[35]

Whilst Coleridge and Schiller can be aligned in this manner, it needs to be kept in mind that what is different about the string of accounts of the potency of the idle mind we have been exploring, when compared to Schiller's overt valuing of idle contemplation, is the danger they position at the very site of the individual's experience of this type of repose. It is in this sense that Cowper's brown study resonates down this line of enquiry. That episode's carefully woven path between the disturbing and the creative, the anarchic and the potent, and the ironic and the earnest, sets not just the tone, but the parameters of Coleridge and Wollstonecraft's subsequent investigations of idle thought. When Coleridge uncovers the paradigm of morality in the individual's encounter with the sensual details of the world, he does so with full acknowledgement of, and in thorough reference to, the risks of such a state. In this sense, poetic activity, or understanding the landscape with sensibility for Wollstonecraft, are depicted as activities that court a kind of alien, anarchic danger in order to retrieve types of knowledge unavailable elsewhere. The individual may profit from such an experience, in the discourse that structures this string of accounts, but he or she runs the risk of being reconstituted in the image of a barely defined, chaotic elsewhere. And while this space may be understood, or conceived of, by means of the imagery of nature (winds, flames, water and so on) – an imagery that might represent what is homely and safe elsewhere – here it is deployed in such a manner as to draw out, consistently and deliberately, what is most fitful, random and foreboding in such terms.

In this respect this series of enquiries must be understood at first to anticipate, and then to echo Schiller's thought, which positioned idle contemplation as the central activity in human life by virtue of the access to moral freedom it made possible. The kind of internal, intense, sensually perplexing activity Cowper and Coleridge show the individual engaging in, a type of experience very close to Schiller's model of idle contemplation, also bears an important relationship with the sublime experiences of nature Wollstonecraft charts. What was 'uncanny' in the brown study and Coleridge's reconstruction of that scene, the manner in which the individual trembled between this world and an undefined elsewhere in those moments, the fitful and foreboding imaginings of the world outside of the speaker: these aspects of what was taking place must be understood to render these episodes as a kind of domesticated sublime experience. The narrator of the 'Effusion' and the protagonist of Wollstonecraft's *Short Residence* both experience a type of encounter in which the grandeur, vastness and intricacy of the natural world at first confront and astound the individual, but then set him or her at play following an identification with, or a thinking beyond, such power or detail. The fireside scenes we have been examining are 'uncanny', therefore, insofar as the same power and magnitude seem to be accessible in the very space most often characterized as homely, safe and contained. Idle contemplation, in the terms of this string of accounts, is both powerful and perplexing, potent and disturbing, no matter whether it is to be experienced in the face of the natural world, or engendered by what is most familiar and quotidian.

To connect this string of accounts in this manner is, importantly, to draw out the manner in which they might all be described, like Rousseau's solitary walks, as reveries. In all these cases, the individual's mind, set at play by the physical parameters of the scene around it, is led, almost involuntarily, to reflections of a significantly wider nature. It may be because we have already encountered Schiller's thorough and focused analysis of this type of phenomenon that we are in a position to pick out the kind of moral sentiments that all these reveries seem to privilege. We must also recognize that, in comparison to the writing of Smith and Ferguson with which we began, idleness is as much a psychological category in these accounts as it was in the thought of Bentham and Schiller. What is different about these accounts in this respect is also significant, however. Where it was possible to read Bentham and Schiller as eventually both working within the parameters of political economy, and thus as writing in the same vein as Book v of the *Wealth of Nations*, it is conspicuous that Cowper and Coleridge offer a fundamental challenge to Smith and Ferguson's models of human nature. Man, in their accounts, is a fundamentally contemplative being, one to whom the area of intellectual life ignored by Smith and Ferguson is of central importance. Moreover, the insight into moral consciousness brought about by such contemplative activity serves to prove this assertion. Social and political consciousness is not to be sought, for Cowper and Coleridge, in man's role in a division of labour, or in a wider economy, but by a careful consideration of the interactions between men and the world in a psychological and spiritual sense. The knowledge to be gleaned from such observation does not offer a model of a 'second nature' with which to balance economic society, as Schiller and Bentham's treatises do, but rather challenges the primary bases of Smith's economic man. If man is fundamentally contemplative, and if he moves towards his moral perfection by performing such contemplative, aesthetic abilities, then organizing society in terms of manual labour, in a system that devalues and restricts ruminative activities, must lead to the degradation of humanity. Cowper and Coleridge's accounts thus depict Smith's human nature, as well as Bentham and Schiller's 'second nature', as false models of human capability.[36]

Furthermore, that it was a reconstruction of the logic of the division of labour that led these enquiries to proceed in the manner they did enables us to say something more precise about the conditions of these reveries themselves. What was latent in the analyses of Smith and Ferguson became somehow explicit and manifest in Cowper's verse. This development suggests that the meditative poetry and prose we have been examining functions, and indeed flourishes, in the wake of such political economy, by taking on exactly the private, individualistic and psychologically interior perspective that was necessarily invisible to the nationwide and schematic stand-points of Smith and Ferguson. What was ignored by those political economic inquiries, the space of interiority or the reality of being alone with oneself, the very terrain that was briefly and accidentally opened up in Smith's individualistic illustrations, can be said to have been necessarily placed in opposition to the discourse of political economy by the very act of its omission.

To describe *The Task* as functioning by means of a similar logic to the analyses of Smith and Ferguson is, therefore, to highlight the manner in which this string of accounts exploits the particular and the individual, those elements which were most problematic to progress by the rules of the division of labour. That *The Task* and the accounts that follow it should do so alongside a convincing and sustained identification of the dangers attendant on the individual's private reflections, moreover – that the psychological category of idleness should be rendered significantly threatening and troubling even in its positive, creative manifestation, in these accounts – means that we should characterize the English thought that anticipates Schiller's inquiry as proceeding even further than he does along the path of understanding the individual's contemplative, idle abilities. In this sense Cowper, Coleridge and Wollstonecraft articulate the connection between the ruminative, the aesthetic and the moral in even more vivid, precise and thorough terms than Schiller does in his *Aesthetic Letters*.

CHAPTER 4

Coleridge's *Pantisocracy*, Biographia *and* Church and State

While Cowper's brown study stands over the string of accounts we have just explored, foreshadowing their rhetoric and setting down the terms in which their fears are to be articulated, to consider Coleridge's thought more generally, as we are to do now, is to encounter a system that seems repeatedly to address, discuss and concern itself with the parameters of idle thought in a whole range of different ways. Thus Cowper's role as an anchor or as a mooring point for Coleridge's ruminations in 'Frost at Midnight' is not one Coleridge turns to very often. Rather, in the years leading up to 'Effusion xxxv' and 'Frost at Midnight', in the various tales and explanations that make up the *Biographia Literaria*, and in the carefully thought-out delineations of *Church and State*, Coleridge can be seen to be developing and staging a conception of poetic capability that departs significantly from Cowper's terminology. The model of poetic activity that emerges from these discussions may be apt to be aligned with the concerns opened up in 'Effusion xxxv' and 'Frost at Midnight', but is also one that leads to a range of concerns markedly distinct from these poems, and that is deployed in a range of radically different contexts, with widely differing objectives.

Although not the most tangible result of Coleridge's acquaintance with Robert Southey, the scheme for 'emigration on the principles of an abolition of individual property' (*Letters*, Vol. 1, p. 94) that arose out of the two young poets' discussions of Rousseau, Godwin, Hartley and Priestley in 1794, is nevertheless significant insofar as it serves to isolate several of the trends in Coleridge's thought that become more pronounced as his career progresses.[1] 'Pantisocracy', as Coleridge christened the plan, was to take place on the banks of the Susquehanna River in northern Pennsylvania, and would be made up of a 'small but liberalized party' of twelve couples (*Letters*, Vol. 1, p. 96), who would labour, according to Thomas Poole's summary, for two to three hours a day: 'The produce of their industry is to be laid up in common for the use of all, and a good library of books is to be collected, and their leisure hours to be spent in study, liberal discussions, and the education of their children.'² If Poole's delineation of the plan made it sound both organized and practicable, however, it should be observed that Southey's version of this combination of activities was rather more haphazard: 'When Coleridge and I are sawing down a tree we shall discuss metaphysics: criticise poetry when hunting a buffalo, and write sonnets whilst following the plough.'³

The simple yet high-flung principles of the scheme, a kind of combination of Poole's composure and Southey's enthusiasm, were matched by the hopes entertained for its effects. Coleridge announced that the 'leading Idea of Pantisocracy' was 'to make men *necessarily* virtuous by removing all Motives to Evil – all possible Temptations' (*Letters*, Vol. 1, p. 114). The plan was to eradicate 'physical Evil' from this miniature society by the removal of any possibility of 'moral Evil' (*Letters*, Vol. 1, p. 154). But for Coleridge this basic premise was also a significant sticking point. After discussing Pantisocracy for '*six* hours' with Dr Thomas Edwards and a Cambridge 'counsellor' named Lushington one evening, Coleridge considered them totally convinced, recording for Southey their declaration of the scheme as 'impregnable'. A paragraph later in this same letter, however, Coleridge is rather more candid with the tactics he used in this discussion:

– But, Southey! – there are *Children* going with us. Why did I never dare in my disputations with the Unconvinced to *hint* at this circumstance? Was it not, because I knew even to certainty of conviction, that it is subversive of *rational* Hopes of a permanent System? (*Letters*, Vol. 1, p. 119)

Children, according to Coleridge's exposition, threaten the Pantisocratic community by the 'prejudices and errors of Society' with which they are already '*deeply* tinged'. Whereas adults have felt the 'ill consequences of their errors' and are thus prepared to attempt living on a different plan, children could not be guaranteed to 'enter into' the '*motives*' of the scheme, as 'repeated experience' has not given them the conviction that things could be otherwise (*Letters*, Vol. 1, pp. 119–20). Moreover, if the moral condition of the children taking part in the plan threatened to undermine its coherence, once embarked on this line of thinking Coleridge did not seem convinced that the case was that different for the adults. Whilst he had campaigned to Charles Heath that all adult members of the scheme were 'highly charged with that enthusiasm which results from strong perceptions of moral rectitude' (*Letters*, Vol. 1, p. 97), to Southey in the wake of this six-hour discussion, he suggested that all 'members of our Community' should be 'incessantly meliorating their Tempers and elevating their Understandings' (*Letters*, Vol. 1, p. 119). The almost frantic tone of these comments, rapidly following the account of Edwards' and Lushington's conversion as they do, gives the impression that, for Coleridge at least, the Pantisocracy would stand or fall on the characters of those participating in it.

What Coleridge suggests to Southey, in order to ensure the character of the female Pantisocrats at least, is 'to be strengthening' their 'minds' and 'stimulating them to literary Acquirements' (*Letters*, Vol. 1, p. 119). Reading and study are to secure the 'moral rectitude' of the community's members, and the success of the community itself. This rather surprising solution to the problem of the potential fallibility of the Pantisocracy, equating as it does morality, good conduct and literary talent, can be explained by reference to what Coleridge says about himself at this time. Two weeks after the six-hour conversion and the account of it given to Southey, Coleridge offers a synopsis of his own vices and virtues, to his brother, the Reverend George Coleridge, in significantly more fatalistic terms:

> There is a Vice of such powerful Venom, that one Grain of it will poison the overflowing Goblet of a thousand Virtues. This Vice Constitution seems to have implanted in me, and Habit has made it almost omnipotent. It is INDOLENCE! ... Like some poor Labourer, whose Night's sleep has but imperfectly refreshed his overwearied frame, I have sate in drowsy uneasiness – and doing nothing have thought, what a deal I had to do! (*Letters*, Vol. 1, p. 125)

To equate vice so explicitly with indolence, and to depict both as so 'implanted' in himself as to obtain omnipotence, serves, amongst other things, to explain the moral attraction of the Pantisocracy for Coleridge. If, as Southey would have it, the Pantisocrats were to be writing sonnets while following the plough, and criticising poetry while hunting buffalo, then they would be unavoidably virtuous by the intensity of their activity. To envisage a society made up entirely of intellectual acquirement and manual labour is, for Coleridge at least, to envisage one as morally constructive as it would be physically productive. While it is only 'indolence' and 'doing nothing' that equate to vice, literary activity, in Coleridge's mind, need never be understood as a kind of leisure, even if we might consider this its primary significance. It is for this reason that in the Pantisocracy, the habits acquired from literature were to be complemented, in the months leading up to their departure, by more manual accomplishments: 'In the course of the winter those of us whose bodies, from habits of sedentary study or academic indolence, have not acquired their full tone and strength, intend to learn the theory and practice of agriculture and carpentry' (*Letters*, Vol. I, p. 97). The Pantisocracy was to be characterized by the combination of academic and manual productivity, and would achieve its value by the essential productivity and (thus) morality of these tasks.

Coleridge's suggestion that in preparation for their emigration the female Pantisocrats supplement their skills with literary acquirements thus serves not only to highlight the dual nature of the activities that would take place in Pennsylvania, but also positions literary activity as holding a very similar status to manual labour, in terms both of morality and of productivity. Coleridge's arguably indulgent portrait of himself as 'Like some poor Labourer' would be realized in the Pantisocratic community. The simile – offering physical labour for literary labour, bodily activity rather than mental activity – would become reality. There Southey's metaphysics and composition would be tasks directly comparable with hunting and ploughing. There Coleridge's indolence – and thus vice – would be an impossibility, when what Poole had characterized as their 'leisure' would be as constructive as their 'industry'.[4]

The high-flung hopes Coleridge held for the Pantisocracy, and the thorough manner in which he went about analysing the principles on which it would be constructed, should not be understood to characterize all his expressions of Pantisocratic enthusiasm from this period, however. In a poem that appeared in the *Morning Chronicle* in December 1794, Coleridge positioned the Pantisocratic promise within a scene melodramatic enough to risk collapsing into comedy.[5] 'Address to a young Jack Ass & it's [*sic*] *tethered* Mother' is made up of the poet speaking to the 'Poor little Foal of an oppressed Race' ('Address', 1),[6] commiserating him on his fortunes, and eventually inviting him into 'the Dell / of high-soul'd Pantisocracy' ('Address', 27–8). What is immediately apparent, in this set-piece, is the opposition between melancholy passivity and a kind of frolicsome, intense activity that is enacted in its progression. The animals are characterized, in the first instance, by their dismal and stationary situation. Just as the foal's 'languid Patience' is what initially attracts the speaker and instigates its address, its mother is 'Chain'd to a Log upon a narrow Spot / Where the close-eaten Grass is scarcely seen, / While sweet around her waves the tempting Green' ('Address', 16–18). At the other end of the poem, when Coleridge pictures the change in the foal's fortune that its inclusion in the Pantisocratic community will bring, the contrast is so striking as to be almost ridiculous:

> Where Toil shall call the charmer Health his Bride,
> And Laughter tickle Plenty's *ribless* side!

> How thou would'st toss thy Heels in gamesome Play
> And frisk about, as Lamb or Kitten, gay –
>
> ('Address', 29–32)

While melancholy passivity has been transformed into 'gamesome Play' here (a state given overtones of quite ungainly enthusiasm by lines 29 and 30), the presence of 'Toil' and 'Health' should also be observed, personified as they are into fellow Pantisocrats. The Pantisocratic community promises to render the labour that the foal's 'moping head' anticipated ('Address', 8–11) no more, and no less, than a compatriot, a fellow citizen with whom to enjoy oneself. Pantisocracy, in this vision, will transform all life's 'Aches' and 'Misery' into 'Joy' and 'Plenty' ('Address', 11, 10, 34).

A comparable but more complicated emphasis on activity, health and joy, is to be found in a poem Coleridge sent to Southey three months before the 'Jack Ass' and rather more serious in tone. The untitled sonnet, the octave of which was later incorporated into the *Monody on the Death of Chatterton*,[7] again stages a kind of before-and-after effect of the establishment of a Pantisocratic community. In the first of these states, the speaker's 'Visionary Soul' is shown to 'dwell / On Joys, that were!', and likewise 'endure to weigh / The Shame and Anguish of the evil Day' with only forgetfulness as a consolation.[8] In the second state, by contrast, after travelling over the 'Ocean swell' (4), the speaker has reached a 'Dell / Where Virtue calm with careless step may stray' (5–6), and where the 'moonlight Roundelay' will be danced in celebration (7). Quite clearly, these lines juxtapose a kind of stagnant motionlessness (represented by a vocabulary of dwelling and enduring) with movement that is both unfettered and spontaneous ('careless step', 'Wizard Passions' (8)). Yet it is to be noted, given all that we have seen of the Pantisocracy so far, that Pantisocratic life is not characterized at all by labour in these lines. Whilst movement is contrasted with inertia, neither state includes any kind of toil or work.

Such difference of emphasis is no doubt a function of the different tone of the sonnet as a whole, when compared to Coleridge's other Pantisocratic writings. The poem ends, for example, with the supposition that after the Pantisocratic transformation of the poet's life, 'Eyes that have ach'd with Sorrow' will, somewhat surprisingly, 'weep' (Sonnet, 9):

> Tears of doubt-mingled Joy, like their's who start
> From Precipices of distemper'd Sleep,
> ...
> And see the rising Sun, & feel it dart
> New Rays of Pleasure trembling to the Heart.
>
> (10–11, 13–14)

What is being worked through and worked out here, it would seem, is the emotional condition of the speaker, his inner life and how the Pantisocracy will affect it. Yet this different and rather more sombre approach has a number of significant effects on the theme of Pantisocracy in the sonnet. First, it serves to position 'doubt' and 'distemper'd Sleep' at the exact point where the virtues of the scheme are being celebrated. By casting a kind of shadow over such celebration, moreover, the low-key or doubt-ridden nature of the sestet also functions to sandwich the Pantisocratic 'Roundelay' between two distinctly melancholy sets of lines. This construction, importantly, is complemented by the nature of the 'Roundelay' itself. Taking place by 'moonlight' and being performed by the 'Wizard Passions' to 'weave an holy Spell' (Sonnet, 8), it would seem to be a struggle to see the whole event as anything other than a kind of magical fantasy scene. It is as if, in the context of the lines that appear before and after it, the Pantisocracy is nothing more than an escape from emotional life. The sonnet as a whole, therefore, renders the Pantisocratic community flimsier than in any of the other sources we have encountered. From this more emotional or personal perspective, the scheme becomes a dream vision, an attempted panacea that somehow never seems to be expected to be completely effective.

What is remarkable about these two poems would seem to be the doubts they write into the Pantisocratic promise. While this effect is achieved in the first case, in the 'Address to a young Jack Ass', by means of melodrama, by rendering the whole scheme so ridiculous as to be almost nonsensical, in the second case, in the sonnet, it as if emotional reality engulfs the scheme, causing it to appear flimsy and magical in comparison to an agenda of real life, 'Shame and Anguish'.[9] These two poems complicate the premises and parameters of the Pantisocracy, therefore, and the effect of their doing so is to undermine, to some extent at least, the systematic seriousness Coleridge established in his letters to Southey and others. The project that aimed at moral perfection and the blissful integration of labour and leisure begins to appear as no more than the product of youthful enthusiasm, from the perspective of this poetry, as what would in fact offer an escape from reality rather than reorder real life on a new plan.

Although this latter perspective proved decisive, in terms of the actual realization of the Pantisocracy, it is nevertheless the case that the scheme's emphasis on the similarities of literary and manual labour, on work as a moral activity that answers the emotional problems of everyday life, is one we will see significantly built upon and echoed as Coleridge's thought progresses.[10] It should be borne in mind in what follows, consequently, that in every picture of the realization of the Pantisocracy scheme, life was to be characterized by activity above all else. Subsistence and leisure were both to be made up of essentially kindred labours that, according to Coleridge's exposition at least, would prove at once morally and physically productive.

Turning to the *Biographia Literaria*, one is struck by a similarity of terminology in that almost every judgement and discussion presented to the reader in this later work seems to be founded on an opposition between activity and passivity.[11] Coleridge's elongated rejection of the philosophy of John Locke and David Hartley (whose systems render the mind a passive recording device of various stimuli and influences), his explanation of the mind as like a 'water-insect' (acting 'by alternate pulses of active and passive motion' (*Biog.*, Vol. I, p. 124)), his acknowledgement of his debt to George Fox and Jacob Behmen (who gave him a 'working presentment' that all 'products of the mere *reflective* faculty partook of DEATH' (*Biog.*, Vol. I, p. 152)), his positioning of the excellence of Shakespeare as lying in his forcing the reader 'into too much action to sympathize with the merely passive of our nature' (*Biog.*, Vol. II, p. 22): these examples, to use but a fraction of those available, construct and utilize a set of priorities in which action stands for what is alive, working, wilful and human, while passivity, when isolated from the active faculties, represents death, delirium and inhumanity.

Of course it would be possible to argue that all these examples are crucial parts of Coleridge's deconstruction of (and case against) Hartley, that for the whole of the first volume of the *Biographia* such is the function of all the material presented to the reader, and that by extending the rhetoric of activity and passivity to the second volume of the text, Coleridge is aiming to illustrate the practical and critical benefits of rejecting such a system. This is one of the senses, indeed, in which the *Biographia* can appear to possess a significant unity of purpose.[12] Yet it is by no means the case that these examples, and the others like them, are devoid of agendas or purposes outside and distinct from this over-arching aim of the whole text. Looking more closely at the manner in which Coleridge deploys the supposition that the Hartleian system figures the mind as entirely passive, what emerges is a preoccupation with identifying a certain type of activity as entirely and particularly unfit to be characterized in this manner.

Let us take the case of Coleridge's pejorative comments on contemporary literary practices that occur in the second chapter of the work. The mass production of literature by stereotyping, in which the same work seems to be varied 'indefinitely' so as to produce '*not* sense' but something 'so like it, as to do well', is most at fault, according to Coleridge, because it 'spares the reader the trouble of thinking; prevents vacancy, while it indulges indolence'. The reader of such works must be understood to be engaged in a kind of sham of attention, according to Coleridge. He or she appears to be occupied, but is not thinking, and so is not active enough to be classed as anything other than indolent. It is for this reason that Coleridge suggests that the difference 'between these and the works of genius, is not less than between an egg, and an egg-shell', for 'at a distance they both look alike'. Since something similar sounds as if it could be said for the task of reading such works, these conditions lead Coleridge to conclude that 'of all trades, literature at present demands the least talent or information' and that 'of all modes of literature' this is most emphatically the case for 'the manufacturing of poems' (*Biog.*, Vol. 1, p. 39).

Turning forwards a few pages in this second chapter, we find Coleridge offering the alternative to this situation, the (in his view) correct estimation of the composition of poetry:

There is no profession on earth, which requires an attention so early, so long, or so unintermitting as that of poetry; and indeed as that of literary composition in general, if it be such, as at all satisfies the demands both of taste and of sound logic. How difficult and delicate a task even the mere mechanism of verse is, may be conjectured from the failure of those, who have attempted poetry late in life. (*Biog.*, Vol. 1, p. 45)

The kind of readerly engagement that prevents 'vacancy' but that is not thereby really activity is contrasted here with the sorts of labour that constitute composition in general, if the work is to satisfy the demands of taste. Whereas the former required a type of attention that could not even be classed as thinking, the latter 'requires an attention' that is both 'long' and 'unintermitting'. The one is not a task but its appearance, while the other is a labour so 'difficult and delicate' as almost to elude classification: its exact parameters are only to be 'conjectured' from the failed attempts of those who underrated its arduousness. What Coleridge has offered the reader is a diptych of types of aesthetic attention, a double view of the correct and incorrect appreciation of the poetic acts of composition and reading – acts, in Coleridge's discussion, of essential similarity. Literature in general, but poetry in particular, is either to be characterized as the lowest form of attention, barely bypassing vacancy, or as the most delicate, difficult and constant task, which (to use Ferguson's terminology) strains and exerts one's abilities to the utmost.

It is possible to point to other moments in the *Biographia* that seem to dramatize different versions of this kind of 'false poetry' argument, moments that serve simultaneously as anti-Hartleian illustrations and further attempts to define the apparently elusive poetic act. In Chapter 6, subtitled in the Princeton edition 'Hartley's System Not Tenable', Coleridge recounts the case of a 'young woman' in Göttingen 'who could neither read, nor write', but who 'was seized with a nervous fever; during which, according to the asseverations of all the priests and monks of the neighbourhood, she became *possessed*, and, as it appeared, by a very learned devil. She continued incessantly talking Latin, Greek, and Hebrew, in very pompous tones and with most distinct enunciation' (*Biog.*, Vol. 1, p. 112). Coleridge's description of and extrapolation from this case is a significant moment in the *Biographia*. By following the logic of its explanation (that the woman had for several years been accustomed to have such languages read to her by her guardian), Coleridge finds himself suggesting that such unconscious memory is a kind of 'dread book of judgement, in whose mysterious hieroglyphics every idle word is recorded'. Further, as reflected in the lofty tone of his introduction of this idea ('And this, this perchance ...'), Coleridge ends the chapter with the suggestion that he 'dare' not 'longer discourse of this, waiting for a loftier mood, and a nobler subject, warned from within and from without, that it is profanation to speak of these mysteries' (*Biog.*, Vol. 1, p. 114). It is as if Coleridge has accidentally led himself to something that almost scares him in the depth of its insight, something significantly 'loftier' and more important than his current theme.

It is significant that Coleridge's treatment of this episode seems to foreshadow the definition of the poetic act that he finally reaches at the close of Chapter 13 (and to which we will have recourse presently). The case offers a portrait of how the Hartleian system construes all acts – but most problematically literary production – as nothing more than reflections and echoes of the myriad of influences and stimuli each individual receives. As Coleridge explains at the very beginning of Chapter 7, 'in Hartley's scheme the soul is present only to be pinched or *stroked*, while the very squeals or purring are produced by an agency wholly independent and alien' (*Biog.*, Vol. 1, p. 117). It is in this view that he jokes that the *Biographia* itself could be said to be written by 'Saint Paul's church' (*Biog.*, Vol. 1, p. 118), and that the 'inventor of the watch did not really invent it; he only looked on, while the blind causes, the only true artists, were unfolding themselves' (*Biog.*, Vol. 1, pp. 119–20). What is wrong with this model, for Coleridge, is that it renders man not a creative agent, but a passive automaton: it entirely negates the will in any act. Thus the case of the possessed woman functions for Coleridge as an image of what creative, literary inspiration would be if Hartley were right. The incessant and pompous Latin, Greek and Hebrew of the girl are not poetic expressions, in that they are unwilled, delirious and automatic. They cannot be said to come from what is defined as a person's 'soul' (in the quotation from Chapter 7, above) since they have not been actively and knowingly created, but are rather accidental echoes of past experience. In this sense, just as the woman herself is not a scholar of these languages, she is not the author of the sentences she has recounted but only the instrument of their reverberation.

Another instance of Coleridge's dramatization of unwilled and hence meaningless expression, one slightly more jocular in tone and context, occurs before he reaches the definitions of poetic creation that all these moments both tend towards and help construct. Amidst his account of his 'tour to the North' with 'the purpose of procuring customers' (*Biog.*, Vol. 1, p. 179) for *The Watchman* in 1796, Coleridge recounts an occasion on which, having reluctantly taken 'half a pipe' of 'herb tobacco mixed with Oronooko', he arrives at an acquaintance's house only to sink 'back on the sofa in a sort of swoon rather than sleep' (*Biog.*, Vol. 1, pp. 182–3). After lying '*deathy* pale and with cold drops of perspiration running down' his face, during which time the 'fifteen to twenty' gentlemen he was meant to be meeting with arrived, the young Coleridge 'awoke from insensibility, and looked round on the party', 'dazzled by the candles which had been lighted in the interim':

> By way of relieving my embarrassment one of the gentlemen began the conversation, with '*Have you seen a paper to day, Mr. Coleridge?*' Sir! (I replied, rubbing my eyes) 'I am far from convinced, that a christian is permitted to read either newspapers or any other works of merely political and temporary interest.' This remark so ludicrously inapposite to, or rather, incongruous with, the purpose, for which I was known to have visited Birmingham, and to assist me in which they were all then met, produced an involuntary and general burst of laughter; and seldom indeed have I passed so many delightful hours, as I enjoyed in that room from the moment of that laugh to an early hour the next morning. (*Biog.*, Vol. 1, p. 183)

In this episode Coleridge deploys the same trope of unmeant, involuntary and thus nonsensical speech with significant comic effect. Whereas the case of the delusional young woman was framed as baffling, Coleridge telling us that it confused 'many eminent physiologists' (*Biog.*, Vol. 1, p. 112), here no explanation can even be looked for, as Coleridge's involuntary expression is so 'ludicrously inapposite to' his considered opinion on the matter. Functioning as one of the several *'anecdotes of the author's literary life'* that constitute his *'Advice to young authors respecting publication'* (*Biog.*, Vol. 1, p. 160), this episode also seems designed to explode graphically the irrationality of the Hartleian system. According to that model, or to Coleridge's caricature of that model at least, this denouncement of newspapers would be considered as much his own expression as the carefully considered and pre-meditated public speaking he was engaged in on this same tour. That this is not the case is made explicit in this instance by the total irreconcilability of the two positions.

What this episode makes apparent more clearly than the case of the possessed woman is that Coleridge's argument against Hartley is founded almost entirely on the latter's omission of the will in his account of human expression. If this element is ignored, or discounted, all speech is given the same status as the young Coleridge's denouncement of newspaper-reading – all speech is rendered the product of a kind of random delirium of sensation and thought. Thus this episode sketches out the manner in which Hartley could be disproved and rejected, in the manner Coleridge seems to want to disprove him, by means of a consideration of what it is to mean what one says, to have opinions. Yet we should note, in this respect, that this anecdote, like the one before it, has slightly different overtones as well. In this case Coleridge sets the scene very carefully, framing his inapposite remark dramatically by intoxication, a *'deathy'* swoon, and candlelight. In the former anecdote, the 'pompous tones' and 'distinct enunciation' also serve to render the woman's delirium distinctly grandiose and artistic. It is as if Coleridge is not just engaged in exposing the missing element in Hartley's system, but is also using this as an occasion to construct his own portrait of poetic creation as an act that is willed or wilful in a very specific way, as a task that would be most degraded if Hartley's system were carried to its logical extreme. These anecdotes are instances of spontaneous, almost other-worldly expression that, by the manner in which they are framed and described, function as examples of what poetic creation would be if it was not willed and deliberate. In both instances, the possibility that we are witnessing genuine poetic inspiration is undermined or exploded by the comic, the melodramatic or the blatantly ridiculous. Coleridge is constructing instances of anecdotal, jocular, false poetry with the purpose, it would seem, of contrasting them with an actual, earnest portrait of the poetic act.

Before considering the portrait that these moments have been building towards directly, it will be helpful to turn away from the *Biographia* for a moment, to a slightly earlier stage in Coleridge's thinking about the connection between the will and poetic activity. In a notebook entry from January 1804, after observing his own lack of inclination to continue 'reading & filling the Margins of Malthus', even though he 'had begun & found it pleasant', Coleridge enters into a train of deliberations on what it is that causes this phenomenon, on what it is, in terms reminiscent of those we have already seen him use in relation to the Pantisocracy, that engenders this 'deep & wide disease' in his 'moral Nature'. That Coleridge's answer to this question comes in the form of his categorization of this task as what he 'OUGHT' to do, as what is his 'Duty' and is thus 'felt as a *command*', and that he comes to the conclusion that '*they most* labor under this defect who are most reverie-ish and streamy', giving himself and his son Hartley as prime examples, serves to define this problem of inclination and morality as one of will, above all else. Since, Coleridge tells us, our education concerning duty begins 'in early Infancy', and since this event serves to separate 'the streamy Nature of the associating Faculty' from what one ought to be doing, from one's 'Duty', this separation operates along the lines of what one must will oneself to engage in, on the one hand, and what one would like to do, naturally and unthinkingly, on the other. One's duty is both morally right and needs to be consciously willed, while one's inclination, what one wants to do when left to one's own devices, is 'reverie-ish', 'streamy', unwilled and, thus, amoral, at the very least, if not actually immoral.[13]

In this example from 1804, idle, unthinking and spontaneous contemplation courts the risk of immorality, in Coleridge's mind, by virtue of its unwilled genesis and its opposition to what must be willed most directly, one's duty. This fact enables us to understand the emphasis on the lack of will in the moments of false poetry we have been considering even more clearly. In a similar vein to Coleridge's thinking about Pantisocratic labour, activity without will is amoral, insofar as it is an idle, unthinking, waste of time – in comparison to what one 'ought' to be doing, at least. To position the will as being accessed and used at moments of apparently spontaneous inspiration, as Coleridge is building towards doing here, is thus to demonstrate the implicit morality in such acts, as well as to represent the task of poetic composition as akin to, rather than in opposition with, one's duty. The Hartleian model of poetry as simply automatic, un-thought association is problematic for Coleridge even in 1804, we might say. The young woman's Latin, Greek and Hebrew are, according to this manner of thinking, a-moral, gratuitous and 'streamy' par excellence, in that they are unwilled and uncontrolled. The younger Coleridge's ridiculous inapposite remark, likewise, stands at a considerable distance from what was his duty, in that situation, precisely because his will was not engaged in its production. Coleridge's 1804 deliberations make clear that the question of whether the will can be identified in an apparently spontaneous act is crucial in determining not only its morality, or the manner in which it relates to what is one's duty and one's inclination, but also its purpose and use. Either, as in the case of the Hartleian illustrations, an act is unwilled and thus undirected, or, as in the case of Coleridge's actual portrait of the poetic act in the *Biographia*, which we will turn to now, it is overtly willed and directly purposive.

Returning to the *Biographia*, one will be disappointed, if one was expecting Coleridge to offer a comparable yet contrasting description of the poetic act of creation in a similarly descriptive form to the 'false poetry' anecdotes we have been examining, an account that would perhaps replace melodrama for drama, bathos for climax. What Coleridge offers the reader is an extremely concise and equally suggestive definition of '*the imagination, or esemplastic power*' (*Biog.*, Vol. 1, p. 295) that has been deferred for at least eight chapters by the time one reaches it in Chapter 13. At that point, moreover, Coleridge's digressionary tactics continue, comically 'playing the role of "English Editor" to his own alter ego of the "Germanic Metaphysical Visionary"'[14] by interrupting his own deduction of the imagination with a fictional 'letter from a friend' (*Biog.*, Vol. 1, p. 300). The result of all this play-acting and procrastination is that the definition, when one finally reaches it, is presented as no more than 'the main result of the Chapter', pared down and isolated from the reasoning that apparently led to it.[15] Instead of the esoteric and atmospheric setting of the young Coleridge's swoon and recovery, the *Biographia*'s actual account of poetic creation occurs with considerably more bathos than either of the 'false poetry' anecdotes we have witnessed.

Whether we consider this laborious and drawn-out process of positioning and de-contextualizing to be part of Coleridge's rhetorical strategy in the *Biographia*,[16] or whether we view such a setting as unfortunate and unavoidable for various reasons,[17] it is nevertheless the case that the definition of the imagination itself can be said to have a resonance within the text disproportionate to its size. This effect is created for the most part by the manner in which the definition serves as a culmination of the terminologies and premises Coleridge has been using and developing for almost the whole of the text's first volume. Coleridge now picks up the argument we saw developing in Chapter 2 (that poetry is the most 'difficult and delicate' task) and combines it with the theoretical vocabulary of his 'deductions from established premises' (*Biog.*, Vol. 1, p. 88) embarked upon in Chapter 5, in order to offer an account of human capability in the kind of terms he shied away from in the wake of his description of the possessed woman. Confronting such territory now head on and significantly without the lofty tone of his comments there, Coleridge begins to define the imagination as follows: 'The IMAGINATION then I consider either as primary, or secondary. The primary IMAGINATION I hold to be the living Power and prime Agent of all human Perception, and as a repetition in the finite mind of the eternal act of creation in the infinite I AM' (*Biog.*, Vol. 1, p. 304). Since Coleridge was formerly 'warned from within and from without' when he approached the connections between the earthly operations of the mind and the 'mysteries' of divine judgement, we could say that the almost stilted tone in which this definition is recited reflects a similar fear. The primary imagination, the completely ordinary 'Agent of all human Perception' is no less than a 'repetition' of the 'act of creation' itself, no less than the 'infinite I AM'.[18] The unadorned matter-of-factness of Coleridge's style, contributing in no small part to the bathos of this moment in the *Biographia*, seems to be directly connected to the transcendent nature of the definition itself. The most ordinary style of perception in human life is, Coleridge suggests, intimately related to what is most quintessentially extraordinary.

In comparison to his treatment of the primary imagination, as Coleridge's definition moves on to the secondary imagination, his tone becomes at least a little less stilted:

The secondary I consider as an echo of the former, co-existing with the conscious will, yet still as identical with the primary in the *kind* of its agency, and differing only in *degree*, and in the *mode* of its operation. It dissolves, diffuses, dissipates, in order to re-create; or where this process is rendered impossible, yet still at all events it struggles to idealize and to unify. It is essentially *vital*, even as all objects (*as* objects) are essentially fixed and dead. (*Biog.*, Vol. 1, p. 304)

The more descriptive and explanatory tone in which this part of the definition is delivered seems to match the more heterogeneous operations of this faculty. Whilst the secondary imagination is 'an echo' of the primary, the manner in which it is portrayed makes it seem rather more powerful by virtue of its multifarious creativity. Furthermore, this creativity, it seems almost impossible not to notice, is depicted in terms of absolute activity. Coleridge's description almost breaks down in order to list the secondary imagination's operations ('It dissolves, diffuses, dissipates'), and the definition ends with the assertion that the secondary imagination is 'essentially *vital*' from the same perspective in which all other objects are 'fixed and dead'. Moreover, just as Nigel Leask has noted the two possibilities for the secondary imagination's action made possible in this definition (either it 'dissolves, diffuses' and 'dissipates', *or* it 'struggles to idealize and to unify', when the former processes are 'rendered impossible'),[19] it should be observed that this characterization serves to magnify the faculty's active capabilities. The secondary imagination seems to exhibit an almost bestial determination to movement, struggling into action even under the severest restraints.

Whereas the primary imagination is a repetition of the ultimate act of creativity, the secondary imagination, by virtue of its association with the 'conscious will', seems to approach even closer to that condition. By dissolving, diffusing and dissipating, it 're-creates' – an act essentially akin to the 'eternal act of creation'. These conditions of the secondary imagination's operation relate directly to Coleridge's argument with, and rejection of, Hartley. In the operation of the secondary imagination, man attains a state as close as he or she can come to divinity. Thus Hartley's evasion of the will as a condition of action and expression severely restricts what man is capable of. Coleridge's now more fleshed-out position renders the willed, deliberate, almost gratuitous harnessing of man's essential creativity not necessary but to be sought after. It is not an essential element of human life, as the operation of the primary imagination is, for example, but an almost self-serving state in which man approaches the perfection of his nature. We might describe the operation of the secondary imagination as a kind of play, in line with Schiller's use of that term. Using the secondary imagination is synonymous, in Coleridge's exposition, with controlling, exploring and setting in motion what is godlike in each individual.[20]

Stepping back from this definition slightly, we can say that the *Biographia* constructs a portrait of human capability in which 'All the organs of spirit are framed for a correspondent world of spirit' (*Biog.*, Vol. 1, p. 242), a portrait split between the two types of imagination and the 'aggregative and associative power' of the fancy (*Biog.*, Vol. 1, p. 293). From this perspective, it is apparent that the secondary imagination, which dissolves in order to recreate, and which playfully explores the connections implicit in all human perception, is the faculty responsible for artistic creativity. It forms new wholes out of sensory data, and creates new objects out of the materials of normal experience.[21] Indeed, once Coleridge finally spells out the details of these faculties at the (anti-) climax of Chapter 13, it becomes the case that to look elsewhere in the *Biographia* is to find hints and suggestions for the operation and use of this specifically creative faculty. In the light of this definition, the account of poetic composition in Chapter 2 might appear to offer a warning that what seems natural and inevitable in the sparseness of definition is in fact 'difficult and delicate'. In Chapter 14, likewise, the first of the text's second volume, Coleridge supplies a description of the poet that suggests that controlling the imagination takes specific abilities and competencies:[22]

> The poet, described in *ideal* perfection, brings the whole soul of man into activity, with the subordination of its faculties to each other, according to their relative worth and dignity. He diffuses a tone, and spirit of unity, that blends, and (as it were) *fuses*, each into each, by that synthetic and magical power, to which we have exclusively appropriated the name of imagination. This power, first put in action by the will and understanding, and retained under their irremissive, though gentle and unnoticed, controul (*laxis effertur habenis*) reveals itself in the balance or reconciliation of opposite or discordant qualities[.] (*Biog.*, Vol. II, pp. 15–16)

In this passage, leaving aside for the moment the obvious Schillerian nature of Coleridge's description, the poetic act is to be understood as a task based around harmony. At the same moment that it subordinates man's faculties to each other, the secondary imagination (if indeed that is what is being described[23]) is to be understood as being impelled and supervised by both the 'will and understanding'. Coleridge's Latin parentheses, a quotation from Petrarch meaning 'carried on with slackened reins', also depicts this operation as a kind of balance of control and relaxation.

In this dense portrait of the poetic act from Chapter 14, the poet is understood as engaging in a task that is to be both controlled and somehow left to its own devices, both restrained and encouraged. Such a characterization of poetic composition is not unique to this moment in the text alone. Turning back to Chapter 7, for example, we find something quite similar in an account of the mind's operations that prefigures Chapter 13's definition. Considering the 'small water-insect' that 'throws a cinque-spotted shadow fringed with prismatic colours on the sunny bottom of the brook', Coleridge suggests that this creature's 'alternate pulses of active and passive motion' are 'no unapt emblem for the mind's self-experience in the act of thinking':

> There are evidently two powers at work, which relatively to each other are active and passive; and this is not possible without an intermediate faculty, which is at once both active and passive. (In philosophical language, we must denominate this intermediate faculty in all its degrees and determinations, the

IMAGINATION. But in common language, and especially on the subject of poetry, we appropriate the name to a superior degree of the faculty, joined to a superior voluntary controul over it.) (*Biog.*, Vol. 1, pp. 124–5)

In this description again, the imagination is described as a faculty aiming at harmony, reconciling active and passive tendencies by being both at once. Further, just as in the extract from Chapter 14 above, Coleridge notes that in the case of poetry, the use of this faculty is characterized by a level of 'controul' over and above that of normal 'thinking'. Once again he combines the notion of control with a description of free and spontaneous movement. The mind, in this example, acts as naturally and instinctively as the 'water-insect'.

These two moments, the one appearing in the text in the immediate aftermath of Chapter 13's definitions, the other prefiguring them and occurring six chapters earlier, cast a similar light over the poetic operation of the secondary imagination. Such a process, the willed but playful use of the essential creativity of human perception, is somehow at once active and passive, a labour insofar as it requires irremissive control, but a relaxation from labour to the extent that such work is carried on with slackened reins. It is a control that is gentle and unnoticed, but still definitely there. Poetic composition, therefore, is simultaneously work and not work. It is made up of creative acts, of blending, fusing, idealizing and unifying, that must be consciously put into action by the will and understanding, that are tasks to the extent that they require constant maintenance and supervision, but that are spontaneous enough to occur as naturally, to the poet, as a water-insect moves across the surface of a brook. These moments depict poetic composition as a type of labour like no other, as something at once difficult but natural, laborious but self-propagating.

Contrasting the portrait these moments construct with the descriptions of the cases of the possessed woman and the delirious younger Coleridge we saw deployed against Hartley, it is possible to see more clearly than ever the extent to which such anecdotes serve as instances of 'false poetry'. In the case of the possessed woman, her incessant, pompous and distinctly enunciated Latin, Greek and Hebrew may offer the appearance of a certain kind of poetic inspiration, but it is apparent, following Coleridge's exposition of the operations of the secondary imagination, that what was spontaneous in the former instance lacked any sort of effort or control, not to mention will. Poetic composition begins by an act of will in cooperation with the understanding, and is then characterized by the labour of supervision, albeit a labour that is gentle enough to be unnoticed. The young woman's delirious and automatic spontaneity stands at a great distance from this description. The former is a careful and playful harnessing of innate abilities, while the latter is a kind of unintended and uncontrolled echo or repetition of experience. In the case of the delirious young Coleridge, the scene may contain all the trappings of a somewhat clichéd image of poetic inspiration, but lacks both the willed instigation of the synthetic powers of the imagination and the subject matter such processes of diffusion and recreation engender. The actual material of the young Coleridge's ejaculation fails to meet the grade of poetic or literary composition for, rather than being a new and deliberate whole created by reconstructing the materials of experience, it is a kind of non-sense completely incongruous with the mind out of which it came.

Thus the *Biographia* as a whole must be understood to contend for the essentially work-like nature of poetic composition. Poetry, in its various and disparate styles of exposition, offers the most dramatic and conclusive demonstration of the incompleteness of Hartley's system. It is a style of thought that is so wilful as to take on the qualities of labour, but at the same time possesses the spontaneity of natural movement. Hartley's system eliminated the possibility of willed poetic composition, therefore, and also put forward a portrait of human capability lacking the process Coleridge sees as the pinnacle of man's achievements. Hartley, in the *Biographia*'s portrait of him at least, reduced all expression to the random patterning of experience at the same time as he degraded the human ability to create new objects out of that same experience.

But the *Biographia*'s depiction of poetry as a specific kind of labour is not only to be connected with Coleridge's treatment of his philosophical reading. Poetry as a kind of work that is both laborious and gentle also bears affinities with the priorities of the Pantisocracy scheme we observed earlier. The latter aimed to render literary acquirements identical with manual labour in terms of morality and productivity, and aimed to render work- and leisure-time constructive in the same way. The *Biographia* takes the case of one literary acquirement in particular, one treated as leisure in Chapter 2's treatment of reading practices, and argues for its work-like nature. Both projects aim to justify the poetic act by aligning it with, and describing it as, manual labour. Alternatively and more sympathetically, one might suggest that Coleridge is engaged, in both projects, in the task of identifying what it is in literary labour that makes it akin to manual labour – identifying the type of intellectual tasks inherent in a non-physical, non-bodily occupation.

It has already been implied that this task is undertaken, at times, in distinctly Schillerian terms. Yet it must also be recognized that the most apparent contemporary German influence in the *Biographia* is not Schiller, but Friedrich Schelling. As modern notes to the text make clear, Coleridge is both paraphrasing and directly translating Schelling for a significant part of Chapters 5 to 13.[24] It is in the context of this apparent reliance, moreover, that the critical task of understanding or explaining the *Biographia* has quite often become the task of aligning Coleridge's judgements in the text most succinctly with Schelling's own work. Hence when Nigel Leask reads Coleridge's description of the secondary imagination in significantly transcendentalist terms, he does so by explicit reference to Schelling:

Secondary imagination is the essential copula between Primary imagination … and fallen consciousness … Without the copula, consciousness remains oblivious to the divine ground of being – unable to 'see all things in God', it perceives only 'fixities and definites', the dualistic limits of the conditioned finite self … In the 1807 *Verhältnis*, Schelling demanded

> How can we, so to speak, spiritually melt this apparently hard form, so that the unadulterated energy of things fuses with the energy of our spirits, forming a single cast?

Coleridge's chapter thirteen definition of secondary imagination answered Schelling's rhetorical question: it 'dissolves, diffuses, dissipates …'. Art represents the purpose and progress of the Absolute, the creative power to dissipate the hard form of 'separated' consciousness, revealing the factitious nature of reality seemingly 'fixed and dead'.[25]

Whether we find the supposition that the secondary imagination reveals the 'factitious nature' of 'fixed and dead' objects plausible, or whether we consider this a step too far from Coleridge's definition itself, which seemed to suggest the opposite, it is apparent that the *Biographia*'s thoroughly documented relationship with Schelling's thought renders the process of reading the text, in this example and in the many comparable to it, almost identical with the search for sources for its various stances and ideas.[26]

Both in opposition to this relationship and in replication of its parameters, there is a group of critics who have attempted to point out how, at several moments of the *Biographia* at least, the search for sources might need to consider Schiller as well as Schelling. Wilkinson and Willoughby, for example, observe the 'close proximity of a number of different, though related, ideas' in the *Biographia* and the *Aesthetic Letters* 'in the few pages surrounding Coleridge's well-known definition of poetic genius in terms of "the balance or reconciliation of opposite or discordant qualities"'. By means of this and other similarities, they question

> whether the unity that Coleridge evolved for himself out of his manifold borrowings, and on which he so clearly put the stamp of his own mind, is not more akin to the aesthetic, psychological, practical temper of a Schiller, whose passion for distinctions he clearly shared, than to the metaphysical system of a Schelling, with its profoundly a-psychological – where not anti-psychological – bias.[27]

John Kooy, in a similar though slightly problematic vein, gives more credence to the fact that Coleridge made efforts to acquire the complete works of Schelling, something he did for no other German writer. He takes the case of Schelling's *System des transcendentalen Idealismus* (1800), the main source text in modern understandings of the *Biographia*, and describes how it was 'written under the twin influences of the Jena Romantics' aesthetic absolutism and Schiller's *Aesthetic Letters*'. In view of this, and of the radical political associations with which Schiller's name was connected in England in the early 1800s, Kooy is attempting to suggest that wherever we see Schelling in the *Biographia* we can basically read Schiller.[28] Despite the questionable nature of this supposition, Kooy proceeds to make compelling connections between Coleridge's 'imitation' and 'copy' and Schiller's 'aesthetic semblance' and 'logical semblance', the *Biographia*'s placing of the pleasure of poetry before its moral effect and the *Letters*' aesthetic's indirect effect on moral action, and Schiller's play drive and Coleridge's 'suspension of disbelief'.[29]

What is clear from these two examples of the attempt to insert Schiller into the scheme of the *Biographia* is that such a task runs up against the sheer fact and volume of Coleridge's reading of Schelling. In order for Wilkinson and Willoughby to question whether Coleridge's tone and temper as a whole are not more akin to Schiller than Schelling they must rhetorically put aside the textual reality of the *Biographia*, just as Kooy must transform Schelling into no more than a lens through which to see Schiller in order to assert the similarity of the *Biographia* and the *Aesthetic Letters*. Even if Coleridge was to consider himself somewhat taken in by Schelling in the years following the *Biographia*'s publication, it is nevertheless the case that Coleridge's reliance on him in the second half of the text's first volume is manifest.[30]

Approaching the relationship between Coleridge and Schiller slightly differently, however, it might be possible to avoid the temptation and the pitfalls of simply suggesting further source material for the *Biographia*. Wilkinson and Willoughby describe two dominant impulses in Coleridge scholarship. On the one hand there is the tendency to find German sources for Coleridge's opinions, several examples of which we have already witnessed. On the other, there is the tendency to observe the similarities even of Coleridge's pre-German thought to Schelling and Schiller. This latter tendency, it will be observed, has already been given rein in my analysis of 'Frost at Midnight' and 'Effusion xxxv'. There, we saw the striking similarities between Coleridge's ideas and the trajectory of the *Aesthetic Letters*, even though Coleridge did not travel to Germany until seven months after 'Frost at Midnight' was composed. Combining this striking coincidence of styles of thought with the critical texts of Schiller's that Coleridge is known to have encountered in Germany – *The Muses' Almanac* of 1797, for example, which contained 'nearly 500 distichs that expressed and commented upon' the 'power of art' and 'aesthetic living'[31] – we reach a point from which Coleridge might be said to have been particularly and specifically prepared to take in the characteristics of Schiller's thought, even without direct knowledge of their main enunciation. If Coleridge had read works related to and offering accounts of the argument of the *Aesthetic Letters*, it would not be a surprise to find the *Biographia* further echoing these parameters, especially given their similarity to Coleridge's own thought even before he encountered them.

To suggest a kind of reconciliation between the two tendencies Wilkinson and Willoughby identify is to position the Schillerian similarities in the *Biographia* as a kind of latent presence more than as any sort of borrowing. As Kooy observes, it can seem as if the Schillerian in Coleridge emerges more when his mind is on practical matters than when he is in the thick of ordering and explaining his studies of Schelling.[32] In the description of the mind as like a 'water-insect' that we encountered in Chapter 7, for example, by describing the mind as made up of 'two powers', which are 'active and passive', and which function by means of 'an intermediate faculty, which is at once both active and passive', Coleridge recalls Schiller's methodology in general terms, rather than any specific passages in the *Aesthetic Letters*.[33] By the manner in which he does so, it would not seem to be much of a leap to equate the imagination, as a faculty mediating between what is active and passive in the mind by being both at once, with Schiller's play drive, reconciling and consummating the opposite functions of the form and sense drives. In the exact same vein as this connection, indeed, just as Schiller's play drive enables man to experience the harmony of his faculties, and hence a type of freedom, Coleridge's imagination, he tells us in Chapter 14, 'brings the whole soul of man into activity, with the subordination of its faculties to each other'. Such 'synthetic and magical power' would seem to align directly with the trajectory of Schiller's thought as we witnessed it in the *Aesthetic Letters*. It seems plausible to say, therefore, that despite the probability that Coleridge had not read the *Aesthetic Letters* in 1817, the *Biographia* depicts the genesis and describes the effects of the secondary imagination in a comparable way to how the *Aesthetic Letters* portray both the origin and the power of the play drive. The connection between the two texts appears more general than specific, more in terms of parameters than details.

In contrast to the vagaries and problems of aligning the *Aesthetic Letters* with the *Biographia*, however, there is another area of Coleridge's thought that almost seems designed to espouse the similarities between his own interests and those of Schiller. Coleridge's last major work, *On the Constitution of Church and State* of 1829, must be understood to echo the *Aesthetic Letters*, whether by coincidence or design, and hence might plausibly be used to argue for Coleridge's knowledge, by the end of his life at least, of Schiller's fullest articulation of his aesthetic priorities. When the *Aesthetic Letters* first appeared in print in Schiller's journal *Horae* in 1795, they ended, significantly, in a footnote to the last paragraph, with Schiller's promise to draft a '*Constitution*' for the 'State of Aesthetic Semblance':

Da es einem guten Staat an einer Constitution nicht fehlen darf, so kann man sie auch von dem ästhetischen fodern [*sic*]. Noch kenne ich keine dergleichen, und ich darf also hoffen, dass ein erster Versuch derselben, den ich dieser Zeitschrift bestimmt habe, mit Nachsicht werde aufgenommen werden.

Since no good State should be without its *Constitution*, it is legitimate to require one for the Aesthetic State too. No such is as yet known to me, and I may therefore venture to hope that a first attempt at one, which I have destined for this Journal, will be received with indulgence.[34]

As Wilkinson and Willoughby observe, in the light of this emphasis on a '*Constitution*' in the *Horae* ending, Coleridge's title itself, in his last major work, seems to replicate the *Letters'* last paragraph, where Schiller draws an analogy between the Aesthetic State, 'the pure Church and the pure Republic'.[35] It is as if, at a first glance at least, Coleridge's *On the Constitution of Church and State* is conceived of as offering a very literal furthering of Schiller's project in the *Aesthetic Letters*.

In terms of the matter rather than just the appearance of this text, one would be disappointed, were one to expect a work of exactly similar style or construction to Schiller's *Letters*. *Church and State* in fact treats its subject not just as a conceptual 'idea' but also as a definite historical reality.[36] This latter, importantly pragmatic emphasis is no doubt a function of the text's overt purpose, that of setting out a detailed and carefully reasoned response to the several Catholic Emancipation Bills that proposed the opening of Parliament to Roman Catholics during the 1820s.[37] Where Schiller sought to trace and deduct the range of human needs and faculties from first causes, thereby positioning what he found as always and already relevant in any human community, Coleridge sets out to decipher such concepts from already-formed societies. Where Schiller's method was abstract and theoretical, Coleridge's seems significantly more practical. Alternatively, and rather less kindly, we could say that where Schiller eventually made use of a kind of play on words between a state of mind and a political or nation-state, Coleridge's approach is significantly more simplistic.

Church and State suggests that a nation or society is to be understood in terms both of its 'civilization' and its 'cultivation'. The former term might be aligned with 'progress' and 'wealth', as Smith sought to explain those terms in the *Wealth of Nations*, for example, while the latter stands in opposition to this perspective in the same way that both Ferguson and Schiller opposed the priorities of political economy. For Coleridge, as for Ferguson and Schiller, the one is often over-developed at the expense of the other:

> But civilization is itself but a mixed good, if not far more a corrupting influence, the hectic of disease, not the bloom of health, and a nation so distinguished more fitly to be called a varnished than a polished people; where this civilization is not grounded in *cultivation*, in the harmonious developement [sic] of those qualities and faculties that characterise our *humanity*. We must be men in order to be citizens. (*C&S*, pp. 42–3)

The similarities to Schiller here are obvious. Not only is cultivation explained as a kind of 'harmonious developement' of 'faculties', but it is also positioned as the essential condition of man's citizen status. Just as Schiller propounded aesthetic freedom as the necessary means to political freedom, inner harmony as the key to a balanced society, Coleridge advocates a specific type of inner development for the good of a nation or community at large.

Yet although Coleridge and Schiller's solutions to the problem of over-civilization are identical in their projected ends, they are significantly different in their actual means. *Church and State*, as its title implies, characterizes these twin impulses of a community's progress as matched by the dual nature of any society. The State, in this model, is that part of society interested in physical property, and in economic or geographical growth. The 'abiding interests, the *estates*, and ostensible tangible properties, not the *persons* as *persons*, are the proper subjects of the *state* in this sense', just as 'it is the depths, breadths, bays, and windings or reaches of a river, that are the subject of the hydrographer, not the water-drops, that at any one moment constitute the stream' (*C&S*, p. 40). The 'National Church', by contrast, is that part of society set aside to consider the population as individuals, the 'water-drops' themselves in the above analogy, and to concern itself with their actual welfare, their cultivation. In Coleridge's terminology the members of this section of society are the 'Clerisy'.

Whilst *Church and State* offers several examples of different societies' versions of the 'National Church' and the 'Clerisy', terms not to be directly equated, even in contemporary England, with the 'Christian Church',[38] it devotes most space to contemporary commercial societies. In the case of these, the list of occupations and roles that constitute the Clerisy becomes quite extensive: 'the sages and professors of the law and jurisprudence; of medicine and physiology; of music; of military and civil architecture; of the physical sciences; with the mathematical as the common *organ* of the preceding; in short, all the so called liberal arts and sciences … as well as the Theological' (*C&S*, p. 46). Coleridge's Church is not to be understood as in any way a narrowly religious institution with specific and limited aims. The account he offers of its objectives and intentions is as various as the list of its constituent members. The Church's 'instructors', made up of the professions above and 'distributed throughout the country, so as not to leave even the smallest integral part or division without a resident guide, guardian, and instructor' (*C&S*, p. 43), are there

> to preserve the stores, to guard the treasures, of past civilization, and thus to bind the present with the past; to perfect and add to the same, and thus to connect the present with the future; but especially to diffuse through the whole community, and to every native entitled to its laws and rights, that quantity and quality of knowledge which was indispensable both for the understanding of those rights, and for the performance of the duties correspondent. Finally, to secure for the nation, if not a superiority over the neighbouring states, yet an equality at least, in that character of general civilization, which equally with, or rather more than, fleets, armies, and revenue, forms the ground of its defensive and offensive power. (*C&S*, pp. 43–4)

This remit for the Clerisy's operations is dauntingly ambitious, even given the realistic touch of aiming for 'an equality' with 'neighbouring states' rather than 'a superiority' over them. It is in the context of this model, however, that Coleridge further expands on the effects of such an individual-based education:

> That in all ages, individuals who have directed their meditations and their studies to the nobler characters of our nature, to the cultivation of those powers and instincts which constitute the man, at least separate him from the animal, and distinguish the nobler from the animal part of his own being, will be led by the *supernatural* in themselves to the contemplation of a power which is likewise super-*human*; that science, and especially moral science, will lead to religion, and remain blended with it – this, I say, will, in all ages, be the course of things. (*C&S*, p. 44)

In this portrait the effect of the Clerisy on a population goes beyond fostering their 'understanding' and 'performance' of their 'rights' and 'duties'. Individual-based cultivation and the study of all the 'liberal arts and sciences' (*C&S*, p. 46) will serve not only to cultivate an interest in religion, a natural 'course of things' in this description, but will do so by unlocking the '*supernatural*' in each individual.

This belief and the language in which it is described marks one of the points at which *Church and State* can be seen to build on the concerns and arguments of the *Biographia*. Coleridge's model of cultivation, in this later work, is not simply to be understood as securing the political capacities of a nation's citizens, but, like Schiller's aesthetic contemplation, also arrogates to itself a form of spiritual or psychological emancipation. The *Biographia* sought to position the processes of poetic composition and reading as acts in which the limits of human capacity are reached, as moments at which man came as close to divine creativity as possible. *Church and State* expounds a system of wide-scale education that will unlock the divinity in each individual. It is as if the difference in remit of these two texts signals Coleridge's attempt to offer the kind of powers he located in the secondary imagination to a community as a whole. Poetry's connection to the essential creativity of the human mind could be said to lead Coleridge, in this text, to propose a different and more inclusive path to something very similar.

This is not the only way in which the *Biographia* and *Church and State* are related. Both works seem to be motivated, or animated, by a desire to posit man's essential activity, and to expose the shortcomings of any system that renders man passive in any significant way. The *Biographia* found man to be degraded by Hartley's system for this very reason. *Church and State* takes issue with the kinds of programmes of social organization that treat men as cogs in a machine of state rather than as individuals:

Shall I proceed with my chapter of hints? Game Laws, Corn Laws, Cotton Factories, Spitalfields, the tillers of the land paid by poor-rates, and the remainder of the population mechanized into engines for the manufactory of new rich men – yea, the machinery of the wealth of the nation made up of the wretchedness, disease and depravity of those who should constitute the strength of the nation! Disease, I say, and vice, while the wheels are in full motion; but at the first stop the magic wealth-machine is converted into an intolerable weight of pauperism! (*C&S*, p. 63)

In this passage we find Coleridge deploying a very similar argument to the one Ferguson and Schiller used against Smith. Coleridge suggests that the side-effects of increased productivity and national wealth are too grave to justify its benefits. Widespread 'wretchedness, disease and depravity' are not worth the 'wealth' of a few men. The list with which this extract begins, 'Game Laws, Corn Laws, Cotton Factories', serves to imply something about the kinds of priorities the contemporary ruling perspective makes necessary. Coleridge's 'hints' are primarily satirical in nature: they serve to foreground a system that is simultaneously ignoring and degrading a whole area of human concerns.

Whilst in one sense we have already seen what it is that Coleridge considers to be missing from this perspective – the consideration of men as spiritual beings, and a system that cultivates their abilities accordingly – glancing at the 'hints' that precede this last quotation, it becomes apparent that, very much like in the *Biographia*, what is at stake in the choice between two systems of organization, for Coleridge, is no less than the correct identification of man as an active being above all else. The 'hints' that precede the last quotation take the form of a spoof of the kind of note-like style we saw Bentham using in his prompts towards the utilitarian way of seeing things:

Education reformed. Defined as synonymous [*sic*] with Instruction. *Axiom of Education so defined.* Knowledge being power, those attainments, which give a man the power of doing what he wishes in order to obtain what he desires, are alone to be considered as knowledge, or to be admitted into the scheme of National Education. Subjects to be taught in the National Schools. Reading, writing, arithmetic, the mechanic arts, elements and results of physical science, but to be taught, as much as possible, empirically. (*C&S*, p. 62)

In this passage Coleridge posits a utilitarian interpretation of Bacon's 'Knowledge is power', suggesting that the correct set of 'attainments' offer 'the power of doing' what one wants 'in order to obtain' what one 'desires'.[39] From a perspective such as Bentham's, it is implied, man desires the exact same domestic and commercial advances the model of political economy promises to the whole nation. Man should be taught 'the mechanic arts', in this view, for it is these that will lead to his advancement, success and thus, apparently, his satisfaction.

Since this spoof of Bentham occurs after the details of the operations and expected results of the Clerisy in Coleridge's exposition, he does not go on to contradict directly the perspective he is sending up here. His critique, for the most part, is implicit rather than explicit. Yet there are moments, like that in the wake of the list of modern governmental concerns we saw above, at which Coleridge seems almost unable to contain his indignation at what it is such a perspective is ignoring. Consequently, this 'chapter of hints' reads as an almost frantic alternation between satire and plain scorn, between indignation and a kind of desperate dark comedy. Immediately following Coleridge's note-like characterization of current 'State-policy' as 'a Cyclops with one eye, and that in the back of the head', for example, the reader is given a glimpse of an apparently more fruitful set of priorities: 'Mean time, the true historical feeling, the immortal life of an historical Nation, generation linked to generation by faith, freedom, heraldry, and ancestral fame, languishing, and giving place to the superstitions of wealth, and newspaper reputation' (*C&S*, p. 67). In the paragraph immediately following this quotation, the contemporary utilitarian priorities that have created this hierarchy are characterized as also engendering 'Talents without genius' and 'a swarm of clever, well-informed men' that is 'an anarchy of minds' and 'a despotism of maxims' (*C&S*, p. 67). What is clear from these moments, and from the spoof of utilitarian education we have just seen, is that Coleridge considers the dominant utilitarian perspective to be eroding the common bonds between men, the notions of 'freedom' and 'ancestral fame' that links them, at the same time as it establishes a society founded on 'talents' (passive accomplishments), rather than 'genius' (the active use of one's innate abilities). '[S]uperstitions of wealth' are replacing a kind of meritocracy of people's abilities, for Coleridge, and, as was the case in the *Biographia*, the danger of such a set of priorities lies in the innate passivity and the mechanical model of human capability it promotes. Man is told, in the prevailing system, that certain mechanical 'attainments' will lead to his satisfaction. Coleridge, in opposition to this, is striving to reconstruct and set about implementing a notion of human 'freedom' inseparable from 'feeling' and 'faith'.

Seeing Coleridge as arguing for the spiritual, religious and 'supernatural' abilities of men is thus seeing him reject a portrait of man as a blank slate on which to impress abilities and accomplishments. In his view, either man is understood as an active being, who uses his 'freedom' and 'faith' in order to interact with others, or he is reduced to a machine, whose desires are as predictable as his mechanical talents. The importance of active 'faith' in Coleridge's portrait of contemporary humanity is made even more apparent as *Church and State* moves past its Bentham-like posturing in order to consider the means to reject this system on a large scale. Addressing himself directly now to the proponents of utilitarian education, Coleridge offers the following contrast:

> It is folly to think of making all, or the many, philosophers, or even men of science and systematic knowledge. But it is duty and wisdom to aim at making as many as possible soberly and steadily religious; – inasmuch as the morality which the state requires in its citizens for its own well-being and ideal immortality, and without reference to their spiritual interest as individuals, can only exist for the people in the form of religion. (*C&S*, p. 69)

Here, religion is conceived of as offering the state what it 'requires', and what the Utilitarians presumably desire for it too, 'its own well-being and ideal immortality'. In positing the national benefits of this type of spirituality-centred education, Coleridge is attempting to prove, like Schiller and Ferguson, that what is beneficial to the individual can also be beneficial to the nation of which he is a part. In Coleridge's scheme, furthermore, since the 'Christian' Church relates to the 'National Church' as does an 'olive tree' to its 'surrounding soil', invigorating and improving the quality of any neighbouring plants (*C&S*, p. 56), implanting religious 'faith' in a nation's citizens is rendered the key both to their, and to their society's, health and strength.

In this sense *Church and State* enters into debates and offers analyses of material far removed from the concerns of the *Aesthetic Letters*, but also represents a significantly more practical attempt to disseminate an essentially similar model of human capability. For both Coleridge and Schiller, the freedom of the mind founded in its potential 'harmony', and the recognition of its transcendental capabilities, will deliver man from a world characterized by passive accomplishments rather than active abilities. One might even be tempted to suggest that if Schiller had constructed a 'constitution' for his Aesthetic State, in accordance with his promise in the *Horae*, it might have looked something like *Church and State*. By harnessing what Coleridge describes as a ready-made and, in any society, always-existing model of the Clerisy or National Church, *Church and State* offers what appears to be a workable method for re-prioritizing contemporary educational practices, for administering a Schillerian second nature to a thoroughly commercial society.[40]

The *Biographia*'s connection to *Church and State* also seems to lie along these lines. While the later work represents a shift of priorities, in that it concerns itself with the active yet contemplative abilities of the mind in general, rather than with poetic composition and the secondary imagination in particular, such a shift is to be understood as one of means rather than ends. That *Church and State* offers a different vessel in order to obtain the same appreciation and use of what is 'supernatural' in the mind, that it sets itself against a prevailing system that renders man a passive, blank slate, and that it posits the centrality of spiritual well-being to human happiness: these considerations, central to the scheme of the work, establish an essential continuity between Coleridge's thinking in this text and the *Biographia*. The earlier work's definition of the secondary imagination, and its concern with the details of poetic composition, can be seen as prototypes for *Church and State*'s interest in human intellectual life more generally. Both texts posit not only the active nature of the contemplative abilities, but also the centrality of these acts to individual and communal life.

We must observe as well in this consideration of the *Biographia* and *Church and State* that even though both works seem to hold some sort of relationship with Schiller's thought – the one in rather general terms, the other perhaps quite specifically – neither can be said to achieve the clarity of connection to the exact dynamics of the *Aesthetic Letters* that we observed in 'Frost at Midnight' and 'Effusion xxxv'. Those poems positioned the aesthetic, compositional experience as a physical entry-point to moral consciousness in a way that is remarkably similar to the *Aesthetic Letters*, but that is not found, in the same form at least, in the *Biographia* or *Church and State*. Pushing the point, we could suggest that the relationship between the creative act and the divine will, in the *Biographia*, is a form of this relationship between aesthetic contemplation and moral awareness. It was, after all, by throwing light on God's 'eternal language' that morality was revealed in 'Frost at Midnight'. Similarly, it could be argued that the fact that the study of the 'liberal arts' engenders the knowledge of how to perform one's 'duties', and unlocks the 'supernatural' in each individual, in *Church and State*, is an instance of this same pattern of ideas. It remains the case, however, that if we consider what is distinctive in Schiller to be this trajectory from the contemplative to the moral, these two examples of Coleridge's thought cannot be said to become significantly more akin to the *Aesthetic Letters* in the wake of Coleridge's time in Germany and study of German sources than those two examples of his pre-German thought.

This is not to say that *Church and State* does not appear to refer directly to the *Aesthetic Letters*, especially as the latter appear in the *Horae* edition. It is as if, by this stage in his career, Coleridge's knowledge of Schiller was deeply interwoven with those themes of his own that he had been working with for the past three decades. *Church and State* might be understood to offer a synthesis of what was Coleridgean even from the Pantisocracy days, or from his lectures in Bristol in the late 1790s, with a way of structuring and framing these concerns borrowed, or inherited, from Schiller.[41] To hold this view of *Church and State* is to see Schiller having some sort of impact on English educational thought in the same way that both he and Coleridge are known to have influenced their own educational systems.[42] Even if *Church and State*'s National Church and localized Clerisy are not the infrastructure suggested in the *Aesthetic Letters*, it could be suggested that they are engendered by the decay of Schiller's system to nothing but the example of a few 'finely attuned souls'.

Returning to the *Biographia*, some sort of connection needs to be drawn between the playfully bathetic nature of Coleridge's description of the secondary imagination there, and the ironic strands of thought we observed in 'Frost at Midnight' and 'Effusion xxxv'. Since those elements equated to a kind of defence against what appeared threatening or radically unknowable in each of those poems' settings, the irony created by the *Biographia*'s stilted recital of its portrait of poetic inspiration, following the grandiose instances of 'false poetry' it has already shown us, appears to be something similar. We might suggest that the *Biographia* needs to play down the implications of its definition of the secondary imagination, because what is accessed in the process it is describing, the process of poetic composition, is uncanny or sublime in the same manner as the experiences described in 'Frost at Midnight' and the 'Effusion'. The poetic act, in this view, is in some sense awe-inspiring or terrifying by virtue of what we might describe as its implicit reference to divine creativity; and the bathetic nature of Coleridge's attempted deduction of the imagination, together with the lack of centre many readers have complained of in the *Biographia* more generally, are to be seen as being caused by the magnitude of that central definition itself. Rather than being a tale without a centre, the text's centre could be said to be engulfed in its own considerable shadow.[43]

Whilst these considerations stand at a considerable distance from what we saw of the Pantisocracy scheme, it is nevertheless the case that there is a distinct line of similarity running through all three of the projects we have considered here. Just as Coleridge's plans for the Pantisocratic community could be related to his concerns about Hartley's system and the manner in which it restricted human capability in the *Biographia*, we have seen that the same emphasis on man as an active, contemplative being animates and impels *Church and State*. The Pantisocracy and the *Biographia* strive to define poetry as labour, or to bring it as close as possible to the condition of work by delineating the manner in which it is a process of willed concentration and 'irremissive' self-supervision, while *Church and State* extends the vocabulary of intellectual activity to human life in general. In this manner, this latest work is a culmination of the trajectory implicit in Coleridge's thought. Poetry was to achieve the status of work in the Pantisocratic community. In the *Biographia*, the work that poetry achieved was to reveal the divine nature of human perception. *Church and State* attempts to open up the knowledge revealed by poetry to a community in general by a specific type of education in the liberal arts.[44]

To characterize Coleridge as being concerned, almost above all else, with demonstrating the active nature of human intellectual life, therefore, is to see him as positing the essential similarity of manual and poetic labour. At the same time it is to see him portraying the contemplative, idle operations of the mind as made up of labours both self-propagating and arduous. Whilst his last major work, *Church and State*, moved away from the delineation of these paradoxical qualities, it did so with a view to offering the products of such labours to a community at large, and with the purpose of demonstrating the centrality of such processes to a nation's security and health. By comparison to the intricacies and intertextualities of the *Biographia*, the Pantisocracy's attempt to align labour and literary accomplishment may seem rather simplistic, or naive, yet it is a task whose arduousness Coleridge continued to probe, despite his and Southey's failure to realize the Pantisocratic community in the way they intended.

Conclusion

Coleridge's *Church and State* aims to house the effects of idle contemplation in an institutional structure designed to be implemented on a national scale. Studying 'the nobler characters of our nature' the population 'will be led by the *supernatural* in themselves to the contemplation of a power which is likewise super-*human*' (*C&S*, p. 44; Coleridge's emphasis). This is Coleridge's solution to the problems Schiller and Ferguson identified in an advanced division of labour. *Church and State* utilizes the separation of employments itself in order to dedicate a whole class of labourers to the cultivation of the population. We should remember, however, that this attempt to treat contemporary ills is to be found in a similar form in the *Wealth of Nations*. Smith observes the necessity of some 'attention of government' in order to form a community's 'abilities and virtues' if they do not happen to be cultivated in the course of their normal activities. His account of this consideration could even be described as more practical than Coleridge's:

> The third and last duty of the sovereign or commonwealth is that of erecting and maintaining those publick institutions and those publick works, which, though they may be in the highest degree advantageous to a great society, are, however, of such a nature, that the profit could never repay the expence to any individual or small number of individuals, and which it, therefore, cannot be expected that any individual or small number of individuals should erect or maintain. The performance of this duty requires too very different degrees of expence in the different periods of society. (*WN*, p. 723)

Smith couches the notion of public cultivation in what would seem to be candid economics. '[P]ublic institutions' and 'public works' are not consistently profitable but 'may be in the highest degree advantageous to a great society'. For this reason they are to be subsidized by the state.

This is an unexpected convergence of Coleridge and Smith's thought. Recapping this part of Smith's argument demonstrates that the *Wealth of Nations* makes use of a notion of cultivation similar to that of *Church and*

State. Smith is concerned at this moment for a community's 'abilities and virtues'. Coleridge and Smith would thus seem to be entirely in accord. Both outline the main concerns of their communities and conclude that an active culture of capabilities and mental powers is to be encouraged. Both could be described as deploying the notion of the whole man as we have seen Schiller use that idea. And yet at the same time we know that Smith and Coleridge are not be equated in this manner. *Church and State* directs all its scorn and rhetoric at systems like Smith's that promote 'wealth' as the goal of societal organization. In 'Frost at Midnight' and 'Effusion xxxv', equally, Coleridge explores the private, individualistic perspective invisible to Smith's enquiry and constructs a portrait of human abilities diametrically opposed to Smith's economic man.

The explanation of this apparent contradiction lies in Smith's style. Appearing to aim at comprehensiveness almost above all else, the *Wealth of Nations* reads as an encyclopedia of economic conditions and tactics. A feature of this comprehensiveness that we had occasion to note above is the inclusion or assimilation of what might be described as classical-republican elements into the work's predominantly political economic agenda. The notion of cultivation figured in the passage above is one such element. Smith could be described as tacking on the educational conditions that ensured the classical citizen's political worth to his otherwise almost completely commercial system.[1] Thus the discrepancy between this concern for 'abilities and virtues' and the type of human nature the rest of the *Wealth of Nations* constructs is significant. The work repeatedly characterizes human life by its labours and activities to such an extent that the repose of contemplation becomes a negative term. Relaxation is the state in which humanity is on hold, in Smith's depiction, not the position from which man cultivates his intellectual talents.

The *Wealth of Nations* thus pays lip-service to the idea of cultivation in its final book but does not orientate human life round the abilities that process would inspire. Coleridge's cultivation, by contrast, is the central ambition of *Church and State*. It is the reason for his institutional approach as well as the animating element of the work. The '*supernatural*' in each of us, properly cultivated, will link generation to generation by 'faith, freedom, heraldry, and ancestral fame' (*C&S*, p. 67). Man's actively contemplative, god-like self will be released by Coleridge's model of nationwide cultivation. The comparison to be made between Coleridge and Smith along these lines is nevertheless an important one for understanding all the texts we have encountered in this study. In this case the solution to the problems caused by advanced specialization is anticipated in the *Wealth of Nations* itself, albeit in a slightly undeveloped form. The notion of the cultivation of passive accomplishments, dramatically put forward in one form or another by Schiller, Coleridge and Mill, is included in Smith's argument without much ceremony at all.

There is also another case in which the political economy of Smith and Ferguson can be seen to contain the possibilities that are subsequently developed against it. In Chapter 2 we observed the similarities of Schiller's characterization of aesthetic contemplation as a state of 'play' to Bentham's state of 'avocation'. Both concepts relied on a notion of paradox. Being at play, for Schiller, was being simultaneously active and passive, at once physical and intellectual but also neither of those things. A continual state of avocation in Bentham's thought was similarly contradictory. Man was conceived of as working at the same time as playing, as being in an enjoyable withdrawal from employment at the same moment that he was continuing to be productive. In Chapter 3 we observed Cowper, Coleridge and Wollstonecraft describing themselves in comparable terms. These writers were in repose in terms of physical relaxation, or mentally relaxed to the extent that they all ceased to control their minds consciously. Yet at the same time these moments of reverie portrayed the mind being set in motion with a surprising intensity. Physical inactivity was again juxtaposed with vigorous mental occupation. A state of pervasive repose was also one of considerable agitation.

Considering these connected parameters in the light of Smith and Ferguson's thought enables us to offer a rationale for their similarity. In Ferguson's *Essay* and in Smith's *Wealth of Nations* we observed how the categories of labour and repose were delimited extremely narrowly. Labour became synonymous with physical activity and was imagined, by Smith especially, as filling almost the entirety of the individual's time. Repose, in this scheme, was the necessary shadow and compensation to a life of labour, the stretch of time in which one recruits one's 'limited' and 'wasting force'. The effect of these definitions was to leave no space, and also thereby to open up the possibility, for the whole host of activities that are neither physical exertion nor complete inactivity. Smith and Ferguson drew attention to an entire area of human life by ignoring and omitting it.

What is distinctive about the activities that belong to this area of human life is that they can be described in opposite terms equally correctly. The intellectual enterprise of producing the *Wealth of Nations*, for instance, might be denominated an active accomplishment by virtue of the manual task of writing the work and the concrete product this process produced. But we might also highlight the contemplative nature of such an undertaking and observe the impossibility of producing a work such as this without imaginatively withdrawing from the society it describes. Without the contemplative abilities of reflection and foresight, the work could never have been produced. Activities left out of Smith and Ferguson's delimitation of labour and repose, therefore, can be described as either active or passive, or indeed as a combination of the two.

It is this ambiguity that is significant for understanding the writers that succeed and oppose Smith and Ferguson's political economy. The notion of paradox that inflects the category of aesthetic contemplation seems to be related to the manner in which contemplative activities are ignored in that discourse. The space between physical activity and passive repose is rendered an indeterminate middle ground by Smith and Ferguson. Passive accomplishments, in that manner of thinking, are neither work nor rest, but somehow both at once. The similarity of this description to Schiller's portrait of being at play, or to Cowper's model of poetic composition, is obvious. The paradoxical parameters of aesthetic contemplation would seem to be anticipated at least, if not somehow prompted, by the limited definitions Smith and Ferguson employ.

The political economic enquiries with which we began this study thus seem to hold an important role in relation to all the texts we have considered. Smith and Ferguson's thought seems to anticipate all the models of human capability subsequently deployed against it. We saw Cowper and Coleridge striving to rewrite the idea of human nature as it appeared in the *Wealth of Nations* by means of a distinctly private, individualistic point of view. Yet we also saw how this perspective was included in Smith's analysis, albeit again in an undeveloped form in comparison to the analyses of Cowper and Coleridge. We saw as well the theme of education become central to the problem of the side-effects of advanced specialization. Bentham focused on the individual's mental accomplishments in much the same way that Coleridge aimed to cultivate the individual's passive abilities. Again however we have seen how Smith's analysis anticipates and includes the notion and many of the parameters of this idea of cultivation.

The various discourses we have studied also bear a direct connection to Wordsworth's 'Gipsies'. The speaker of that poem strove to demonstrate that his intellectual activities were labours, in comparison to the physical inertia of the gypsies at least. The play of poetic energies was aligned with work by virtue of its intensity and latent productivity. We have now seen several different versions of this claim. In Schiller's description, aesthetically orientated intellectual activity is marked out from other human engagements by two things: its employment of both sides of man's sensuo-rational nature and the intensity of its experience. The *Aesthetic Letters* create an implicit hierarchy of engagements and position aesthetic contemplation as the most important and stimulating type of human activity. It is this hierarchy, replicated implicitly by Cowper for instance, that enables poetic composition to be described as a type of work. Since manual labour as Smith and Ferguson understood it was both limited and limiting, identifying a human activity that is fully engaging means that it can be described as more work-like than work itself. Aesthetic contemplation and poetic composition become, in this comparison, the most intense and directly creative acts in which an individual can be engaged.

Distinct from this type of comparison, however, there is also another important way in which one of the writers we have considered attempts to render aesthetic activities work-like. In 'Effusion xxxv', Coleridge's 'idle flitting phantasies' end the poem as the objects of considerable embarrassment. Rather than being the subject of the poet's continued exaltation, Sara's 'reproof' causes him to regret their occurrence and to play down the value he attributed to them at the moment when he felt their intensity. The logic that stands behind this sense of guilt can be traced in Coleridge's ruminations on the will. Considering 'streamy', un-willed and uncontrolled association to be lacking in morality compared to the kinds of tasks that align with one's duty, the 'uncall'd and undetain'd' thoughts Coleridge experiences in the poem are to be understood as dangerously amoral. The problem facing Coleridge is how idle thought, so central to his descriptions of the activity of the poet, can be rendered a more moral activity.

The solution to this problem, as we saw in the *Biographia*, is to identify the operation of the will in the workings of the secondary imagination. When the type of idle thought that goes into poetic composition can be described as needing 'irremissive, though gentle and unnoticed, controul' (*Biog.*, Vol. II, p. 16), it becomes a much more moral activity for Coleridge. Because the will both instigates and subsequently monitors the play-like operations of the secondary imagination, it is no longer problematic that idle thought may appear to be entirely uncontrolled, as is the case in the 'Effusion', for example. The *Biographia* assures us that the will is constantly active in this process. Poetic composition is to be understood as akin to both one's duty and one's inclination. It is both pleasurable and work-like, at once idle and active.

The argument of Wordsworth's 'Gipsies' is thus replicated and enlarged upon in both Coleridge's identification of the operation of the will in aesthetic contemplation and the kind of comparisons of poetic work and manual work deployed by Schiller and Cowper. The intense contemplation represented by Wordsworth's careful use of poetic diction is work-like by virtue of its intensity and because of its deliberate genesis. The speaker of 'Gipsies' may not make direct use of Coleridge's version of this argument, but the poem contains many of the elements necessary for its implementation. 'Gipsies' also functions very much like the analyses of Schiller and Cowper. The poem dramatically contrasts different types of human engagement, introduces the category of idle contemplation, and then stylistically and thematically contends for the greater intensity and worth of this style of thought. Were it not for the tone of indignation that characterizes the whole text, the speaker of Wordsworth's 'Gipsies' could be aligned quite unproblematically with Cowper's persona in *The Task*.

In reference to 'Gipsies', one should also note the pastoral flavour of the literature this study has considered. The emphasis on the import of leisure as opposed to labour, and the notion of the insight engendered by communion with nature, cast Cowper and Wollstonecraft's rural reveries, much like Coleridge's Pantisocracy thought and Cowperian poetry, into the realms of the pastoral. These works, from this perspective, offer observations on the workings of commercial society from the telling distance of rural idleness, suggesting that the relationships described there can teach us about life at the centre of that society in much the same way that the relationship between shepherd and sheep, as William Empson observes, might function as a kind of serious parody of that between ruler and populace.[2] It is significant, however, that there is a key element of Cowper and Coleridge's versions of this mode that moves the poetry we have considered here beyond the generic boundaries of the pastoral. Where Empson, for instance, describes that genre as functioning by means of an apparent narrative naivety, so that its works can play the role of being both 'about' and 'by' the rustic or labouring community,[3] the ironic elements we had occasion to observe in 'Effusion xxxv', or in the brown study, move the register of those poems into importantly distinct territory. Such territory might be described as that of a philosophy similar to that of Schiller, or even one more critical than a work such as the *Aesthetic Letters* because of its ability to detach itself from the Rousseauvian model of the natural. Thus when Coleridge voices the counter-argument to his tentative 'And what if all of animated nature …' in the form of his wife's disapproval, that poem also moves into a position from which it can critique the assumptions of the pastoral and its depiction of what is seemingly natural in man's connection with his environment. Cowper's serio-comic identification of the workings of his faculties in the brown study performs something of a similar role, albeit in a less developed manner. These observations allow us to say that the poetry this study has considered both replicates and analyses a kind of ideology of leisure. It is concerned with the possibility of founding a system of thought on the opposite assumptions to those of political economy, but also with the problems in doing so. That this quandary is portrayed by a subtle exploration of the conditions of the pastoral, moreover, renders the idea of distance from the site of commercial society itself significantly problematic.

The final element of the texts we have been considering here that I want to highlight is the relationship between the German-language enquiry of Schiller and the network of English-language texts we have been exploring rather more thoroughly. It is not simply the case that Schiller's writing provides a set of theories applicable to the English poetic practitioners we have been studying. In Chapter 3, on the contrary, we observed how the interconnected portraits of human capability put forward by Cowper, Coleridge and Wollstonecraft could be described as constructing an even more thorough portrait of aesthetic contemplation than the *Aesthetic Letters*. These writers not only positioned various types of moral consciousness as accessible to the contemplative individual, but also identified the dangers attendant on idle thought with compelling precision and consistency. In Chapter 4, similarly, we observed how the similarities of Coleridge's pre-German thought to the parameters of the *Aesthetic Letters* made the question of the influence of Schiller ultimately indecipherable in Coleridge's work. It was not clear whether the priorities of *Church and State* were prompted by Coleridge's reading of Schiller or by the concerns he had held since his Pantisocracy days.

These points of similarity between the *Aesthetic Letters* and many of the other sources we have studied, often occurring where influence cannot be established, render the question of Schiller's relationship to the English-language writing we have considered problematic. The *Aesthetic Letters* stand over all the texts here in terms of valuing and positioning aesthetic contemplation within a scheme of man's intellectual and physical engagements. More clearly than any other writer, Schiller makes idle thought the answer to the problems of advanced specialization. Yet something important can be achieved by recalling some of the connections we have made in this investigation. Firstly, there were the internal similarities of Smith and Ferguson's thought and *The Task*. The *Wealth of Nations* and that poem both aimed to define and delimit labour and leisure, and both thereby highlighted the types of activities that do not fit into those terms. Cowper, of course, took this logic to its next stage, making explicit what was only latent in Smith and Ferguson. Secondly we should remember Cowper's clear and focused influence on Coleridge and Wollstonecraft. The clarity and precision of his ruminations on idle thought led those two writers to replicate the brown study's characteristics and thus to continue *The Task*'s investigation into aesthetic consciousness.

These connections allow us to suggest that the British thought we have considered reaches its position of greatest similarity to Schiller without the direct influence of the *Aesthetic Letters*. A chain of shared logic, of cause and effect, from Smith to Coleridge renders idle contemplation the central activity in human life by virtue of the moral and aesthetic possibilities it opens up. The passive accomplishments, accessed most clearly in a private, contemplative setting, become the answer to the problems of advanced specialization, and then become imbued with fundamentally connected aesthetic and moral consequences.[4] What is clear in describing these developments is the importance of Cowper and of *The Task*. It is that poem that investigates idle contemplation explicitly in these terms. It is that poem that considers aesthetic contemplation in such detail and with such subtlety that its parameters are made clearly visible to Coleridge and Wollstonecraft. Whilst Coleridge may have had his own reasons for exploring the details of poetic composition, it is Cowper who charted this territory in detail a decade before Coleridge began his investigation. In the texts we have considered, it is Cowper who moved British thought alongside Schiller's idealism, ten years before the publication of the *Aesthetic Letters*.

Epilogue: Wordsworth and Kingsley

I want to end this study by taking a brief look at what happens to the notion of aesthetic contemplation in the wake of Coleridge, Cowper and Schiller. To do this I want to consider Charles Kingsley's novels *Yeast* and *Alton Locke* alongside Wordsworth's 'Three years she grew in sun and shower', and take a slightly more detailed look at how John Stuart Mill's writing negotiates the discrepancies between its utilitarian and aesthetic influences. This analysis will enable us to see that far from being emancipated from the political problems that motivated its invocation and deployment by Schiller, aesthetic contemplation maintains a tense and fraught relationship with contemporary social reality. Turning our attention to Kingsley's writing will also put us in a position to assess the impact of the model of idle thought developed by Wordsworth, Cowper, Coleridge and Wollstonecraft.

First serialized in *Fraser's Magazine* in 1848, *Yeast: A Problem* would seem to have a dual aim. In addition to depicting the social and political problems that lead, in Kingsley's opinion, to a degraded morality amongst the lower classes, the novel also concerns itself with movement of the 'young men and women' of the 'day' 'either towards Rome, towards sheer materialism, or towards an unchristian and unphilosophic spiritualism'. In Kingsley's hands, importantly, these problems are connected. The novel describes the solution to the lower classes' troubles as the 'real living belief' that all members of society should feel as opposed to the spurious 'belief-in-believing' he sees as prevalent.[1] It is one of the categories of forces that Kingsley depicts as pulling in the opposite direction from this apparently spurious type of belief that is of particular interest to the present study, however. In the class of 'unchristian and unphilosophic spiritualism' falls a type of aesthetic contemplation very similar to that described by Wollstonecraft and Coleridge. This model of aesthetic consciousness, moreover, is portrayed in the novel by direct reference to Wordsworth.

The poem around which *Yeast* constructs this model is Wordsworth's 'Three years she grew in sun and shower'. Composed in 1798 and published in the second edition of the *Lyrical Ballads* in 1800, 'Three years she grew' is the fourth of the five 'Lucy' poems (in Wordsworth's final ordering of them at least). The poem describes the three-year-old Lucy being taken in by Nature, whose explanation of the qualities this union will engender makes up thirty-four lines of the forty-two-line poem. The poem's final stanza, returning to the speech of the narrator, makes clear that Nature's taking of Lucy to him- or herself[2] is synonymous with, or is the narrator's way of describing, the child's death:

> Thus Nature spake – The work was done –
> How soon my Lucy's race was run!
> She died, and left to me
> This heath, this calm and quiet scene;
> The memory of what has been,
> And never more will be.
> ('Three years', 37–42)

This stanza thus casts a radically new light over Nature's speech, rendering the natural world that the narrator looks out over both a further means to realize Lucy's growth into 'A lady' ('Three years', 6) and a physical trace of every one of her features and attributes. What seemed to be a description of the natural education Lucy would receive in reality becomes an account of her total union with nature, a sublimation insofar as it is both the consummation of Lucy's 'loveli[ness]' ('Three years', 2) and a destruction of her physical form.

The actual details of Lucy's 'education' make up the entirety of Nature's speech and the majority of the poem. Here, for example, are the poem's fourth and fifth stanzas:

> The floating clouds their state shall lend
> To her; for her the willow bend;
> Nor shall she fail to see
> Even in the motions of the Storm
> A beauty that shall mould her form
> By silent sympathy.
>
> The stars of midnight shall be dear
> To her; and she shall lean her ear
> In many a secret place
> Where rivulets dance their wayward round,
> And beauty born of murmuring sound
> Shall pass into her face.
> ('Three years', 19–30)

Nature's speech up to this point in the poem has given an intricate, unpredictable and infinitely variable flavour to Lucy's interactions with the speaker. Picturing Lucy 'in rock and plain, / In earth and heaven, in glade and bower' ('Three years', 9–10), as alternately powerful, 'sportive' and 'restrain[ed]' ('Three years', 12–13), the poem represents the child's relationship with Nature as everything at once, as a potentially limitless series of gifts and responsibilities. But the fourth and fifth stanzas function differently. Constructed almost identically, both beginning their second line with 'To her' and both ending with a description of how 'beauty' shall enter into the child, these stanzas figure Lucy's relationship with Nature in a similar and consistent manner. In both cases Lucy is shown to interact instinctively and gracefully with Nature, achieving things that would seem to require effort or correct activity with spontaneous ease. Lucy will not 'fail to see' the beauty that will 'mould her form' even in the apparently forlorn 'motions of the storm', although the manner in which this achievement is phrased makes failure sound like a definite possibility. Likewise the child will discover 'many a secret place' without hardship and will thus transform a kind of esoteric aural 'beauty' into a physical attribute able to 'pass into her face'. These stanzas thus depict Lucy's interaction with Nature as akin to Cowper's relationship with the woodland of *The Task*'s final book. In that episode, 'wisdom', hard-won over a sustained period of time in normal conditions, was achieved instantly, spontaneously and apparently without effort. The simple grace of this process rendered it at once calming and exhilarating for Cowper. Wordsworth's Lucy, in comparison, seems to gain additional grace by being the object of Nature's description rather than the subject speaking. The powers, sympathies and beauties she receives seem entirely natural to her, rearing her to a 'stately height' ('Three years', 32) by the end of Nature's speech.

Framing this description with the calm understatement of a pensive narrator, 'Three years she grew' is simultaneously an ideal portrait of a child's aesthetic education at the hands of Nature and a justification and interpretation of mortality. The poem describes an ideal relationship with Nature at the same moment that it makes the price of such a connection the individual's death. It depicts a narrator whose appreciation and contemplation of the natural world are also his longing for death, since a state even more attractive than Cowper's woodland meditation is on offer to the individual who will let him- or herself be taken into nature. Hence the poem depicts Wollstonecraft's desire to 'expand' into an unknown 'element' in even more detail than the Scandinavian Letters. Wordsworth gives this impulse a physical, aural and moral goal.

The aspect of 'Three years she grew' that *Yeast* draws upon most directly is one that aligns the poem with Coleridge's 'Effusion' and Cowper's brown study. At the beginning of the poem's second stanza, Nature introduces its multifarious description of the activities Lucy will engage in with the assertion that 'Myself will to my darling be / Both law and impulse' ('Three years', 7–8). This pronouncement renders the catalogue of activities and abilities that follow considerably problematic. Although Lucy will be able to 'spring' around the landscape and will be lent the 'state' of 'floating clouds', for example, neither of these engagements will be the object of the child's free will in this light. Nature, rather, will prescribe every activity that occupies her and every capacity she develops. The education to be received by Lucy in the poem is thus one of control above all else. Lucy will not even be given the slightest 'impulse' in this process. She is to be entirely directed, lacking control over even her smallest actions. Importantly, therefore, the Lucy reared to a 'stately height' in the poem will also be barely human. She will not have the capacity to impel her own activity, but will be a slave to Nature.

Casting a kind of macabre light over all the action of 'Three years she grew', this denial of Lucy's free will recalls the state described by Coleridge in 'Effusion xxxv'. In that poem, the narrator's 'idle flitting phantasies' were engendered the moment he ceased to control his mind consciously. His 'indolent and passive brain' could neither 'call' up thoughts nor 'detain' them. In the brown study similarly, it was when Cowper's 'understanding' took 'repose', temporarily giving up its supervision of the mind's activity, that his 'Fancy' could explore thoughts 'ludicrous and wild', apparently of its own choosing. The extent to which the style of thought that took place in the brown study was distinct from the operations of the poet's free will was underlined by the fact that the episode came to a close as Cowper was 'restore[d]' to himself. We could say, consequently, that one of the main features of Coleridge's and Cowper's portraits of idle thought that gave them dangerous and perplexing overtones has been picked out by Wordsworth. In all three cases, the mind is controlled by proxy, by a force that can be neither seen nor estimated. In all three cases, therefore, the subject being described is both raised above normal human capability and rendered disturbingly unhuman.

Kingsley's most clear rewriting of this motif occurs in *Yeast*'s third chapter, in the immediate aftermath of the novel's introduction of the theme of social problems. Lancelot, the novel's protagonist, is informed of the squalor in which the neighbouring peasantry live by Kingsley's Carlyle-like gamekeeper, Tregarva. When the first of many conversations

Epilogue: Wordsworth and Kingsley

between these two figures comes to a close, as Lancelot sits down to fish on a 'buck-stage' over the river, the subject Tregarva has introduced into the novel, instead of dominating the protagonist's thoughts, is forced out of his mind, against his will, by another stimulus:

> Lancelot sat and tried to catch perch, but Tregarva's words haunted him. He lighted his cigar, and tried to think earnestly over the matter, but he had got into the wrong place for thinking. All his thoughts, all his sympathies, were drowned in the rush and whirl of water. He forgot everything else in the mere animal enjoyment of sight and sound. Like many young men at his crisis of life, he had given himself up to the mere contemplation of Nature till he had become her slave; and now a luscious scene, a singing bird, were enough to allure his mind away from the most earnest and awful thoughts. He tried to think, but the river would not let him. It thundered and spouted out behind him from the hatches, and leapt madly past him, and caught his eyes in spite of him, and swept them away down its dancing waves, and let them go again only to sweep them down again and again, till his brain felt a delicious dizziness from the everlasting rush and the everlasting roar. (*Yeast*, p. 48)

Lancelot's repeated 'contemplation of Nature' has made him its 'slave'. Attempting to think, the physicality of the scene before him inhibits his brain from controlling itself. Even the 'most earnest and awful thoughts' cannot resist the allure of the river as it encompasses him with the intensity of its movement. Although Lancelot's interaction with nature will presently be equated with 'Three years she grew' by direct quotation, at this stage Kingsley's description brings Wollstonecraft's waterfall strongly to mind. Kingsley's protagonist interprets the physical movement of water very differently however. For Wollstonecraft the relentless crashing of the cascade caused her thoughts to rise above her cares and move towards a higher plane of existence and a new level of insight. Such a tendency, moreover, was a positive and enlightening transformation, emancipating her from a whole host of everyday troubles. In this scene of Kingsley's, on the contrary, the river's ability to remove thought from the details of the everyday becomes problematic by virtue of the importance of those thoughts. Rather than engendering new insight in Lancelot, the river can only draw him narrowly into its physicality. The type of object that was a source of reverie for Wollstonecraft becomes only an end in itself for Kingsley's protagonist, an intense physical experience that leads nowhere.[3]

The imagery with which Kingsley continues his description seeks to draw out this pointlessness by characterizing the river as a kind of artificial presence in comparison both to the thoughts upon which Lancelot is attempting to focus and the landscape around it:

And then below, how it spread, and writhed, and whirled into transparent fans, hissing and twining snakes, polished glass-wreaths, huge crystal bells, which broiled up from the bottom, and dived again beneath long threads of creamy foam, and swung round posts and roots, and rushed blackening under dark weed-fringed boughs, and gnawed at the marly banks, and shook the ever-restless bulrushes, till it was swept away and down over the white pebbles and olive weeds, in one broad rippling sheet of molten silver, towards the distant sea. (*Yeast*, pp. 48–9)

The river here seems to be an entity significantly distinct from the 'banks', 'roots' and 'boughs' around it. Kingsley's language in this passage gives it the quality of artifice, as if it were an intricate carving made up of 'fans', 'snakes', 'glass-wreaths', 'crystal'. Furthermore, by attacking the landscape around it – 'gnaw[ing]' the bank, shaking the 'bulrushes' – this gaudy, seductive presence seems to act as a hostile force in relation to the rest of nature. Sweeping down the landscape 'in one broad rippling sheet of molten silver', the river before Lancelot thus seems to withdraw his thoughts from social problems by means of a kind of allure of artificial refinement. This river represents a facet of the natural world that opposes its counterparts, an aspect of nature that inhibits Lancelot's seemingly natural interest in the welfare of his fellow men in much the same way that it attacks the landscape around it.

The river is not the only element of the scene before Lancelot that withdraws his thoughts from their desired subject, however. Kingsley's description of this moment concludes by focusing the reader's attention on the other natural objects surrounding his protagonist:

Downwards it fleeted ever, and bore his thoughts floating on its oily stream; and the great trout, with their yellow sides and peacock backs, lunged among the eddies, and the silver grayling dimpled and wandered among the shallows, and the may-flies flickered and rustled round him like water fairies, with their green gauzy wings; the coot clanked musically among the reeds; the frogs hummed their ceaseless vesper-monotone; the kingfisher darted from his hole in the bank like a blue spark of electric light; the swallows' bills snapped as they twined and hawked above the pool; the swifts' wings whirred like musket-balls, as they rushed screaming past his head; and ever the river fleeted by, bearing his eyes away down the current, till its wild eddies began to glow with crimson beneath the setting sun. The complex harmony of sights and sounds slid softly over his soul, and he sank away into a still day-dream, too passive for imagination, too deep for meditation, and

> Beauty born of murmuring sound,
> Did pass into his face.
> (*Yeast*, p. 49)

Kingsley's quotation of 'Three years she grew' in this context renders Wordsworth's 'Beauty' a mixed blessing. The 'complex harmony' of which it is made up is deployed as a network of seductive, tranquillizing distractions for Lancelot. '[K]ingfisher[s]', 'frogs', 'may-flies', 'swifts' and 'swallows' complement the intricacy of the river's movement to create a 'delicious dizziness' in Lancelot's mind. Importantly however, this mental state, described in this final passage as a 'still day-dream', acts as a kind of narcotic on the protagonist. '[T]oo passive for imagination' and 'too deep for meditation', Lancelot is paralysed by the physicality of the scene around him until the sun sets over the 'glow[ing]' river 'eddies'. The 'murmuring' beauty that passes into the protagonist's face is thus synonymous with intellectual and physical apathy in the face of social problems, an apathy that causes him to waste the hours this scene takes up in pointless, undesired, but seductive reverie.

Kingsley's use of Wordsworth in this scene should be understood to be carefully focused, therefore. 'Three years she grew' has been chosen and recreated at this moment in the novel precisely because of this notion of the power nature can wield over the individual. Wordsworth's poem directly questions the model of aesthetic consciousness developed by Schiller, Coleridge and Cowper in a manner only hinted at in the writing of the two last named. In 'Three years she grew' aesthetic contemplation does not open up the possibility of other types of knowledge, and does not bring about moral consciousness in the individual concerned. Rather, as is the case for the narrator of the poem, this style of idle thought is depicted as a morbid, self-serving and narrow reverie. As Lucy's interaction with Nature has been reduced to being the object of an omniscient control, the narrator's imaginative justification of the child's death can only offer him 'The memory of what has been'. Comparing this outcome to the kind of conclusions found in Coleridge's 'Effusion' or 'Frost at Midnight' must lead one to characterize Wordsworth's version of the aesthetic reverie as vain and limited.

It is precisely this notion of narrowness, restriction and vanity that Kingsley seems to be most interested in, moreover. In his hands, aesthetic contemplation withdraws the mind from social and moral thought. Nature becomes the site at which the individual is inhibited from engaging in deliberate contemplation and is instead robbed of his or her mental self-control. The 'mere contemplation of Nature' has become a kind of idol for Lancelot, to be worshipped for its own sake rather than for the knowledge it can engender and the action it can inspire. It is as if the reveries of Coleridge and Cowper have been misinterpreted, understood merely as an engagement with the physical landscape rather than as a means to engender a particular style of intellectual and moral thought. In Kingsley's hands, further, such an act of contemplation takes place without the individual's instigation even, as in this case, when he desires to consider some other subject matter or some more pressing topic. What was a welcome and partially voluntary state – the individual ceasing to control his or her mind – is described by Kingsley as a kind of imposition on the individual, a tyranny of aesthetic contemplation that can be as vain as it is unwanted.

This set of beliefs about the attractions and the failings of aesthetic contemplation does more than simply inform Lancelot's behaviour at this moment in the novel, however. The model of this specific type of idle thought, rather, illustrated through Kingsley's use of 'Three years she grew', should be understood to inform the development of *Yeast*'s plot as a whole. The novel's romantic subplot, for instance, which takes place between Lancelot and Argemone, pits religious belief against the protagonist's aesthetic 'spiritualism'. Importantly, moreover, Kingsley depicts Argemone as significantly more drawn to Lancelot's aesthetics than he is to her faith. Take this description from the novel's tenth chapter:

> As One higher than them would have it, she took a fancy to read Homer in the original, and Lancelot could do no less than offer his services as a translator … And step by step Lancelot opened to her the everlasting significance of the poem; the unconscious purity which lingers in it, like the last rays of the Paradise dawn; its sense of the dignity of man as man … She could not but listen and admire, when he introduced her to the sheer paganism of Schiller's Gods of Greece; for on this subject he was more eloquent than on any. He had gradually, in fact, as we have seen, dropped all faith in anything but Nature; the slightest fact about a bone or a weed was more important to him than all the books of divinity which Argemone lent him – to be laid by unread. (*Yeast*, pp. 130–1)

The intellectual exchange taking place between Lancelot and Argemone in this passage is distinctly lopsided. The books that inspire and reflect the latter's faith are accepted but not taken seriously by Lancelot, while his every word is absorbed by Argemone. Further, the protagonist's passion lies in aesthetic pursuits above all else: the poetry of Homer, the writing of Schiller, not to mention anything to do with the physicality of the natural world. Whilst it is not strictly the case that the novel will attempt to expose the vanity of these pursuits, Kingsley is at pains to describe Lancelot's gradual conversion from using his aesthetics as an idol to a genuine belief in the power and centrality of true religious faith. At this stage in the novel, then, the aesthetic appears as an arena of the protagonist's intellectual employment that is not misguided exactly, but that should not consume the entirety of his considerable energies and talents. Even more importantly perhaps, aesthetic pursuits are again depicted as seductive and alluring, even to a figure like Argemone possessed of a sound and admirable religious faith.

Another moment at which Kingsley deploys the aesthetic to rather ironic effect occurs in the novel's thirteenth chapter, when Tregarva takes Lancelot to witness a local village fair in order to let the protagonist experience a manifestation of lower-class life. This episode, which culminates with Lancelot feeling 'utterly down-hearted' about 'the poor', is also the occasion on which Kingsley gives the reader a glimpse of his protagonist's thinking on the potential solutions to the moral failings he has witnessed:

> He had expected, as I said before, at least to hear something of pastoral sentiment, and of genial frolicsome humour; to see some innocent, simple enjoyment: but instead, what had he seen but vanity, jealousy, hoggish sensuality, dull vacuity? drudges struggling for one night to forget their drudgery. And yet withal, those songs, and the effect which they produced, showed that in these poor creatures, too, lay the germs of pathos, taste, melody, soft and noble affections. 'What right have we', thought he, 'to hinder their development? Art, poetry, music, science – ay, even those athletic and graceful exercises on which we all pride ourselves, which we consider necessary to soften and refine ourselves, what God has given us a monopoly of them? – what is good for the rich man is good for the poor. Over-education? And what of that? What if the poor be raised above 'their station'? What right have we to keep them down? How long have they been thralls in soul, as well as in body? (*Yeast*, pp. 194–5)

Lancelot's potential solution to the 'hoggish sensuality' and 'dull vacuity' he has witnessed is aesthetic education. He considers 'Art, poetry, music' and 'science' to be the basis of moral behaviour, suggesting, albeit only to himself, that the depravity he has witnessed could be solved on the model of beauty, by refined and 'graceful' activities.

In addition to noting the Schillerian flavour of these thoughts of Lancelot's, we should also observe the manner in which Kingsley, as narrator, treats them. As the protagonist's train of thinking comes to a close, the novel's narrator innocently observes the manner in which Lancelot and Tregarva's ruminations differ at this moment:

> Tregarva's meditations must have been running in a very different channel, for he suddenly burst out, after long silence –
> 'It's a pity these fairs can't be put down. They do a lot of harm; ruin all the young girls around, the Dissenters' children especially, for they run utterly wild; their parents have no hold on them at all.' (*Yeast*, p. 195)

In comparison to Lancelot's attempts to formulate a solution to what the pair have witnessed, Tregarva's thoughts are significantly more pragmatic. He would like to see physical action with a clearly defined end rather than education on the suppositions of idealist psychology. Indeed, if one compares Lancelot's aesthetic solution to the details of the problems outlined in his first conversation with Tregarva, the route of art and poetry becomes even more outlandish. Here, Tregarva is speaking first:

> 'Are men likely to be healthy when they are worse housed than a pig?'
> 'No.'
> 'And worse fed than a hound?'
> 'Good heavens! No!'
> 'Or packed together to sleep, like pilchards in a barrel?'
> 'But, my good fellow, do you mean that the labourers here are in that state?'
> 'It isn't far to walk, sir. Perhaps some day, when the May-fly is gone off, and the fish won't rise awhile, you could walk down and see.' (*Yeast*, p. 45)

Physical problems of subsistence of the kind Tregarva implies function in the novel as a direct rebuttal of Lancelot's aesthetic impulses and hopes. Kingsley juxtaposes such economic and social reality with the network of beliefs we have observed in Cowper, Coleridge and Wollstonecraft, which imagines the contemplation of nature as the activity that will refine and moralize man. In Kingsley's hands the two completely fail to match. The former is a crisis of physical conditions and of the responsibilities of rural landowners, while the latter functions as a seduction and a narcotic. Aesthetic contemplation holds no purchase over social problems in this portrait, and the plot of *Yeast* as a whole is concerned with charting Lancelot's conversion from aesthetic 'spiritualism' to genuine faith and to political activity motivated by that faith.

I want to turn away from *Yeast* now, and consider Kingsley's very much connected novel, *Alton Locke, Tailor and Poet: An Autobiography*, first published in 1850. Although this latter text does not make direct reference to Wordsworth's poetry in the way that *Yeast* does, I want to read Kingsley's use of river- and seascapes in this novel in light of the connections we have already witnessed between waterside contemplation and 'Three years she grew'. On the evidence of *Alton Locke*, reveries taking place in sight of and above water seem to be connected, in Kingsley's mind, to Wordsworth's poem.[4] In this way, this second novel of Kingsley's can be read as exploring aspects of 'Three years she grew' not touched on by the action of *Yeast*, and, vice versa, the novel can be opened up by reading it through Wordsworth's poem.

Epilogue: Wordsworth and Kingsley

Alton Locke commences by foregrounding a significant juxtaposition or discrepancy. The novel's protagonist occupies a position comparable to that described by Coleridge in 'Frost at Midnight'. He is, in his own exposition at least, a born poet, but one bereft of the sights and sounds that he desires to experience: 'the little scraps of garden before the doors, with their dusty, stunted lilacs and balsam poplars, were my only forests; my only wild animals, the dingy, merry sparrows, who quarrelled fearlessly on my window-sill, ignorant of trap or gun' (*Alton Locke*, p. 5).[5] Connecting a poetic sensibility with natural objects like this might lead one to expect the novel to describe the poet's gradual and climactic attainment of them. Yet *Alton Locke* does not do this. Kingsley rather depicts the manner in which his protagonist's class and profession clash with, dilute, rub up against and confound his poetic endeavours and ambitions. The vexed relationship between Alton's poetry and a whole series of his other obligations render the protagonist's poetic character both problematic and elusive. In this way the comparison with Coleridge that the novel's opening suggests is misleading. *Alton Locke* is much less about poetic achievements and poetic sensibility than it is about the objects that inhibit such activity and such a state of mind.[6]

Kingsley's depiction of the aesthetic capabilities of his protagonist can be pinned down, however, in part at least, by reference to Wordsworth's 'Three years she grew'. Let us turn, for example, to *Alton Locke*'s deliberate anticlimax, its account of 10 April 1848, on which the Chartist petition was to be presented to Parliament. In that episode, following the confirmation of his cousin's engagement to Lillian, Alton finds himself in a delirium of feelings and thoughts on Waterloo Bridge:

> I buried myself in a recess of the bridge, and stared around and up and down.
> I was alone – deserted even by myself. Mother, sister, friends, love, the idol of my life, were all gone. I could have borne that. But to be shamed, and know that I deserved it; to be deserted by my honour, self-respect, strength of will – who can bear that? ...
> 'What drives the Frenchman to suicide?' I asked myself, arguing ever even in the face of death and hell – 'His faith in nothing but his own lusts and pleasures; and when they are gone, then comes the pan of charcoal – and all is over ... Those old Romans, too – why, they are the very experimentum crucis of suicide! As long as they fancied that they had a calling to serve the state, they could live on and suffer. But when they found no more work left for them, then they could die – as Porcia died – as Cato – as I ought. What is there left for me to do? outcast, disgraced, useless, decrepit –' (*Alton Locke*, p. 238)

The description that follows these desperate thoughts separates Alton's situation into a quandary of duty and inclination:

I looked out over the bridge into the desolate night. Below me the dark moaning river-eddies hurried downward. The wild west-wind howled past me, and leapt over the parapet downward. The huge reflection of Saint-Paul's, the great tap-roots of light from lamp and window that shone upon the lurid stream, pointed down – down – down. A black wherry shot through the arch beneath me, still and smoothly downward. My brain began to whirl madly – I sprang upon the step. – A man rushed past me, clambered on the parapet, and threw up his arms wildly. – A moment more, and he would have leapt into the stream. The sight recalled me to my senses – say, rather, it re-awoke in me the spirit of mankind. I seized him by the arm, tore him down upon the pavement, and held him, in spite of his frantic struggles. (*Alton Locke*, pp. 328–9)

This episode is constructed with strikingly similar materials to the fifth stanza of 'Three years she grew'. There is the motif of the narrator morbidly and silently staring out at the scene before him, his thoughts torn between his physical situation and objects that are no more ('I was alone – deserted even by myself'). There is the foregrounding of the nocturnal setting that takes place in both this scene and the poem's fifth stanza: Wordsworth's 'stars of midnight' become Kingsley's 'desolate night'. And likewise there is the river, described in *Alton Locke* in terms that echo Wordsworth's. The poet's 'secret place', for example, has been translated into a buried 'recess of the bridge' in the novel. Kingsley's 'dark moaning river-eddies', likewise, recall the 'murmuring' 'rivulets' that 'dance their wayward round' in 'Three years she grew'.

The effect of this allusion on this moment in the novel is complex. In general terms, the spectre of 'Three years she grew' raises the question of the kind of education and cultivation Alton has received up until this point in his life (the novel, after all, is a first-person *Bildungsroman*). In 'Three years she grew' Lucy was imagined as receiving an aesthetic and naturalistic education par excellence, a programme in which every epitomized and pure aspect of Nature was infused into the child spontaneously and gracefully. The effect of this process was to produce a 'lady' in Nature's 'own' image: 'hers shall be the breathing balm / And hers the silence and the calm / Of mute insensate things' ('Three years', 16–18). The protagonist of *Alton Locke*, by contrast, has been educated amongst a paucity of natural objects. The 'little scraps of garden' that fill the place of Lucy's 'glade and bower' gave way, early in his childhood, to the stench, filth and moral depravity of his tailors' workroom:

I recoiled with disgust at the scene before me … A low lean-to room, stifling me with the combined odours of human breath and perspiration, stale beer, the sweet sickly smell of gin, and the sour and hardly less disgusting one of new cloth. On the floor, thick with dust and dirt, scraps of stuff and ends of thread, sat some dozen haggard, untidy, shoeless men, with a mingled look of care and recklessness that made me shudder. The windows were tight closed to keep out the cold winter air; and the condensed breath ran in streams down the panes, chequering the dreary out-look of chimney tops and smoke. (*Alton Locke*, pp. 23–4)

The 'secret' vantage point Lucy has over her dancing 'rivulets' is hence not simply replicated but also parodied by Alton's 'recess in the bridge'. The latter, appearing to be a solitary hiding place from the hardships and struggles of the city, turns out to be invaded by those ills almost as soon as Alton occupies it. Jemmy Downes, a one-time fellow tailor of the protagonist, interrupts Alton's morbid reverie by his attempt to put an end to his own troubles.

While the Thames flowing under Waterloo Bridge may serve as an image of nature penetrating to the heart of the city in *Alton Locke*, then, it is a nature robbed of the associations that structure Lucy's mind. The 'beauty born of murmuring sound' that will 'pass into her face' becomes a 'howl[ing]', 'moaning', downward-dragging 'lurid stream'. The unambiguous connotations of the river are further highlighted by the 'black wherry' that Alton sees passing under the bridge. There seems to be no other way to interact with the river than to be dragged downwards by it, pulled along relentlessly and inevitably. It is a constant, persistent force, motioning 'still and smoothly downward'. This is the nature that has educated Alton, dragging him downwards, whirling madly like a river-eddy, rather than 'rear[ing]' him up to a 'stately height'. Where Lucy's river was but one object in a landscape of mountains, rocks, plains and bowers, Alton's Thames is a rare symbol of a natural world obscured at all other times by 'chimney tops and smoke'. In this connection indeed we should note that Alton interprets the reflection of St Paul's as a series of 'great tap-roots'. Buildings have taken the place Nature held for Lucy and, since it is the reflection of St Paul's that shines upon the stream, the effect of this substitution is to render nature 'lurid' and 'moaning' rather than 'danc[ing]' and 'murmuring'.

In addition to foregrounding the idea of Alton's education, Kingsley's subtle reference to Wordsworth in this scene also draws out the choice Alton is faced with at this moment, and indeed in the course of the novel as a whole, between his duties and his inclinations. In 'Three years she grew' the position the narrator reveals himself to be in by the poem's final stanza can be expressed as a choice between what he desires and what he ought to do. On the model of Lucy's supposed experience of Nature, and on the evidence of the narrator's morbid fascination with the 'calm and quiet scene' before him, the narrator would seem to want to join Lucy in being swallowed up by the landscape. His contemplation of the 'heath' in front of him and the description of Lucy's death that, by the end of the poem, one must attribute to the narrator, mean that it is death in nature that is being considered and weighed up in the poem. The narrator's intense appreciation of Nature's variety, purity and grace, demonstrated in the cataloguing of powers and attributes that make up the poem, becomes almost synonymous with death. Nature's secret places and silent sympathies are only to be fully accessed in death. The narrator seems to yearn for the same fate that has befallen Lucy. By contrast with this seemingly intense desire, Wordsworth's narrator's duty might be expressed as his life outside this realm of morbid contemplation. What the narrator ought to do is re-establish his ties with other human figures than Lucy, continue his life without being consumed by the deathly fascination with nature that impels the poem. 'Three years she grew' thus opposes life and death, humanity and nature, along the lines of its narrator's duty and inclination, respectively.

This scheme, importantly, seems to function as an almost exact template for the moment in *Alton Locke* we are considering. That Alton is contemplating suicide is made explicit for the reader by the catalogue of historical justifications for ending one's life that pass through the protagonist's mind at the beginning of the episode. Thus when we read 'My brain began to whirl madly – I sprang upon the step', it is clear what is about to happen. Alton's desire, at this moment, is to plunge into this lurid version of nature, to terminate his existence in the moaning, eddying symbol of his life up to this point. As Lucy died into the symbol of her perfection, and as Wordsworth's narrator wants to be swallowed up by the force that took Lucy, Alton wants to submit to the wild, howling forces of nature that have both characterized and beset his life.

In opposition to this distinct and intense desire, Alton's duty must also be seen to exert its influence on the scene. And again, in this case, 'Three years she grew' serves as a paradigm. Just as Wordsworth's narrator's duties were to humanity, life and the world outside his memory of Lucy, Alton's obligations, prompted in him by his friendship with Sandy Mackaye and John Crossthwaite, are to his fellow tailors and to men of his class more generally. It is for these people that he writes poetry, out of obligation to these people that he all but squanders his aristocratic connections, and for the benefit of these people that he will eventually write his autobiography. On Waterloo Bridge this responsibility to humanity takes the form of Jemmy Downes, attempting to throw himself into the river at the exact moment Alton is contemplating the same act. This event, shaking the protagonist out of his morbid delirium, also marks the end of Kingsley's recreation of 'Three years she grew'. Alton's dream of yielding to the world that thwarts his actions is ended and replaced by his duty to his co-worker.

It is in this sense that both Wordsworth's poem and this episode in *Alton Locke* end on a note of quotidian bathos. Wordsworth's 'calm and quiet scene', contrasted implicitly with the frequent and varied activities of Lucy in the poem, places the narrator's world of everyday concerns at a considerable distance from his imaginative justification of the child's death. In *Alton Locke*, similarly, although Jemmy Downes gives the episode a kind of symmetry by replicating the frantic tone that characterized Alton's thoughts on burying himself in the bridge, it is in a mood of everyday sensibleness that the protagonist calms him:

> 'What is there left on earth to live for? The prayers of liberty are answered by the laughter of tyrants; her sun is sunk beneath the ocean wave, and her pipe put out by the raging billows of aristocracy! Those starving millions of Kennington Common – where are they? Where? I axes you', he cried fiercely, raising his voice to a womanish scream – 'where are they?'
>
> 'Gone home to bed, like sensible people; and you had better go too.' (*Alton Locke*, p. 329)

Jemmy's series of questions would not be out of place in the mouth of Alton at the beginning of the episode. Yet the protagonist's attempts to appease his friend signal the switch that has taken place in his state of mind. From indulging his morbid desires, he returns to acting in accordance with his duty to his fellow men: 'The sight recalled me to my senses – say, rather, it re-awoke in me the spirit of mankind.' Both 'Three years she grew' and this moment in *Alton Locke* thus represent a moment of reverie that is at once morbid and desirable, but that is then classified as indulgent. Both episodes depict a kind of momentary, contemplative pause in the individual's adherence to his obligations.

This moment on Waterloo Bridge thus replaces Wordsworth's intensely idealized natural landscape with a kind of sham of nature, with a river that can only reflect the lurid sights around it, and that seems only able to make sounds in accordance with the moral depravity through which it runs. There are moments in *Alton Locke*, however, in which its protagonist is allowed to consider more rural and natural landscapes. These moments, furthermore, sparse as they are in Alton's narrative, can be seen to reopen and continue the novel's dialogue with 'Three years she grew'. Take, for example, the novel's penultimate scene, as Alton, crossing the Atlantic with Crossthwaite and his wife, stares out across the nocturnal seascape:

> Hark! again, sweet and clear, across the still night sea, ring out the notes of Crossthwaite's bugle – the first luxury, poor fellow, he ever allowed himself; and yet not a selfish one, for music, like mercy, is twice blessed … Well – thank God! at least I shall not be buried in a London churchyard! It may be a foolish fancy – but I have made them promise to lay me up among the virgin woods, where, if the soul ever visits the place of its body's rest, I may snatch glimpses of that natural beauty from which I was barred out in life, and watch the gorgeous flowers that bloom above my dust, and hear the forest birds sing around the Poet's grave. (*Alton Locke*, pp. 388–9)

This passage both mirrors the scene on Waterloo Bridge and functions in a similar manner to Wordsworth's poem. At night, looking across water from an elevated position, stimulated by the noises around him, Alton once again envisages his own death. Yet here, just as the sounds to be heard are 'sweet and clear' rather than deathly and ghostly, and just as the water beneath him is 'still' rather than eddying, the end Alton imagines is more serene. This death, indeed, would seem to have affinities with Lucy's own as the narrator imagines it in 'Three years she grew'. Both are made up of activities that constitute interaction with nature. Alton's 'soul' will 'visit' the site of 'its body's rest', 'snatch glimpses' of nature and listen to birds sing, just as Lucy will 'spring' around the landscape, see beauty 'in the motions of the storm' and 'lean her ear' to the river. In both, likewise, nature is an active agent, 'bloom[ing]' spontaneously or 'spring[ing]' around the landscape, rather than simply reflecting the city's woes and failings as the Thames does in the earlier scene. This episode offers a less troubled recreation of Wordsworth's poem, therefore. Kingsley's protagonist is about to attain a state akin to that of Wordsworth's Lucy.

But Kingsley's use of Wordsworth's poem at this moment is not as simple as such a sense of resolution might imply. We should note, for example, that this idyllic solution to Alton's problems and desires has come at a price. The protagonist's political, literary and personal actions on behalf of his fellow labourers are significantly compromised by his exile to America. Political engagement of the kind Alton engages in, albeit problematically, for the duration of the novel would seem to be precluded by this geographical location. The sense of aesthetic satisfaction that Kingsley's allusion to Wordsworth throws over this moment thus serves to highlight the incompatibility between aesthetic and political desires. Alton would seem to have to choose between the macabre, morbid and seemingly futile aesthetic experience that took place in the midst of political struggle on Waterloo Bridge on 10 April, and the less complicated, more reassuring, idyllic reverie that occurred before his arrival in America. The former was characterized by a dizzying, twisted Nature, which seemed to confound Alton at the same moment that it educated him; the latter a more classical, Wordsworthian Nature, whose simple reassurances overtly contradict the complexities of the protagonist's political, metropolitan life. The choice is between political engagement and political withdrawal, but also between a disturbing and perplexing aesthetic life and one of almost clichéd predictability and satisfaction.

Alton's choice has already been made for him by this stage in the novel, of course. But it is in the light of these alternatives that the protagonist's 'LAST WORDS', a three-verse poem that also concludes the novel, attempt to bridge the gap between exile and engagement.[7] Beginning with a repeated direction to 'weep' for 'pauper, dolt, and slave' (*Alton Locke*, p. 389), echoing Alton's reverie above the Thames in its second stanza ('Down, down, down, and down'), and then concluding with a kind of call to arms, with a return to action in the name of humanity, the poem encapsulates the movement of the novel as well as the stages of 'Three years she grew'. It is the poem's final stanza that addresses the theme of political engagement most directly:

> Up, up, up, and up,
> Face your game, and play it!
> The night is past – behold the sun! –
> The cup is full, the web is spun,
> The judge is set, the doom begun;
> Who shall stay it?
> (*Alton Locke*, p. 390)

The staccato, repetitively energetic pace of the last four lines of this verse represent Alton's attempt to invoke action on the part of his future readers. 'The night' that characterized the reveries on Waterloo Bridge and above the Atlantic is 'past'; the new day of struggle and toil for the good of man has arrived. In this poem and in his autobiography as a whole Alton is thus attempting to effect political activity and political reform from his idyllic rural retirement. The protagonist's Wordsworthian leisure is being used to motivate action in the midst of political unrest.

Kingsley is to be understood, therefore, as exploring the connections between a certain kind of political engagement and aesthetic experience in these moments, the two maintaining a complicated relationship. Alton's political activity and urban locale do not so much inhibit his aesthetic life as render it fraught, macabre and perplexing. His experiences on Waterloo Bridge thus bring Cowper's brown study to mind once again. Both seem physically dangerous to the same extent that they are stimulating. Both, moreover, acquire a kind of allure and resonance by virtue of the sense of danger they contain. It is in this manner that Alton's political engagement offers a more interesting spectacle in the novel than his eventual withdrawal into, and death in, nature. Kingsley portrays aesthetic consciousness in thrall to urban social degeneration as a more intriguing and idiosyncratic state than the poet acting instinctively and spontaneously in nature.[8]

In order to explore this relationship between aesthetic and political life in *Alton Locke* further, I want to leave the novel aside for a moment and turn to an alternative attempt to formulate this connection, which occurs in the writing of John Stuart Mill. Mill's *Autobiography*, as we saw earlier, focuses largely on the author's education at the hands of his father and his subsequent 'self-education', even though the work was not published until after Mill's death in 1873. The aspect of Mill that is most pertinent to this consideration of Kingsley's writing is the relationship he describes between these two periods of his development. You will remember that in the former, as the rough caricature goes, Mill was impressed with an astonishing course of classical and more practical accomplishments. Mastering Latin and Greek at an early age, he was also given significant responsibilities in the preparation of his father's *Elements of Political Economy*, published in 1821 when the younger Mill was fifteen. The period that Mill describes as his 'self-education', by contrast, corresponds, in the caricature at least, to his discovery of more aesthetic accomplishments, to the poetry of Wordsworth in particular and the notion of the 'passive susceptibilities' more generally. It is worth looking at these two periods in slightly more detail, however, for the attribution of political economic ideas to one side of Mill's development and aesthetic ideas to the other is not as accurate as an overview of the *Autobiography* might make it seem.

In the *Autobiography*'s first chapter, Mill's account of his 'Childhood, and Early Education', one finds the following:

> But though these exercises in history were never a compulsory lesson, there was another kind of composition which was so, namely writing verses, and it was one of the most disagreeable of my tasks. Greek or Latin verses I did not write, nor learnt the prosody of those languages. My father, thinking this not worth the time it required, contented himself with making me read aloud to him, and correcting false quantities. I never composed at all in Greek, even in prose, and but little in Latin: not that my father could be indifferent to the value of this practice, in giving a thorough knowledge of those languages, but because there really was not time for it. The verses I was required to write were English. When I first read Pope's Homer, I ambitiously attempted to compose something of the same kind,

Epilogue: Wordsworth and Kingsley

and achieved as much as one book of a continuation of the *Iliad*. There, probably, the spontaneous promptings of my poetical ambition would have stopped; but the exercise, begun from choice, was continued by command.⁹

The aspects of the young Mill's education described here are not what the reader already acquainted with his case in outline would expect. In the first stage of Mill's education he was required to write poetry by his father and had himself already begun to do so by choice.

Reading on, indeed, one finds that the list of poetic subjects Mill read, translated into verse and composed after, is extensive:

> He generally left me to choose my own subjects, which, as far as I remember, were mostly addresses to some mythological personage or allegorical abstraction; but he made me translate into English verse many of Horace's shorter poems: I also remember him giving me Thomson's 'Winter' to read, and afterwards making me attempt (without book) to write something myself on the same subject … Shakespeare my father had put into my hands … Milton … Goldsmith, Burns, and Gray's 'Bard' … perhaps I may add Cowper and Beattie … I remember his reading to me (unlike his usual practice of making me read to him) the first book of *The Fairie Queene* … the metrical romances of Walter Scott … I read at his recommendation and was intensely delighted with[.]¹⁰

Mill's list goes on to pick out more specific short poems from various authors he read at this time, but the overall pattern is clear. Far from being bereft of aesthetic materials, the young Mill was led to acquire a literary knowledge of considerable depth and to practise poetic composition in a range of styles as well as on subjects of his own choosing. Even more importantly, perhaps, Mill is clear that these endeavours were a source of happiness and enjoyment to him. Walter Scott 'intensely delighted' him and Pope's Homer sufficiently inspired him to write his own version of it.

Less academic aesthetic experiences were not denied to Mill either. In addition to describing the regular rural walks he took with his father, the *Autobiography* also gives an account of the kind of sights that made an impression on the young student. This is Mill's description of Bentham's house in Devonshire, which Mill spent some time at:

> The middle-age architecture, the baronial hall, and the spacious and lofty rooms, of this fine old place, so unlike the mean and cramped externals of English middle class life, gave the sentiment of a larger and freer existence, and were to me a sort of poetic cultivation, aided also by the character of the grounds in which the Abbey stood; which were riant and secluded, umbrageous, and full of the sound of falling waters.¹¹

The young Mill, in this description, was by no means blind to aesthetic pleasures, finding Ford Abbey and its grounds to be a 'poetic cultivation' of sorts. In the south of France, likewise, where Mill spent some time staying with Bentham's brother, the mountain scenery apparently had a similar effect: 'This first introduction to the highest order of mountain scenery made the deepest impression on me, and gave a colour to my tastes through life.'[12]

With these experiences in mind, let us turn to Mill's description of the deep questioning of his own beliefs and upbringing that took place in 1826. Mill explains his crisis as follows:

'Suppose that all your objects in life were realized; that all the changes in institutions and opinions which you are looking forward to could be completely effected at this very instant: would this be a great joy and happiness to you?' And an irrepressible self-consciousness distinctly answered, 'No!' At this my heart sank within me: the whole foundation on which my life was constructed fell down. All my happiness was to have been found in the continual pursuit of this end. The end had ceased to charm, and how could there ever again be any interest in the means? I seemed to have nothing left to live for.[13]

Mill is about to claim, famously, that this deep indifference to the cause of social reform was caused by a lack of cultivation of his feelings in his educational programme. Yet the reader who has noted Mill's considerable literary education and his apparent 'poetic cultivation' at Ford Abbey will find this a curious explanation. Mill's education would seem to have been as generous in terms of aesthetics as it was in political and social topics. Following the educational models of Schiller and Coleridge, Mill ought to be in as good a position as anyone to feel deeply for the cause in which he professedly believes.

Mill's solution to this puzzle takes the form of opposing one aspect of his education to another. On the one hand there is 'analysis', the main instrument, he now tells us, given to him by his education for considering ideas and connections. 'Analysis', in the portrait Mill paints of it, is destructive above all else: 'The very excellence of analysis (I argued) is that it tends to weaken and undermine whatever is the result of prejudice; that it enables us mentally to separate ideas which have only casually clung together: and no association whatever could ultimately resist this dissolving force.'[14] It is made clear in this description that the opposite of analysis, in Mill's mind, is 'association', that network of beliefs that Bentham and James Mill inherited from David Hartley. Mill separates association into two strands. Association by education, firstly, connects sensations of pleasure or pain with certain objects or manners of doing things by a process of repeated training, as it were. This is the type of upbringing Mill says he received from his father, telling us that it is particularly effective at producing lasting associations of a negative kind.[15] Secondly, however, there is also association by feeling, a connection whose genesis is not described by Mill, but that, in his account, has the strength and permanence to resist the destructive powers of analysis.

As is implied in these definitions, Mill concludes that his education was made up of too much analysis and not enough cultivation of his emotional associations, leaving him in the position of having no opinions that were both deeply held and deeply felt:

> My education, I thought, had failed to create these feelings in sufficient strength to resist the dissolving influence of analysis, while the whole course of my intellectual cultivation had made precocious and premature analysis the inveterate habit of my mind. I was thus, as I said to myself, left stranded at the commencement of my voyage, with a well equipped ship and a rudder, but no sail; without any real desire for the ends which I had been so carefully fitted out to work for: no delight in virtue or the general good, but also just as little in anything else.[16]

This interpretation, importantly, serves to discount the effects of the young Mill's aesthetic activities, covering up their existence as much as possible. Analysis was so predominant in his upbringing, both chronologically and quantitatively, he now concludes, that it easily undid any development his feelings underwent.

The method Mill eventually finds of counteracting this supposed shortcoming is the cultivation of what he denominates the 'passive susceptibilities' or 'the internal culture of the individual' in addition to those faculties that his education had fostered:

> I never turned recreant to intellectual culture, or ceased to consider the power and practice of analysis as an essential condition both of individual and of social improvement. But I thought that it had consequences which required to be corrected, by joining other kinds of cultivation with it. The maintenance of a due balance among the faculties, now seemed to me of primary importance.[17]

Mill now depicts his education as only half-complete. Analysis must be complemented and balanced by 'passive' cultivation, the ability to understand juxtaposed with materials that enable one to feel as well. The reader is thus invited at this point to remember Mill's early education as one thing only. It was a course in the 'power and practice of analysis', a programme rigidly focused on the means to social improvement.

As we learnt in the context of Schiller's thought, it is aesthetic objects that Mill associates with 'passive' cultivation. By the fostering of an aesthetic sense he hopes to redress his educational imbalance. The *Autobiography* thus goes on to explain how it was the poetry of Wordsworth that drew Mill out of his emotional crisis and enabled him to understand the type of happiness that an individual should strive for:

> I felt that the flaw in my life, must be a flaw in life itself; that the question was, whether, if the reformers of society and government could succeed in their objects, and every person in the community were free and in a state of physical comfort, the pleasures of life, being no longer kept up by struggle and privation, would cease to be pleasures … I needed to be made to feel that there was real, permanent happiness in tranquil contemplation. Wordsworth taught me this, not only without turning away from, but with a greatly increased interest in, the common feelings and common destiny of human beings. And the delight which these poems gave me, proved that with culture of this sort, there was nothing to dread from the most confirmed habit of analysis.[18]

Aesthetic contemplation, in this model, the type of reverie Wordsworth depicts in 'Three years she grew' or elsewhere, has the strength and depth to resist any type of analysis. '[T]ranquil contemplation', for Mill, is a 'permanent' condition of human life, the negligence of which leaves men bereft of the foundation of their 'happiness'.

This, of course, is Mill's version of Schiller's 'whole man'. Inherited from Coleridge most directly in the *Autobiography*, this aspect of Mill's thought presents intellectual life much as Schiller conceived of it. The practice of analysis, the activity that confirmed Mill's political economic interest and utilitarian orientation, needs to be complemented, in the mature Mill's thought, with more aesthetic and inward accomplishments, just as Schiller found the products of over-intellectualization to be lacking in the qualities that an aesthetic education would engender. For Mill, as much as for Schiller, the product of the combination of these two strands of thought would be the rounded individual, the figure able to understand both legislation and contemplation, both political economy and poetry. Balance becomes Mill's 'creed'[19] following his experiences in 1826 in much the same way that 'harmony' is the goal of the *Aesthetic Letters*.

In Mill's thought, consequently, this motif is not unique to the *Autobiography* alone. His essays *On Bentham and Coleridge*, for example, written in 1838 and 1840 and first published in the *London and Westminster Review*, read the two men as expounding entirely antithetical beliefs:

> It would be difficult to find two persons of philosophic eminence more exactly the contrary of one another. Compare their modes of treatment of any subject, and you might fancy them inhabitants of different worlds. They seem to have scarcely a principle or a premise in common. Each of them sees scarcely anything but what the other does not see.[20]

Yet the thesis of Mill's two essays taken together is that, much like the seemingly opposed powers of analysis and association by feeling, Bentham and Coleridge are actually two sides of one more complete unit: 'We hold that these two sorts of men, who seem to be, and believe themselves to be, enemies, are in reality allies. The powers they wield are opposite poles of one great force of progression … Each ought to hail with rejoicing the advent of the other.'[21] Combining these opposites for Mill, as was the case in the *Autobiography*, leads to a more complete picture of human life and a fuller appreciation of the manner in which the 'great force of progression' functions.[22]

Mill's 'Inaugural Address' on becoming Rector of the University of St Andrews, also touched on above, sets things out similarly. Mill describes the branches of knowledge that ought to be taught in a university at considerable length, finally adding the 'aesthetic' to the 'intellectual' and the 'moral'. In this manner, Mill offers a model of a rounded and harmonious education, asserting that the university will offer an 'opportunity for gaining a degree of insight into subjects larger and far more ennobling than the minutiæ of a business or a profession'.[23] The 'Inaugural Address' thus constructs a portrait of human occupations very similar to that found in the *Aesthetic Letters*: 'The more prosaic our ordinary duties, the more necessary it is to keep up the tone of our minds by frequent visits to that higher region of thought and feeling, in which every work seems dignified in proportion to the ends for which, and the spirit in which, it is done.'[24] The aesthetic occupies a higher sphere of life than our everyday 'duties' here, Mill finding the latter in need of balancing by the former. Further, in much the same way that Schiller connected the aesthetic to the moral, Mill places aesthetic education behind virtuous living:

There is … a natural affinity between goodness and the cultivation of the Beautiful, when it is real cultivation, and not a mere unguided instinct. He who has learnt what beauty is, if he be of a virtuous character, will desire to realize it in his own life – will keep before himself a type of perfect beauty in human character, to light his attempts at self-culture.[25]

Once the 'passive susceptibilities' have been catered for, in the *Autobiography* and in this 'Inaugural Address', the individual will not only be completely rounded, but will desire to 'realize' beauty in his own life by being 'virtuous'. Mill's aesthetic also recalls the kind of concerns that characterized Bentham's *Chrestomathia* in that it will resist the dissolving powers of analysis at the same time as catering for the individual's happiness and moral well-being. The 'internal culture of the individual' will lay the responsibility for one's enjoyment, mental security and virtue in the powers of 'tranquil contemplation'.

This recurrence of the motif of 'harmony' and of the notion of the half-complete or lopsided intellect in Mill's thought is significant. Mill presents an individual's aesthetic and analytic capabilities as holding the potential, above all else, to be combined. In possession of either an aesthetic sense or an analytic mind, man is an unfinished educational product in this scheme of things. The businessman with whom he illustrates the 'Inaugural Address' and Mill himself before 1826 are both in need of further tuition before they can be presented as rounded and balanced individuals. Once this extra passive cultivation has taken place, however, that is precisely what they are. Mill depicts harmony, happiness, psychological tranquillity and virtuous behaviour as the rewards of any individual who cares to balance out his or her faculties. The *Autobiography* and the 'Inaugural Address', moreover, both position discord, incompleteness and considerable depression as the necessary results of psychological lopsidedness, of the individual whose 'passive susceptibilities' have not been taken care of.

It is by picking out this aspect of Mill's thought that his writing can be placed in dialogue with *Alton Locke*. According to Mill's educational programme, the protagonist of *Alton Locke* would be the epitome of the whole man. It is he who is both tailor and poet, he who can labour manually but is also endowed with a fully developed aesthetic appreciation of the world. In Schiller's terms, Alton ought to have an attitude to the objects before him that render his work not drudgery but a willed contribution to a society founded on equal rights. In Mill's terms, similarly, Kingsley's protagonist has all the means to be happy and satisfied. He has both the aesthetic abilities necessary to find 'permanent happiness' in 'tranquil contemplation' and the occupational responsibilities that will give his literary activities the quality of leisure.[26]

Far from being two halves of Alton's harmonious existence, however, we have already seen the manner in which Kingsley renders his protagonist's aesthetic life at odds with political engagement in the cause of social reform. Alton's contemplation is not tranquil and untroubled, and by no means engenders happiness in him. Equally, his eventual attainment of a location and style of contemplation that might recreate this relationship is depicted, by Kingsley, as confounding the politics that had been the focus of his life. *Alton Locke* would thus seem designed to contend for the incompatibility of the two intellectual employments Mill depicts as complementary. Just as Alton's reverie on Waterloo Bridge can only parody Wordsworth's description of Lucy's death in nature, the protagonist's attempts to publish his poetry through his connection with Dean Winnstay also encapsulate this relationship between social reform and aesthetics. The Dean's criterion for helping Alton with publication is that he give up, both in his life and in his verse, his 'bitter tone against the higher classes' (*Alton Locke*, p. 152). The lines in Alton's poetry being referred to by the Dean, however, are 'the very pith and marrow of the poems' for the novel's protagonist:

> They were the very words which I had felt it my duty, my glory, to utter. I, who had been a working man, who had experienced all their sorrows and temptations – I, seemed called by every circumstance of my life to preach their cause, to expose their wrongs – I to quash my convictions, to stultify my book, for the sake of popularity, money, patronage! (*Alton Locke*, p. 182)

Although in this quandary it is the market for poetry rather than poetic activity itself that inhibits the politics of Alton's verse, the protagonist's aesthetic impulses are nevertheless in conflict with the politics of his society. The 'pith and marrow' of Alton's aesthetic expression are politically unacceptable to those who will enable him to labour by his aesthetic impulses.[27]

Alton Locke should thus be understood to construct an important counter-argument to the trajectory of Mill's thought, as well as to that of Schiller and Coleridge. In addition to his new delight in Wordsworth, Mill's 'self-education' is almost synonymous in the *Autobiography* with his discovery of, and alignment with, Coleridge's writing and the German tradition we have seen him introduce into British thought. In the months and years following his crisis in 1826, Mill records the manner in which he begins to understand, and subsequently takes on, many of the positions held by Coleridge, Goethe and the 'other German authors' he read at that time.[28] Since the consequence of Mill's interest in these figures is his adoption of the notion of the whole man that we traced in Schiller's writing, Mill and Kingsley can be placed in direct opposition to one another. The one considers human life to approach closer and closer to an image of harmony the more attention is paid to the inner man. The other takes the case of the labouring classes and contends for the fundamental incompatibility of the cultivation of the inner man and his outward life and circumstances. Mill formulates aesthetic and political life as complementary. Kingsley depicts the manner in which they conflict. The latter is thus to be seen as focusing on the concrete conditions of English social life in order to chart the manner in which the operations of the world differ from the portrait given of it by idealist psychology.

Mill's *Autobiography* should not be understood to represent the story of its author's education entirely as a movement from incompleteness to wholeness and harmony, however, and in this way it holds a final pertinence for this topic. Paying close attention to the manner in which Mill describes the stages of his development in fact reveals similar complexities and contradictions to those depicted in *Alton Locke*.[29] As Mill describes the gradual transformation of his opinions that took place as a consequence of his crisis, for example, the social existence he presents to the reader also undergoes significant changes. In 1829, in the immediate aftermath of his conversion to Wordsworth, Mill describes his withdrawal from the 'Debating Society' he engaged in with several of his friends as follows:

> After 1829 I withdrew from attendance on the Debating Society. I had had enough of speech-making, and was glad to carry on my private studies and meditations without any immediate call for outward assertion of their results. I found the fabric of my old and taught opinions giving way in many fresh places, and I never allowed it to fall to pieces, but was incessantly occupied in weaving it anew. I never, in the course of my transition, was content to remain, for ever so short a time, confused and unsettled. When I had taken in any new idea, I could not rest till I had adjusted its relation to my old opinions, and ascertained exactly how far its effect ought to extend in modifying or superseding them.[30]

Mill's account of this period is interesting in several ways. Firstly, the aesthetic and passive sensibilities he has been led to cultivate would seem to conflict with his habitual 'speech-making'. In this new intellectual manifestation, Mill is more inclined to prolonged 'private studies and meditations' than to expressing his thoughts in public as soon as they arise. Secondly, this new passive and ruminative Mill also depicts himself as too busy contemplating to engage in other activities. He was 'incessantly occupied' in this period, he tells us. He 'could not rest' till his internal matrix of beliefs had been entirely modified. Passive cultivation of the type Mill has learnt from aesthetic materials, from the tranquil contemplation that they promote, has not only led him to favour internal modification over outward expression, therefore, for this period of time at least, but has also made him too busy to engage in debating on political matters. The passive susceptibilities would seem to preclude, or at least hamper, political activity.

Turning further through the *Autobiography*, Mill's domestic arrangements towards the end of his life also promote a similar idea. Following his wife's sudden death in 1858, Mill 'bought a cottage as close as possible to the place where she [was] buried', near Avignon in France, living in it for the remainder of his life with his step-daughter, Helen.[31] Much like Bentham's Ford Abbey, this house served as a rural retirement from which to escape London life. Further, in much the same way that Bentham's home provided 'riant and secluded' grounds, Mill's house was the site at which he engaged in distinctly rural pastimes. In a letter to William Thornton, for instance, Mill describes the 'vibratory' and other facilities he and Helen created there. The former is apparently –

> a pleasant covered walk some 30 feet long where I can vibrate in cold or rainy weather. The terrace, you must know, as it goes round two sides of the house, has got itself dubbed the 'semi-circumgyratory'. In addition to this, Helen has built me a *herbarium* – a little room fitted up with closets for my plants, shelves for my botanical books, & a great table whereon to manipulate them all. Thus you see with my herbarium, my vibratory & my semi-circumgyratory I am in clover.[32]

These rural pastimes, the background to his time as Member of Parliament for City and Westminster (1865–8), serve, in the context of the *Autobiography*, to raise the question of a necessary complement to, but also respite from, political activity. Mill's withdrawal from his Debating Society was justified by his new-found desire for passive contemplation. These rural activities seem to balance an interest in politics with more ruminative and solitary occupations. In the light of his classification of socio-political speculation as 'active' and aesthetic cultivation as 'passive',[33] therefore, Mill's politics in these years would seem to be both supported and balanced out by his rural rumination. The two cannot be engaged in at the same time, but must be alternated indefinitely.

If we add to these considerations the details Mill gave us of his education at the hands of his father, what emerges is not a portrait of the balanced nature of political and aesthetic activity, so much as an account of how the two seem to compete with and almost preclude one another. Mill's early education was made up, in his primary description of it, of both aesthetic and socio-political tasks and activities. In addition to sketching out the whole 'science'[34] of political economy in note form from his father's lectures – the notes were then used by James Mill to write his *Elements of Political Economy* – Mill also spent a considerable amount of time reading and composing poetry. So whereas he subsequently classifies his intellectual crisis as being the result of a lack of passive, aesthetic education, after reading Mill's account of his desire for rumination rather than action later in the *Autobiography* one might reasonably consider such a crisis to be the result of the fundamental incompatibility of the materials of his education.³⁵ Contending overtly for the harmonious alliance of aesthetic and political thought and activity, the *Autobiography* also records the relationship of these two poles of intellectual life more subtly. In this unacknowledged subtext aesthetics and politics do not seem able to be combined at the same time. The two concerns are almost mutually exclusive, the mature Mill being only able to practise one at a time, contemplating rather than debating, or enjoying rural pleasures rather than politics. Whereas Schiller suggested that the aesthetic attitude would inform political life, therefore, the mechanic's task being transformed by his constant attitude of aesthetic semblance, Mill depicts the two as opposites and alternatives. The styles of thought it takes to ruminate and to debate cannot be carried out at the same time, for Mill, just as rural activities are to be separated from political engagement.

The reason for this discrepancy between the thought of Schiller and Mill, importantly, lies in the notion of paradox that inflected the category of being 'at play' in the *Aesthetic Letters*. Schiller characterized intellectual life as either sensual or rational, as either passive or active, but then described how the aesthetic was both at once, both sensuo-rational and somehow, paradoxically, both active and passive. Once man has been balanced out by means of an aesthetic education in Schiller's model, consequently, he can unite the poles of his nature in one act. Holding an aesthetic attitude to the object at hand renders one simultaneously active and passive, in Mill's terms both political and aesthetic. Mill's thought lacks this category. Aesthetics and politics are never combined in either his description of his own life, or that of human life more generally. The two, rather, are complementary alternatives, needing to be juxtaposed chronologically in order to balance out the individual, but unable to be sublimated into a new whole that is both at once and thereby a new state. The businessman of the 'Inaugural Address' must 'visit' the 'higher region of thought' that the aesthetic represents, as Mill indeed visits his rural retirement, but cannot combine his two intellectual occupations at the same time. Mill's inheritance of the parameters of German and Coleridgean thought thus misses out the key notion that mediates between the poles of intellectual life. Where Coleridge and Schiller posit the consummation of man's potential, Mill depicts him fluctuating between propensities, never combining his aesthetics with his politics.

Yet it is apparent that by paying attention to the more practical aspect of the *Aesthetic Letters*, rather than to the abstract ideals of Schiller's model of human behaviour, Mill could be understood in rather more positive terms. For in Schiller's description the pure category of aesthetic contemplation was not so much an ambition as a paradigm. The reality portrayed by the *Aesthetic Letters* was one in which the state of pure determinability could only be approximated, man having to leave it in order to act in any way and thereby becoming temporarily unbalanced, psychologically speaking, in any act. When Mill depicts himself, or the businessman of the 'Inaugural Address', as 'visiting' higher regions of thought, therefore, we could understand him as offering a considerably more practical version of the same relationship Schiller describes. The aesthetic represents an ideal state of harmony, but man must constantly flit between physical engagements and intellectual states. The aesthetic pleasures that Mill positions in the background to his political activities could thus be understood as a kind of Schillerian safeguard to all his activities.

The way in which Mill's relationship with Schiller is understood is important to understanding the connections that can be made between his thought and Kingsley's writing. To describe Mill as omitting the element of the *Aesthetic Letters* that mediates between the different activities of life, firstly, is to read Mill in a manner that could be quite aptly aligned with *Alton Locke*. Both texts polarize intellectual life between aesthetic and political impulses, in this view, and both present the two as ultimately irreconcilable. Mill's text does not provide a paradigm for Alton's quandary between his desire for aesthetic contemplation and political activity, instead offering a portrait of a man with the means to enjoy both. Mill's aesthetic pleasures occur in his French rural exile but he then returns to London in order to engage in political activity. Kingsley's protagonist's exile into nature is only to be achieved in death, and is synonymous with his withdrawal from the political scene. Both texts, therefore, could be described as offering a more negative portrait of political activity than Schiller's *Aesthetic Letters*. Both portray socio-political problems as untouched by the aesthetic education of their protagonists. Alternatively, however, if we consider Mill's writing to enact an essentially practical dissemination of Schiller's portrayal of human life, Mill and Kingsley must be seen to differ on the relation between political and aesthetic activity. Where Kingsley posits their incompatibility, Mill considers them two parts of the human whole. *Alton Locke* depicts an aesthetic sphere thrown into turmoil by its protagonist's politics. Mill's *Autobiography* describes the manner in which aesthetic activity rounds, completes and gives emotional depth to one's political beliefs.

In contrast to the impotence of aesthetic thought over political activism in *Alton Locke*, therefore, we should remember that Kingsley depicts his protagonist's aesthetic relationship with the world as being almost entirely subsumed by his position in the social matrix. Alton's reverie on Waterloo Bridge is transformed from a serene appreciation of nature's power over man to a macabre, tortured admission of his own eddying existence. The most resonant and interesting spectacle of the novel is hence created by the power Alton's social position holds over his aesthetic life. The latter is represented by a howling wind and a lurid stream where one would expect it, given Alton's status as a 'poet', to fit the pattern of Wordsworth's 'Three years she grew'. The aesthetic is thus in thrall to the political in *Alton Locke*. It is no longer a realm of unfettered possibility from which to learn freedom by example, as it was for Schiller. In Kingsley's portrait, one's aesthetic appreciation of the world is structured entirely by the social and political relationships that characterize one's life. It is for this reason that Alton is so struck by Guido's image of St Sebastian, which he encounters in Dulwich Gallery, a portrait in which the saint, arms bound behind him, displays an arrow in his side while expressing a kind of emotional rhapsody on his face. The protagonist's aesthetic impulses relate, above all the other images on display, to a portrayal of what Richard Menke has called the 'martyred ... body undergoing simultaneous physical agony and spiritual transcendence'.[36] It is his own powerless situation that Alton's aesthetic sense is drawn to. Kingsley's aesthetic is thus a realm of restraint rather than of Schillerian freedom. The style of contemplation that offered Coleridge and Wollstonecraft insight into their moral situations, provides, to the protagonist of *Alton Locke*, only a series of images of the futility of his social position and the impotence of his political struggles.

Both *Alton Locke* and *Yeast* thus depict socio-political problems as almost entirely unaided by the aesthetic powers of their protagonists. In the earlier novel, Lancelot's keen interest in the contemplation of nature was portrayed in a variety of ways but was in no uncertain terms a seductive distraction from the spiritual belief that could motivate and achieve real social change. Not that the novel demonstrated these effects; Kingsley concerned himself rather with ironic accounts of aesthetic contemplation and of the relevance of aesthetic education to contemporary social conditions. It is in this sense that *Yeast* sets itself against the trajectories both of Schiller's *Aesthetic Letters* and of the type of analysis of aesthetic contemplation to be found in Coleridge's 'Frost at Midnight'. The style of idle thought that brought about moral consciousness and hence political progress is dismissed, by Kingsley, as seducing the mind away from its real obligations and as engendering only a kind of vain worship of the physical intricacy of nature. Whilst its materials and social focus are slightly different from those of *Alton Locke*, then, *Yeast* comes up with similar conclusions. In both novels, aesthetic powers are not the means to effect political action. In both, similarly, aesthetic contemplation is described as significantly less potent, and as significantly less rewarding, than in the portraits offered of it by Cowper, Coleridge and Wollstonecraft. Kingsley's novels could thus be described as foregrounding the thoroughly pastoral connotations of an aesthetic psychology founded in nature-contemplation, and as challenging that genre's purchase over the urban scene of political life.[37]

We have also seen that by paying attention to different aspects of Mill's *Autobiography*, the relationship between aesthetic and political thought that this text would seem to describe is transformed radically. Mill suggests that aesthetics and politics are two sides of one whole, but also depicts their intellectual consideration as two distinct tasks, both able to carried out by the same individual but not able to be combined into one act or attitude. *Alton Locke* also focuses its attention on this interaction. Placing the novel in the context of Mill's thought thus enables us to register the manner in which the former denigrates aesthetic contemplation, rendering it consistently subservient to political activity. In Kingsley's hands in both novels, therefore, Wordsworth represents a distinctly apolitical aesthetic, one of undiluted, pastoral contemplation in nature; of complete, and occasionally forced, withdrawal from the scene of political and social challenges. Both *Yeast* and *Alton Locke* thus invoke the kind of aesthetic consciousness we have seen in Cowper, Coleridge and Wollstonecraft only to describe its social irrelevance. Kingsley depicts the aesthetic sense in thrall to political reality at the same time as recreating the charges made against Schiller's thought. The two novels classify Wordsworthian aesthetic contemplation as nothing but a retreat from the scene of political action into a world of intellectual pleasures. Kingsley thus uses Wordsworth to draw out the indulgence of the reverie taking place in 'Three years she grew' as well as the tyranny aesthetic contemplation can exert over other types of thought. For the speaker of that poem, as much as for Lancelot and Alton, the aesthetic contemplation of nature may be one's inclination, but holds no connection to one's duty.

The relevance of all these texts for this investigation as a whole thus lies in the reception they offer to the idea that aesthetic consciousness contains the power to transform man's moral and hence political life. Just as Schiller's project is implicitly questioned by these texts, the model of human life common to Coleridge, Cowper, Wollstonecraft and Wordsworth undergoes a thorough analysis in the thought of both Kingsley and Mill, emerging as more of an idealized portrait of human engagements than any sort of plan for action, as more of a mythically pastoral model than a realist study. No longer the occupation that unites and justifies all others, aesthetic contemplation becomes simply a specialization of its own in Kingsley's analyses, a geographically and generically separated sphere of intellectual activity. Kingsley thus denies to the aesthetic category what Raymond Williams describes as the 'dynamic function' that both characterized and motivated its invocation.[38] Aesthetic contemplation is rendered an ideology of leisure that seeks to justify its separation from specialized labour. In this sense the motif of specialization that Smith used to characterize life in an advanced division of labour could be seen to exert its influence over the category of the aesthetic as well, by the middle of the nineteenth century. The trajectory of British thought that anticipated, echoed and in many ways departed from Schiller's analysis in his *Aesthetic Letters* might thus be said to flounder in the thought of Kingsley. In *Yeast* and in *Alton Locke*, it is the intricate and dangerous aspects of idle contemplation, picked out by Cowper, Wollstonecraft and Coleridge, that characterize aesthetic experience. No longer the risk needing to be taken in order to access the image of moral consciousness, these elements, to Lancelot and Alton, represent the separation of aesthetic thought from every other element of human life.

Notes

INTRODUCTION

1. W. Wordsworth, *The Brothers* in W. Wordsworth and S. T. Coleridge, *Lyrical Ballads*, ed. R. L. Brett and A. R. Jones (London: Routledge, 1991), pp. 135–50.
2. W. Wordsworth, 'Gipsies' in Poems in Two Volumes, *and Other Poems, 1800–1807*, ed. J. Curtis (New York: Cornell University Press, 1983), pp. 211–12.
3. W. Wordsworth, *'Home at Grasmere*, MS. B' in *Home at Grasmere*, ed. B. Darlington (New York: Cornell University Press, 1977), pp. 38–106.
4. D. Simpson, *Wordsworth's Historical Imagination* (New York: Methuen, 1987), p. 33.
5. *Biog.*, Vol. II, p. 136 n. 3.
6. Simpson offers a convincing reading of these lines, observing how uncharacteristic words such as 'Vesper' and 'fulgent' are in Wordsworth's work, and explaining their presence as complex allusions to Milton: see Simpson, *Wordsworth's Historical Imagination*, pp. 30–3.
7. As we will see, Schiller's writing of the *Aesthetic Letters* was shaped to a considerable degree by his reading of Ferguson.

I   THE DIVISION OF LABOUR

1. It is worth noting that in this quotation, and indeed in all the texts we will be considering in this chapter at least, the individual in question is always male. While I will be following the terms used by both Smith and Ferguson in my own analyses, if one wanted to explore the relation of these ideas to contemporary female labour or female life more generally, a good starting point would be Priscilla Wakefield's *Reflections on the Present Condition of the Female Sex: With Suggestions for Its Improvement* (London: printed for J. Johnson; and Darton and Harvey, 1798), which both organizes itself around and begins by direct reference to Smith:

   He does not absolutely specify, that both sexes, in order to render themselves beneficial members of society, are equally required to comply with these terms ['that every individual is a burthen upon the society to which he belongs, who does not contribute his share of productive labour']; but since the female sex is included in the idea

of the species ... their sex cannot free them from the claim of the public for their proportion of usefulness. (pp. 1–2)
2. Compare Plato, *The Republic*, ed. G. R. F. Ferrari (Cambridge: Cambridge University Press, 2000), 369e–370b.
3. Compare F. Hutcheson, *A System of Moral Philosophy*, 3 vols. (Glasgow: R. and A. Foulis, 1755), Vol. I, pp. 288–9; and H. Home, Lord Kames, *Sketches of the History of Man*, 4 vols. (Basil: J. J. Tourneisen, 1796), Vol. III, pp. 4–5.
4. For more on the relationship between these two areas of the work, see S. Copley, 'Introduction: Reading the *Wealth of Nations*' in S. Copley and K. Sutherland (eds.), *Adam Smith's* Wealth of Nations*: New Interdisciplinary Essays* (Manchester: Manchester University Press, 1995), pp. 19–20.
5. Compare K. Marx, *Economic and Philosophic Manuscripts of 1844* in K. Marx and F. Engels, *The Marx–Engels Reader*, ed. R. C. Tucker (London: W. W. Norton, 1978), pp. 66–125 (p. 95); and *Capital: A Critical Analysis of Capitalist Production*, 3 vols. (Moscow: Foreign Languages Publishing House, 1954), Vol. I, pp. 354, 362–4. It will be observed, in what follows, that this study does not strive to make any extended use of Marx's critique of Smith, or for that matter of an overtly Marxist approach to the categories of labour or progress (though it does, later, draw on a Marxist tradition of interpreting pastoral literature). Such an absence is intentional, this work seeking to reconstruct the debate over the status, dangers and rewards of idle thought it identifies, and to put contemporary terminology to use in its analysis where possible. (It should also be noted that it is my intention to continue my account of idle contemplation beyond 1830 in a subsequent work, and that such a project would deal with Marx's thought at length.)
6. S. Fleischacker, *On Adam Smith's* Wealth of Nations*: A Philosophical Companion* (Princeton: Princeton University Press, 2004), p. 79. In this vein, Istvan Hont and Michael Ignatieff also consider Smith to be more concerned about the administration of justice than the creation of liberty for the labouring classes he describes; see their 'Needs and Justice in the *Wealth of Nations* Nations: An Introductory Essay' in I. Hont and M. Ignatieff (eds.), *Wealth and Virtue: The Shaping of Political Economy in the Scottish Enlightenment* (Cambridge: Cambridge University Press, 1983), pp. 1–44.
7. It is possible, of course, in line with the subservient position Smith allots to education in the *Wealth of Nations*, to see him as advocating a system of education that inhibits the stultifying effects of specialization but ensures that mechanical workers are not thereby enlightened enough significantly to question their place in such division, just as Bernard Mandeville had advocated subsistence wages for the poor in order to ensure that their function as labourers was not altered. For more on Mandeville's economics, see M. M. Goldsmith, *Private Vices, Public Benefits: Bernard Mandeville's Social and Political Thought* (Cambridge: Cambridge University Press, 1985).
8. It is the power Smith bestows on the division of labour that led to the favourable reception the *Wealth of Nations* received on its publication. Whilst Sir James Steuart's *An Inquiry into the Principles of Political Oeconomy*, 2 vols.

(London: A. Millar and T. Cadell, 1767), published a decade earlier, was repeatedly criticized for his advocacy of the intervention of statesmen in commercial concerns, Smith's work was praised for its overall message of liberty, a result of his commitment to a division of labour that could seemingly sort out all the interrelations of various parts of the economy naturally. Of course, Smith's success was also down to the specificity and thoroughness of his economic analysis: despite continuing to be of central importance to economic writers decades after its publication, the work was found to be less economically relevant to both continental and later British economic conditions. For more on the reception and context of the *Wealth of Nations*, see *WN*, pp. 1–60.

9. See, for example, *WN*, p. 378, where it is suggested that man has a natural 'predilection' for the tranquillity of agricultural work as opposed to urban employment, and *ibid.*, p. 760, where, amid an account of university teaching practices, Smith states that it is 'in the interest of every man to live as much at his ease as he can'.

10. For two slightly different accounts of the reception the *Essay* received both on its publication and in the years to come, see F. Oz-Salzberger, 'Introduction' in A. Ferguson, *An Essay on the History of Civil Society Society*, ed. F. Oz-Salzberger (Cambridge: Cambridge University Press, 1995), pp. vii–xxv; and D. Forbes, 'Introduction' in *Essay*, pp. xiii–xli. Oz-Salzberger finds the *Essay* to have met with widespread immediate acclaim and to have exerted considerable influence on several aspects of speculative thought in subsequent decades, while Forbes suggests that Ferguson's reputation was established very much sooner in Germany and America than in Britain, and is slightly less positive about the actual influence of his ideas.

11. It is in the same vein as this thought that Priscilla Wakefield suggests that the 'many branches of science' in which 'women may employ their time and their talents' would be 'beneficial' to both 'themselves and to the community' (Wakefield, *Reflections*, pp. 8–9); and indeed Wakefield places a similar emphasis on labour to Ferguson, telling us, for example, that 'Labour is the price of knowledge, as indeed it is of every other valuable possession which is placed within our attainment; neither health, nor the activity of the intellectual powers, nor even pleasure itself can be enjoyed unless purchased by exertion' (*ibid.*, p. 79).

12. John Pocock also notes that Ferguson's portraits of savage and barbarian characters are marked by their alternative states of complete indolence and intense energy: a feature, I would suggest, of the relief-like nature of human behaviour in Ferguson's thought. See J. G. A. Pocock, *Barbarism and Religion*, 4 vols. (Cambridge: Cambridge University Press, 1999), Vol. II, pp. 331, 337.

13. See, for example, S. Copley (ed.), *Literature and the Social Order in Eighteenth-Century England* (London: Croom Helm, 1984), pp. 13–14; and J. G. A. Pocock, *The Machiavellian Moment: Florentine Political Thought*

and the Atlantic Republican Tradition (Princeton: Princeton University Press, 1975), pp. 486–7.
14. Of the many speculative investigations into the various means of organizing and controlling a society that take place as a result of this tension between civic and economic priorities, Steuart's *Principles of Political Oeconomy* seems to come up with the most extreme and progressive stance, suggesting that 'Were the principle of public spirit carried further [than its current state]; were a people to become quite disinterested; there would be no possibility of governing them. Every one might consider the interest of his country in a different light, and many might join in the ruin of it, by endeavouring to promote its advantages' (quoted in Copley, *Literature and the Social Order*, p. 122). In the light of this idea, it should be remembered that the *Wealth of Nations* is not as progressive or as anti-classical-republican as it could be.
15. See *WN*, p. 684; and N. Parker, 'Look, No Hidden Hands: How Smith Understands Historical Progress and Societal Values' in Copley and Sutherland, *Adam Smith's* Wealth of Nations, pp. 126, 142 n. 7.
16. It is worth observing at this point the relative understandings of 'duty' and 'inclination' implied in these two alternatives, for these terms are pertinent to many of the other writers considered in this study. For Smith, commercial society's importance is reflected in the junction of duty and interest it substantiates – following one's self-interest (one's inclination) by labouring and trading leads to the advancement of one's society (one's duty) in the form of its economic prosperity. Smith moves the category of duty towards that of inclination, in other words, placing the former as the direct and near result of the latter. For Ferguson, on the other hand, classical society is also to be understood as an alignment of duty and inclination, but in a form that moves one's inclination towards one's duty. If man is inherently civic and noble, then his interest is to reach the perfection of his nature by promoting society's good (the latter being the most direct mechanism that can enable the former). Interest moves towards duty as man is described as a naturally dutiful entity. We will have occasion to note the importance of these terms again in what follows.
17. In line with this position, indeed, Ferguson rejects any supposition of a state of nature entirely (see *Essay*, pp. 1–10) and even recognizes virtuous behaviour to make itself felt in the thick of the self-interest of commercial society: 'Even while the head is occupied with projects of interest, the heart is often seduced into friendship; and while business proceeds on the maxims of self-preservation, the careless hour is employed in generosity and kindness' (*Essay*, p. 37).
18. Pocock, *Barbarism and Religion*, Vol. II, p. 336; compare Pocock, *The Machiavellian Moment*, p. 501. The abundance of Ferguson's observations concerning Native Americans is demonstrated by the number of references in the *Essay*'s index to the subject: see the twenty-one separate topics under the 'North American Indians' entry. For Ferguson's judgement that man is endowed with the same qualities in his rudest as in his most polished

state, see *Essay*, p. 94: 'With all these infirmities, vices, or respectable qualities, belonging to the human species in its rudest state; the love of society, friendship, and public affection, penetration, eloquence, and courage, appear to have been its original properties, not the subsequent effects of device or invention.'
19. A further orientation of Ferguson's use of classical models for his analysis of modern commercial society might be the political and intellectual climate in the wake of the Seven Years' War (1756–63), the most tangible results of which were the emergence of Britain as the most powerful colonial power in the world and the expansion of her empire. As Pocock remarks, the end of this war was the 'appropriate moment, according to all the conventions of the classical vocabulary, at which to utter warnings against the fate of Rome, transformed from a republic to a despotism by the conquest of an empire' (Pocock, *The Machiavellian Moment*, p. 510). This context obviously connects to Ferguson and Smith's involvement in Scots militia debates during and after the Seven Years' War (through the Poker Club, of which they were both members) and the ways in which their writings either reflect or ignore these preoccupations: a topic that is beyond the remit of this chapter but certainly connected to it. For a thorough analysis of Ferguson's thinking and activity relating to the militia issue and the manner in which the publication of the *Wealth of Nations* may have influenced the defeat of Lord Mountstuart's Scots Militia Bill of 1775, see R. B. Sher, 'Adam Ferguson, Adam Smith, and the Problem of National Defense', *Journal of Modern History*, 61 (1989), 240–68.
20. Pocock, *The Machiavellian Moment*, pp. 441, 494–5. In the migration of classical republicanism from Renaissance Italy to the Britain of the seventeenth and eighteenth centuries, as John Barrell notes, 'the ability of the disinterested citizen to grasp the true interests of society had come to be identified as a function of his ownership of landed property'; see J. Barrell, 'The Public Prospect and the Private View: The Politics of Taste in Eighteenth-Century Britain' in S. Pugh (ed.), *Reading Landscape: Country, City, Capital* (Manchester: Manchester University Press, 1990), p. 28.
21. For an account of the extremely positive reception the *Theory* received in 1759 and afterwards, see D. D. Raphael and A. L. Macfie, 'Introduction' in *TMS*, pp. 25–32.
22. This is the so-called 'Adam Smith Problem'.
23. Nicholas Phillipson reads the process of the sufferer being calmed slightly differently, finding that 'the pleasure we get from mutual sympathy smacks as much of the relief we feel when the anxieties generated by the encounter are over as of disinterested or spontaneous pleasure'. The relief Phillipson identifies could be said to be comparable with the repose I am highlighting; compare N. Phillipson, 'Adam Smith as Civic Moralist' in Hont and Ignatieff, *Wealth and Virtue*, pp. 179–202 (pp. 184–5).
24. 'Inclination' is conceived of by Ferguson in terms extremely close to 'duty', in other words.

25. Hont and Ignatieff, 'Needs and Justice', p. 2, record that this contention was a 'scandal' at the time of the text's publication.
26. For Ferguson's version of this idea, see *Essay*, p. 183.
27. Barrell, 'The Public Prospect and the Private View', p. 31.
28. Fleischacker observes another rhetorical use of the subjunctive in the *Wealth of Nations* – that it phrases and enters entirely into the suppositions of counter-arguments at great length in order to engage fully with and then refute them: see Fleischacker, *Adam Smith's* Wealth of Nations, pp. 4–11. Smith's subjunctive could also be read rather more widely, it should be observed: in comparison to *The Theory of Moral Sentiments*, for example, the later work would seem to be almost entirely conjectural, Smith constantly writing as if he were imagining how a society would operate if self-interest were the only impulse of its members.
29. J. Barrell, *English Literature in History 1730–80: An Equal, Wide Survey* (London: Hutchinson, 1983), pp. 45–50.
30. See F. Nietzsche, 'On the Uses and Disadvantages of History for Life' in *Untimely Meditations*, ed. J. P. Stern (Cambridge: Cambridge University Press, 1983), pp. 57–123.

2 UTILITARIAN EDUCATION AND AESTHETIC EDUCATION

1. That the educational and penal thought of Bentham functions as a concrete framework for reform, and thus realization, means that, in comparison to my analysis of Smith and Ferguson's predominantly speculative systems (and indeed in comparison to the way in which I will deal with Schiller), it will be necessary, in what follows, to contextualize utilitarian education by means of contemporary social developments, in particular the impetuses to, and realizations of, penal reform in the 1770s and 1780s. The reason for using Schiller as a counterpart to Bentham in this chapter is twofold, as has already been implied. On the one hand Schiller's *Aesthetic Letters* constitute the most complete contemporary statement of opposition to both Bentham's premises and aims; yet on the other, as we will see subsequently, Schiller's thought also exerts significant influence on British educational and aesthetic enquiries.
2. See J. Bentham, 'Outline of a Work Entitled Pauper Management Improved', *Annals of Agriculture and Other Useful Arts*, 30 (1798), 89–176, 241–96, 393–424, 457–504.
3. Howard was made Sheriff of the county of Bedford in 1773, and found a whole host of injustices taking place in the gaol. Some defendants, for example, 'whose prosecutors did not appear against them; after having been confined for months', were 'dragged back to gaol, and locked up again till they should pay *sundry fees* to the gaoler, the clerk of assize, &c': see J. Howard, *The State of the Prisons in England and Wales, with Preliminary Observations, and an Account of Some Foreign Prisons* (Warrington: W. Eyres, 1777), p. 1.
4. *Ibid.*, pp. 72–3.

5. M. Ignatieff, *A Just Measure of Pain: The Penitentiary in the Industrial Revolution, 1750–1850* (New York: Pantheon, 1978), p. 53. I am indebted to Ignatieff for just about all of the background to Bentham's thought that appears here; see especially Ignatieff's third chapter on 'The Ideological Origins of the Penitentiary'.
6. *Ibid.*, p. 67; it is this system of beliefs that makes possible a consensus of any sort, in these two decades, between a pious religious reformer such as Howard and the non-religious Bentham on the make-up of the penitentiary, as we will see.
7. J. Bender, *Imagining the Penitentiary: Fiction and the Architecture of Mind in Eighteenth-Century England* (Chicago: University of Chicago Press, 1987), p. 23.
8. Howard, *The State of the Prisons*, p. 79.
9. Many more of the Panopticon project's practical considerations are expressed in a slightly troubling manner by Bentham. In Letter VII, for example, a rationale for 'gagging' is offered, where it is necessary, in the following terms: 'Punishment, even in its most hideous forms, loses its odious character, when bereft of that *uncertainty*, without which the rashest desperado would not expose himself to its stroke' (*Writings*, p. 49).
10. Bentham refers to this event, in the *Panopticon* letters, as follows: 'I AM come now to the article of *pecuniary economy*; and as this is the great rock upon which the original penitentiary-plan I understand has split, I cannot resist the temptation of throwing out a few hints relative to the mode of management, which I look upon as the most eligible in this view' (*ibid.*, p. 51).
11. Howard, Eden and Blackstone's original proposal for the 1779 Penitentiary Act in fact 'called for the creation of a whole network of "hard labor houses"'. Ignatieff notes that the phrase was 'discarded' 'at some moment in 1778' in 'favor of "penitentiary"'. Whilst this change, in his account, brought about a notable change in the rhetoric of the proposals, the idea that work must be a punishment persisted for these three thinkers: see Ignatieff, *A Just Measure of Pain*, pp. 93–4.
12. Bentham, 'Pauper Management Improved', p. 139; the phrase is also used by Janet Semple in her analysis of the Panopticon as penitentiary, *Bentham's Prison: A Study of the Panopticon Penitentiary* (Oxford: Clarendon Press, 1993).
13. William Blackstone, quoted in Ignatieff, *A Just Measure of Pain*, p. 94; the junction of duty and interest was to pervade the operations of the Panopticon further than this, in Bentham's plans, for, since it would be in the inspector/manager's interest to get the most work possible out of the inmates, and since this would be achieved, in Bentham's view, by letting them like their work, the inspector's duty of care would be aligned, in the Panopticon, with his interest in profit.
14. Quoted by M. Božovič, 'Introduction' in *Writings*, p. 4.
15. J. Bentham, *Panopticon; or, The Inspection-House* (Dublin: Thomas Byrne, 1791), p. 150.

16. J. Howard, *An Account of the Principal Lazarettos in Europe* (Warrington: W. Eyres, 1789), pp. 162, 18, 169.
17. Bentham, *Panopticon; or, The Inspection-House*, pp. 143, 151; also quoted by Semple, *Bentham's Prison*, pp. 89–90, whose account of the question of solitary confinement I am largely following.
18. Bentham, *Panopticon; or, The Inspection-House*, p. 145; Semple, *Bentham's Prison*, p. 130. 'Promiscuous association' was just about the most commented-upon and lamented feature of old-style gaols, one that the Penitentiary Act was at pains to eradicate.
19. Ignatieff, *A Just Measure of Pain*, p. 58; for a detailed account of Howard's religious background and the impact this had on other reformers, see *ibid.*, Chapter 3, pp. 44–79.
20. Indeed, his preference for the word 'Panopticon' over 'penitentiary' signals this difference in aim, penitentiary having 'connotations of religious and spiritual repentance quite alien from Bentham's thought'; see Semple, *Bentham's Prison*, pp. 49–50.
21. Semple records Bentham's beliefs that the 'overwhelming corrupting influence in the lives of the poor that tempted them into crime was idleness' and that 'the cure for idleness was work'; see *ibid.*, pp. 93, 155.
22. See Ignatieff, *A Just Measure of Pain*, p. 112.
23. For more on Bell and Lancaster, as well as the connections between their systems and the *Chrestomathia*, see M. J. Smith and W. H. Burston, 'Introduction' in *Chrestomathia*, pp. xi–xxix, who also outline the stages of planning the school underwent, including the hope that it would be erected in Bentham's garden at Queen's Square Place. Bentham's eventual maintaining of this offer only under innumerable (and rather ridiculous) personal and legal conditions was what led ultimately to the scheme's failure in 1821.
24. The clarity of the opposition between these examples of the thought of Schiller and Bentham should by no means be considered a coincidence, for Schiller's formulation of the themes of his *Aesthetic Letters* was greatly influenced by his reading of Ferguson and his negative treatment of an advanced division of labour (see E. M. Wilkinson and L. Willoughby, 'Introduction' in *Aesthetic*, pp. xxxi–xxxii). Bentham and Schiller might thus be described as reacting, albeit quite differently, to the same tradition of British political economy. This fact serves as a further demonstration of the pertinence of Schiller's thought for the network of texts this study considers, positioning the *Aesthetic Letters* in the group of systems of thought inflected by the writing of Smith and Ferguson.
25. Translations, unless stated otherwise, are Wilkinson and Willoughby's, as they appear in *Aesthetic*; this dual-text edition is also the source for the longer quotations, which I will give in the original as well.
26. My translations.
27. See J.-J. Rousseau, *A Discourse on the Origin of Inequality* in *The Social Contract and Discourses*, ed. G. D. H. Cole (London: Everyman, 2001), pp. 31–126.

28. My translation.
29. Nathan Bailey's *Dictionary English–German and German–English, oder englisch–deutsches und deutsches–englisch Wörterbuch*, 2 vols. (Leipzig and Züllichau: Friedrich Frommann, 1797), it should be noted, offers no translation for 'Vernünftelei', instead describing it as 'bad Vernünfteln', referring to the entry above, which classifies 'Vernünfteln' as reasoning 'too nicely, subtilely, sophistically'; see Vol. II, p. 531.
30. M. J. Kooy, *Coleridge, Schiller and Aesthetic Education* (Basingstoke: Palgrave, 2002), p. 108.
31. My translations.
32. Bailey's 1797 *Dictionary* records 'benehmen' as 'to deprive' or 'to abate'; see Vol. II, p. 75.
33. It is for this reason that Wilkinson and Willoughby warn against reading Schiller as advocating 'a recoil into the timeless world of beauty' or an 'apolitical retreat into the ivory tower of aestheticism', as they say Georg Lukács did, for example; see *Aesthetic*, p. xv.
34. See, for instance, I. Kant, *Kritik der Urtheilskraft* (Berlin: Druck und Verlag von Georg Reimer, 1913), p. 197.
35. For an example of a reading that points out the features of Kant's analysis that tend towards this connection between the aesthetic and the moral, see Kooy, *Coleridge, Schiller and Aesthetic Education*, p. 102; I am also indebted to Kooy for his identification of the pertinent elements in Kant's project to an analysis of Schiller.
36. We should also remember that, whereas for Kant the objects associated with the aesthetic were primarily natural ones – the third Critique devoting very little space to a consideration of art objects – for Schiller, the latter are distinctly and almost exclusively the target of the aesthetic impulse.
37. In one sense, of course, the proposal of the aesthetic as the solution to apparently economic or political problems should not strike us as surprising if we bear in mind that in classical societies, as both Smith and Ferguson remark, it was the cultivation of 'musick' (in its broadest sense, meaning all arts inspired by the muses) that was understood to maintain the citizen's political comprehension and prowess. See, for example, Smith's observation that ancient Greek education was split into 'gymnastic exercises' and 'musick', the latter being designed to 'humanize the mind, to soften the temper, and to dispose it for performing all the social and moral duties both of publick and private life' (*WN*, p. 774). The manner in which the *Aesthetic Letters* focus on the very problems debated by Smith and Ferguson is made less surprising when we consider the influence and reception Ferguson enjoyed in Germany. Just as Duncan Forbes considers Ferguson's thought to have been initially more successful in Germany than it was in Britain (see above, p. 175), it is widely acknowledged that Schiller's antipathy to the division of labour was brought into focus by his reading of Ferguson.
38. A. Ryan, 'Introduction' in J. S. Mill and J. Bentham, *'Utilitarianism' and Other Essays*, ed. A. Ryan (London: Penguin, 1987), p. 10.

39. See J. S. Mill, *Autobiography*, ed. J. Stillinger (Oxford: Oxford University Press, 1971), pp. 38, 83–6, 142; a fuller analysis of Mill's account of this opposition is to be found in my Epilogue on 'Wordsworth and Kingsley', below, pp. 141–72.
40. J. S. Mill, 'Inaugural Address Delivered to the University of St Andrews' in *Essays on Equality, Law, and Education*, ed. J. M. Robson, Vol. XXI of *Collected Works of John Stuart Mill*, 33 vols. (Toronto: University of Toronto Press, 1984), p. 251.
41. Kooy, *Coleridge, Schiller and Aesthetic Education*, p. 111.
42. See *Aesthetic*, p. liii.
43. In line with this apparent decay of the ambitions of the *Aesthetic Letters*, it is worth noting that Schiller's project as a whole is susceptible to what Kooy terms 'ironic … inver[sion]'. Kooy records Friedrich Schlegel's contention with Schiller that the 'psychic dissonance which for Schiller was an object of regret, to be overcome through aesthetic experience and eventually replaced by a sense of wholeness, was for Schlegel nothing less than aesthetic consciousness itself, escape from which was not only not possible but undesirable' (Kooy, *Coleridge, Schiller and Aesthetic Education*, pp. 20–1).

3 COWPER, COLERIDGE AND WOLLSTONECRAFT

1. The term 'A brown study' comes from the 'Argument of the Fourth Book'; see *Task*, p. 140.
2. M. Priestman, *Cowper's Task* (Cambridge: Cambridge University Press, 1983), p. 7; D. Griffin, 'Redefining Georgic: Cowper's Task', *ELH*, 57:4 (1990), 865–79 (pp. 871–2).
3. Kevis Goodman, *Georgic Modernity and British Romanticism: Poetry and the Mediation of History* (Cambridge: Cambridge University Press, 2004), pp. 9, 90, 97–8, 104; for a fuller articulation of the phrases 'history-on-the-move' and the 'apprehension of historicity', see Goodman's 'Introduction' on 'Georgic Modernity: Sensory Media and the Affect of History' (pp. 1–16), as well as her chapter on Cowper, 'Cowper's Georgic of the News: The "Loophole" in the Retreat' (pp. 67–105).
4. For transcripts of alternative versions of the poem, see S. T. Coleridge, *The Complete Poems*, ed. W. Keach (London: Penguin, 1997), pp. 231–3, 515–17.
5. S. T. Coleridge, 'Frost at Midnight' (1808), 26.
6. Coleridge, 'Frost at Midnight' (1817), 19–22.
7. Coleridge, 'Frost at Midnight' (1829), 17–23.
8. S. T. Coleridge, 'Effusion XXXV', in *The Complete Poems*, pp. 85–6; for the final version of the poem, 'The Eolian Harp', see S. T. Coleridge, *Poetical Works* I, ed. J. C. C. Mays, Vol. XVI of *The Collected Works of Samuel Taylor Coleridge*, 23 vols. (Princeton: Princeton University Press, 2001), pp. 231–5. For a more detailed analysis of the initial textual context of 'Effusion XXXV' than I will give, together with an account of how this might relate to its subject matter and later reception, see P. Magnuson, '"The Eolian Harp" in Context', *Studies in Romanticism*, 24:1 (1985), 3–20.

9. Stephen Bygrave describes this passage as 'a dislocation from the dramatic present of the poem, disguised by the fact that this other habitual activity, though introduced as an analogy ("thus ... as ...") is rendered, like the rest of the poem, in the present tense' (S. Bygrave, *Coleridge and the Self* (London: Macmillan, 1986), p. 109); amongst other effects, this technique serves to foreground the poet's aloneness for the duration of the events of these lines, and the presence of Sara for their re-telling in the poem's present.
10. For a detailed account of the textual variations of this poem, see J. Stillinger, *Coleridge and Textual Instability* (Oxford: Oxford University Press, 1994), pp. 27–43.
11. P. Magnuson, 'The Politics of "Frost at Midnight"', J. Thompson, 'An Autumnal Blast, a Killing Frost: Coleridge's Poetic Conversation with John Thelwall', *Studies in Romanticism*, 36:3 (1997), 427–56 (p. 434); *Wordsworth Circle*, 22:1 (1991), 3–11.
12. Magnuson (connectedly) reads this phrase as containing reference to Burke's concept of the origin of revolution; see *ibid.*, p. 10.
13. 'FM', 46; Coleridge, 'Frost at Midnight' (1829), 41.
14. 'FM', 46–7; Coleridge, 'Frost at Midnight' (1829), 41–2.
15. 'FM', 48; Coleridge, 'Frost at Midnight' (1829), 43.
16. These observations could be used to extend Kevis Goodman's reading of the sociability of idle thought in the brown study to 'Frost at Midnight'. In both episodes associative contemplation seems to be a means by which rural withdrawal from society can invoke the random sociability of political engagement. The role of strangeness, and of the stranger, in both texts thus bears an important connection to the central motif of Schiller's thought that this chapter is tracing (that of the aesthetic encounter invoking moral consciousness). It should be noted, however, in this connection, that Coleridge's earlier 'Effusion xxxv' could not be described in similar terms, a fact that suggests this is not a consistent feature of Coleridgean idle contemplation in this period in the same way as the ironic withdrawal or the identification of physical danger.
17. Compare Peter Barry's reading of this passage, which highlights the sexual nature of Coleridge's language: P. Barry, 'Coleridge the Revisionary: Surrogacy and Structure in the Conversation Poems', *The Review of English Studies*, 51 (2000), 600–16 (pp. 604–5); Bygrave also offers some observations on the erotic overtones of the harp: see Bygrave, *Coleridge and the Self*, pp. 109–10.
18. 'FM', 35, 41–3; Coleridge, 'Frost at Midnight' (1829), 35, 36–9.
19. It has been observed (see, for example, D. Wu (ed.), *Romanticism: An Anthology* (Oxford: Blackwell, 1994), p. 42n) that the motif of reposing, either voluntarily or involuntarily, 'Midway the hill of science', recalls Coleridge's position 'on the midway slope / Of yonder hill' in the 'Effusion' (26–7). 'Frost at Midnight' had not been written when Barbauld wrote 'To Mr S. T. Coleridge'.
20. For more on this tradition, see E. Bohls, *Women Travel Writers, Landscape and the Language of Aesthetics, 1716–1818* (Cambridge: Cambridge University Press, 1995).

21. J.-J. Rousseau, *The Reveries of the Solitary Walker* (Dublin: Whitestone, Lynch, et al., 1783), pp. 167–346 (pp. 176–7); and *Les Rêveries du promeneur solitaire* (Paris: Librairie Jules Tallandier, 1969), p. 35: 'Mon corps n'est plus pour moi qu'un embarras, qu'un obstacle, et je m'en dégage d'avance autant que je puis.'
22. The similarities between Rousseau and Cowper in this respect make clear that in one sense the genre of all the texts we are considering here is the reverie.
23. M. A. Favret, *Romantic Correspondence: Women, Politics, and the Fiction of Letters* (Cambridge: Cambridge University Press, 1993), p. 104.
24. It is no doubt as a result of these juxtapositions that the *Letters* acquire their reputation for extraordinary seductiveness: William Godwin observed that 'If ever there was a book calculated to make a man in love with its author, this appears to me to be the book' (quoted in *Short Residence*, p. 239); for more on this aspect of the letters, see H. Guest, *Small Change: Women, Learning, Patriotism, 1750–1810* (Chicago: University of Chicago Press, 2000), pp. 303–4.
25. Wollstonecraft lived in France between 1792 and 1795.
26. While Guest suggests that this passage 'clearly influenced Coleridge in the composition of "Frost at Midnight"' (Guest, *Small Change*, p. 309), Thompson also draws out the conceptual similarities between that poem and Thelwall's 'To the Infant Hampden', written in October 1797. Coleridge is known to have read both sources; for the influence of Thelwall, see Thompson, 'An Autumnal Blast'; and for a record of his reading of Wollstonecraft, see S. T. Coleridge, *Notebooks*, ed. K. Coburn and M. Christensen, 5 vols. (London: Routledge, 1990), Vol. I, entry 261.
27. For a slightly different reading of these two paragraphs, see Guest, *Small Change*, pp. 309–10; or for a different take on the types of movement at work in the *Letters*, see M. A. Favret, '*Letters Written during a Short Residence in Sweden, Norway, and Denmark*: traveling with Mary Wollstonecraft' in C. L. Johnson (ed.), *The Cambridge Companion to Mary Wollstonecraft* (Cambridge: Cambridge University Press, 2002), pp. 209–27.
28. The phrase 'to snap the chain of thought' also occurs in 'Letter XXIII': see *Short Residence*, p. 342. If we were to look for evidence of Wollstonecraft's knowledge of the brown study elsewhere, we should note that seventeen separate extracts from Cowper occur in her anthology *The Female Reader*, of 1789, twelve of which are taken from *The Task*. One of the longest of these, entitled 'An Evening's Invocation to Winter' is from Book IV of *The Task*, ending just one-and-a-half verse paragraphs from the beginning of the brown study episode: see M. Wollstonecraft, *The Female Reader*, Vol. IV of *The Complete Works*, ed. J. Todd and M. Butler, 7 vols. (New York: New York University Press, 1989).
29. It could be suggested, in this connection, that this difference in the extent to which Cowper, Coleridge and Wollstonecraft's reveries are resolved or contained in the texts lies either in the generic distinctions to be made

between meditative poetry and travel writing, or in the differences of gender between the speakers of these texts. On the latter subject, it is striking that commentators have frequently read the speakers of the poetry we are considering here as feminized: for a recent example, see Barry, 'Coleridge the Revisionary'.

30. Guest, *Small Change*, p. 308; in this sense, of course, the final letters could be said to function in a similar manner to Cowper's ironic postscript in the brown study, pointing out, in this case, that these moments were mere fantasies.
31. Also quoted in *ibid.*, p. 308.
32. Coleridge, 'Frost at Midnight' (1829), 51–8; 'FM', 56–63.
33. Coleridge, 'Frost at Midnight' (1829), 58–62; 'FM', 63–7.
34. These lines are also importantly related to the passage that makes up the second verse paragraph of the poem: in recognizing himself in the other, in flirting with identification with the stranger, be it 'townsman', 'aunt' or 'sister', the young poet was anticipating God's message as it is figured in this passage, and the connection it posits between all objects.
35. It should also be noted, however, that if one wanted to follow Friedrich Schlegel's ironic critique of Schiller's project as a whole (see Chapter 2, n. 43), 'Frost at Midnight' could be read as replicating Schlegel's emphasis on the productivity, and thus essentiality, of psychic dissonance, as opposed to psychic wholeness, the desired outcome of Schiller's aesthetic project. That it is a 'calm' that 'disturbs / And vexes meditation', that it is the ruminative powers of the individual in crisis, in other words, that leads to the moral insight of the poem's penultimate verse paragraph, ties the aesthetic consciousness of the poem to the problematic fragmentation of modern mental and spiritual powers that Schiller's work is at pains to overcome. It is as if, in this view, the poem's moral insight could not have been brought about without the fragmented experiences that commence the poem. Even following this observation, however, 'Frost at Midnight' could still be described as moving from the experience of psychic dissonance to that of wholeness, as overcoming Schlegel's position to replicate that of Schiller.
36. Despite the essentiality of Cowper and Coleridge's thought in this respect, it is nevertheless conspicuous that these texts also remain open to being read as in thrall to the premises and logic of political economy, in its insistence on the creativity, or purposiveness, of contemplation. In the creative overtones of the brown study, or in the moral consciousnesses of 'Frost at Midnight' and 'Effusion xxxv', one could read the economic paradigm of productivity: that is, of judging an act or an object only by its value to commercial society. This is the case here because, like Schiller's politically motivated aesthetic detour, Cowper and Coleridge's moral consciousness is announced as 'useful', in the widest terms. Once again, in other words, thought that sets itself against the premises of political economy could be said to struggle to evade the style of thinking that characterized Book v of the *Wealth of Nations*. A dispute with political economy, in this view, seems

unable to separate itself successfully from that discourse's terminology and classification; or, phrased another way, the comprehensiveness of the *Wealth of Nations* can be read as anticipating any debate about its details.

4 COLERIDGE'S PANTISOCRACY, *BIOGRAPHIA* AND *CHURCH AND STATE*

1. For more on the matter of these discussions, see R. Holmes, *Coleridge: Early Visions* (London: Penguin, 1989), p. 62.
2. T. Poole, quoted in Holmes, *Coleridge*, p. 72; and D. S. Malachuk, 'Labor, Leisure, and the Yeoman in Coleridge's and Wordsworth's 1790s Writings', *Romanticism on the Net*, 27 (2002), paragraph 14, available online at www.erudit.org/revue/ron/2002/v/n27/006564ar.html. Last accessed 10 May 2010.
3. Southey, quoted in Holmes, *Coleridge*, p. 75.
4. In this connection, it should be observed that the reports of contemporary American life Coleridge read in his research for the Pantisocracy scheme tended to exaggerate the amount of leisure time inhabitants there enjoyed. J. P. Brissot de Warville's *Travels in the United States* of 1794, for example, states, as Malachuk reports, that an American farmer 'works scarcely two hours in a day for the support of himself and family', passing 'most of his time in idleness, hunting or drinking' (see Malachuk, 'Labor, Leisure, and the Yeoman', paragraph 13). Clearly the immoral flavour of two of these three activities was to be corrected by the Pantisocracy's emphasis on literature, which would be at once leisure and labour.
5. The poem was printed on 30 December 1794, in issue 7867.
6. In addition to appearing in the *Morning Chronicle* in 1794, the fact that Coleridge also sent the letter to Southey means that it appears in his *Letters*, Vol. 1, pp. 142–3.
7. Lines 140–7; for details of the sonnet's initial attribution to Southey, when it first appeared in print, see *Letters*, Vol. 1, p. 104 n. 2.
8. S. T. Coleridge, untitled sonnet in *Letters*, Vol. 1, p. 104, lines 1–2, 3–4.
9. If one wanted to identify an emotional episode the sonnet might be motivated by, one would be struck by the fact that it first appears in a letter to Southey that begins by reference to Coleridge's deliberations between Sara Fricker and Mary Evans: see *Letters*, Vol. 1, pp. 103–4; and, for a detailed description of both relationships, Holmes, *Coleridge*.
10. While the Pantisocracy was not realized by Coleridge and Southey, as Holmes observes, 'the Susquehanna scheme did become a reality in other hands, and had considerable influence on radical thinking in England at this time': see Holmes, *Coleridge*, p. 89.
11. The *Biographia* met with generally unfavourable reviews on its publication in 1817: just as Hazlitt remarked that only 'some things' in it were 'readable' (W. Hazlitt, 'Coleridge's Literary Life' in *Complete Works of William*

Hazlitt, ed. P. P. Howe, 21 vols. (Bungay: Chaucer Press, 1933), Vol. XVI, pp. 115–38), many others found it 'obscure' and far too 'metaphysical'. For more details of these reviews, and for details of the text's composition, see *Biog.*, Vol. I, pp. lxv–lvii.

12. In accordance with the largely pejorative reviews the *Biographia* received on publication, many readers, both then and since, have found it to be unbalanced, or at least made up of quite unconnected parts (see F. Burwick (ed.), *Coleridge's* Biographia Literaria*: Text and Meaning* (Columbus: Ohio State University Press, 1989), p. vii). In contrast to this trend, there are also those who argue for various types of consistency in the text. Thomas Vogler, most notably, considers the work as a whole to be a deliberately and ironically empty 'philosophical sandwich', constantly playing with the readers' expectations of Coleridge as author: see T. Vogler, 'Coleridge's Book of Moonlight' in Burwick, *Coleridge's* Biographia Literaria, pp. 20–46.

13. S. T. Coleridge, *Notebooks*, ed. Coburn and Christensen, Vol. I, entries 1832, 1833; this association of what is 'reverie-ish' with what is amoral clearly functions as a kind of unpacking of the logic behind Coleridge's 'Effusion XXXV', which we examined in the previous chapter. If Sara, as auditor of the poem, objected to the 'streamy' nature of the poet's deductions from his 'idle flitting phantasies', then we might say that this is because they could be described as amoral by virtue of the absence of the will in their creation. If, in other words, Coleridge could prove that the will was engaged, even unconsciously, in such moments of reverie, then he would be in a position to reject Sara's classification of his ruminations there as blasphemy, and, in turn, invest the poetic act with all kinds of significances. This, of course, is largely what the *Biographia* does, as we will see.

14. Burwick (describing Vogler and using Carlyle's terms), *Coleridge's* Biographia Literaria, p. ix.

15. Coleridge states that the 'Chapter' itself is 'reserved for that future publication, a detailed prospectus of which the reader will find at the close of the second volume' (*Biog.*, Vol. I, p. 304). No such 'prospectus' appears there.

16. As N. Reid, 'Coleridge and Schelling: The Missing Transcendental Deduction', *Studies in Romanticism*, 33:3 (1994), 451–79 (p. 452); J. F. Solomon, 'Annotating the Annotations: A Philosophical Reading of the Primary and Secondary Imagination' in Burwick, *Coleridge's* Biographia Literaria, p. 138; and Vogler, 'Coleridge's Book of Moonlight' do, for example.

17. As Engell and Bate do, for instance, in their account of the *Biographia*'s conception: see *Biog.*, Vol. I, pp. xli–cxxxvi.

18. This definition, it should be noted, is in one sense a standard restatement of an idea common to Kant, Schelling and others; for more on this heritage in the context of this definition, see *ibid.*, pp. lxxxv–lxxxvi.

19. N. Leask, *The Politics of Imagination in Coleridge's Critical Thought* (London: Macmillan, 1988), p. 139. Leask reads the existence of two

alternative courses of action for the secondary imagination as problematic, suggesting that Coleridge's definition creates a tension that was 'simply not present as a problem in Schelling's account of aesthetic mediation' (for more on Leask and Schelling, see below); he also extrapolates from these options to show the different possible (political) functions of art in relation to history: see pp. 139–40.

20. It should be noted that in reading the secondary imagination in this manner I am, to some extent at least, carrying over the terminology Coleridge uses in his definition of the primary imagination. The style in which, and length at which, the secondary imagination is depicted give the impression that it is some sort of intensification, or more complete development, of the primary, that is. If one were to set more store by the word 'echo' than I have done, however, one might conclude that the secondary imagination is a more restricted, less developed or somehow less active form of the primary imagination.

21. This is certainly the way it has been read in almost all critical accounts: see, for example, Leask, *The Politics of Imagination*, p. 136; Solomon, 'Annotating the Annotations' pp. 138–49; and *Biog.*

22. Coleridge could be said to anticipate the relationship of these and other moments in the *Biographia* to the definitions at the end of Chapter 13 when he states, in Chapter 4, that 'were it … fully ascertained, that this division [between the fancy and the imagination] is no less grounded in nature, than that of delirium from mania [for example], [i]t would in its immediate effects furnish a torch or guidance to the philosophical critic; and ultimately to the poet himself' (*Biog.*, Vol. II, pp. 84–5).

23. While this passage occurs after Coleridge's division of the imagination into primary and secondary, it is most often assumed to have been written before that definition. In accordance with this opinion, Coleridge's reference to 'the preceding disquisition on the fancy and the imagination', which introduces this quotation, is dismissed as not referring to the Chapter 13 definitions (see *Biog.*, Vol. II, p. 15 n. 4, for example). If we wanted to challenge this chronology, as, for instance, Norman Fruman has done (see S. T. Coleridge, *Biographia Literaria*, ed. N. Leask (London: J. M. Dent, 1997) p. xlvii), or if we simply wanted to read the text for what it has appeared to say since its first publication, we might assume that Coleridge is referring to his Chapter 13 definition. At the very least, we should note that if the standard chronology is correct, Coleridge nevertheless did not see fit to change the references to the imagination in Volume II after adding the bulk of the material that makes up Volume I.

24. The relationship between Coleridge and Schelling should not be understood as a modern discovery, however. Coleridge's daughter, Sara, was the first to point towards Schelling as the source for many of her father's ideas. For more on this topic, see the 'Introduction' and extensive notes in *Biog.*

25. Leask, *The Politics of Imagination*, pp. 137–8.

26. These two processes become almost synonymous if one happens to read from the current Princeton edition of the *Biographia*, where every known link to Schelling is matched by exhaustive quotations and translations of this 'source material'.
27. *Aesthetic*, pp. clxix–clxx.
28. M. J. Kooy, *Coleridge, Schiller and Aesthetic Education* (Basingstoke: Palgrave, 2002), pp. 124, 128, for example; in general terms, Kooy rather overstates the case for Coleridge's knowledge of Schiller, discounting any similarities there might have been between the two thinkers before Coleridge encountered Schiller's writing, and talking of Coleridge as if he was familiar with the *Aesthetic Letters* after having demonstrated that such familiarity cannot be proved at this time: see pp. 62, 99, for instance. For a similar assessment of Kant's changing political valence between 1790 and 1818, see D. M. Baulch, 'The "Perpetual Exercise of an Interminable Quest": *The Biographia Literaria* and the Kantian Revolution', *Studies in Romanticism*, 43:4 (2004), 557–81 (p. 566).
29. Kooy, *Coleridge, Schiller and Aesthetic Education*, pp. 113, 116, 123.
30. For reasons for Coleridge's eventual rejection of Schelling's system, see *ibid.*, p. 125.
31. *Ibid.*, p. 84.
32. *Ibid.*, p. 123.
33. Engell and Bate, in their edition of *Biographia*, reference Schiller, *Aesthetic*, pp. 150–2, 208–10 as two possible sources for this passage, although the similarities are not particularly obvious: see their note at *Biog.*, Vol. I, p. 124.
34. *Aesthetic*, p. 300; the German original is not quoted by Wilkinson and Willoughby, but can be found at *Die Horen, 1795*, 6. Stück, ed. J. Kühlne, available online at www.wissen-im-netz.info/literatur/schiller/herausgeber/horen/1795/06/02.htm, last accessed 10 May 2010. In the *Horae* edition, the *Letters*' last paragraph was part of this final footnote; see also Kooy, *Coleridge, Schiller and Aesthetic Education*, p. 148 (*Horae* is Kooy's translation of the journal's original title, *Die Horen*).
35. Wilkinson and Willoughby in *Aesthetic*, p. cliv.
36. It is this sometimes strange mixture of styles that has led to some commentators remarking on the difficulty of *Church and State*. Peter Allen, for example, describes the text as 'brilliantly suggestive and maddeningly elliptical', 'a perplexing mixture of political commentary, social theory, and historical analysis': see P. Allen, 'S. T. Coleridge's Church and State and the Idea of an Intellectual Establishment', *Journal of the History of Ideas*, 46:1 (1985), 89–106 (p. 89).
37. For more on the context out of which *Church and State* emerges, see S. T. Coleridge, *On the Constitution of Church and State*, ed. J. Barrell (London: J. M. Dent and Sons, 1972), pp. viii–xxxi; while Coleridge was in favour of the Bill only, as Barrell summarizes, 'if it were accompanied by securities to protect the institutions which are the subject of this book from any attempt

by Rome to establish a political base in England' (p. ix), it was actually passed, in 1829, before *Church and State* was published.
38. Although the 'National' and 'Christian' Churches are not the same thing in contemporary England, their similarity or cohabitation is, for Coleridge, 'a blessed accident, a providential boon', and 'a grace of God' (*C&S*, p. 55).
39. This is Colmer's reading: see *ibid.*, p. 62 n. 3.
40. Indeed, the influence *Church and State* enjoyed on English educational thought is considerable. As Barrell summarizes, 'it was felt in Disraeli's Young England movement, in the Broad Church, and in the Christian Socialism of F. D. Maurice; for a while it "humanized" the Utilitarianism of John Stuart Mill; Newman, Kingsley, Thomas and Matthew Arnold were all much indebted' (in Coleridge, *Church and State*, ed. Barrell, p. xxiv). Despite such influence, however, it should be noted that it is possible to react to the suggestions of *Church and State* in less positive terms: just as Allen reads the work as propounding 'a social mechanism essential for achieving rule by consent' ('S. T. Coleridge's Church and State', p. 95), Leask finds 'the function of cultivation' to be 'to instil reverence rather than enlightenment', and suggests that Coleridge is hoping to '"let sleeping dogs lie" by inculcating devotion ... rather than knowledge and critical inquiry' (*The Politics of Imagination*, p. 218).
41. Leask, in this connection, points to similarities between the themes of Coleridge's Bristol lectures in the 1790s and the concerns of *Church and State*: see Leask, *The Politics of Imagination*, pp. 34–45.
42. See above for Coleridge's influence on English educational thought, and for Schiller's impact on the same area of German intellectual life. See Kooy, *Coleridge, Schiller and Aesthetic Education*, p. 82, who records, for example, Coleridge's meeting with Wilhelm von Humboldt, a vocal 'supporter and correspondent of Schiller', who 'articulated' the gist of the *Aesthetic Letters* in 1809 'in terms relevant to the founding of the new university in Berlin'.
43. The most interesting of those readers who have found the *Biographia* to be centre-less is Vogler, who relates the text to Swift's *Tale of a Tub*, and finds that its 'foundation, cornerstone, keystone' is 'not there in the place where it was repeatedly announced and long expected – an absence made so emphatic as to be almost the *presence* of nothingness': see Vogler, 'Coleridge's Book of Moonlight', p. 31. For two alternative readings of this idea of the 'gap' in the *Biographia*, see K. Wheeler, *Sources, Processes and Methods in Coleridge's* The Biographia Literaria (Cambridge: Cambridge University Press, 1980); and C. M. Wallace, *The Design of the* Biographia Literaria (London: Allen and Unwin, 1983); both of whom see such a space as an invitation for the reader actively and imaginatively to participate in deciphering the text.
44. Malachuk reads this connection similarly, describing the 'politicized leisure' of the Pantisocracy, which offered the space for civic contemplation, as 'foreshadowing' the 'more sophisticated republicanism' of *Church and State*: see Malachuk, 'Labor, Leisure, and the Yeoman', paragraph 22.

CONCLUSION

1. Of course a description such as this ignores the interest the *Wealth of Nations* demonstrates in classical-republican modes of thought more generally. As we saw, and as scholars such as J. G. A. Pocock and Stephen Copley have observed (see above, pp. 24–8), Smith's text functions by repeated reference to the benefits of the classical organization of society.
2. W. Empson, *Some Versions of Pastoral* (London: Hogarth Press, 1986), p. 12.
3. *Ibid.*, pp. 6, 12–13.
4. Whilst, as stated, it has not been this study's ambition to pursue a Marxist analysis of its material, this chain of logic does offer significant comment on Marx's reading of the division of labour. At first glance, that is, this pattern of development would seem to conform to Marx's description of the manner in which specialization's separation of mental and manual work allows systems of thought to turn against contemporary economic society, even though, for Marx as for Smith, it is only under those economic conditions that consciousness could develop in that manner (see K. Marx, 'The German Ideology' in Marx and F. Engels, *The Marx–Engels Reader*, ed. R. C. Tucker (London: W. W. Norton, 1978), p. 159). Such developments, however, on a more sustained consideration, also serve to question the assumption in Marx's writing that it is to 'active', labouring life, rather than to 'what men say, imagine [or] conceive', that one must look in order to find the explanation of the separated consciousness's attempts at spirituality (*ibid.*, p. 154). The thought of Coleridge and Cowper, for example, in fact asks what might follow if we positioned man's contemplative and aesthetic faculties as primary, rather than his abilities to labour and to trade. This is to say that many of the texts considered by this study reject the premise, shared by both Smith and Marx, that man's labour represents the only significant facet of human ability, his contemplation being only that facet's shadow for Smith, and spume for Marx (see *ibid.*, p. 159). In so doing, importantly, they also offer the possibility of rejecting the materialist assumption itself.

EPILOGUE

1. *Yeast*, pp. 9–10.
2. For a more gendered reading of Wordsworth's poem than I will give here, see M. B. Ross, 'Naturalizing Gender: Woman's Place in Wordsworth's Ideological Landscape', *ELH*, 53:2 (1986), 391–410: Ross asserts that the 'psychology' of the poem 'requires that nature be masculine' (p. 396). For an account of the poem's relationship with the other four Lucy poems, see F. C. Ferguson, 'The Lucy Poems: Wordsworth's Quest for a Poetic Object', *ELH*, 40:4 (1973), 532–48; and for a reading of the poems in line with the ideas this study analysed in Cowper's brown study, see R. Adelman, 'Idle Thought in Wordsworth's Lucy Cycle', *Romanticism*, 17:1 (2011).

3. In this sense, Kingsley could be understood to be rejecting the tentative sociability that Kevis Goodman's reading uncovered in the model of thought to be found in the brown study (see Chapter 3, n. 16).
4. If one wanted to extend this connection, the significance of water in Kingsley's later children's novel, *The Water Babies* (1863), could be plausibly aligned with the network of ideas to be found in the river- and seascape scenes of *Yeast* and *Alton Locke*. Note, for example, Kingsley's description of the may-flies surrounding Lancelot (above, p. 146) as 'like water-fairies, with their green gauzy wings'.
5. Compare this quotation to Coleridge's 'For I was reared / In the great city, pent 'mid cloisters dim, / And saw nought lovely but the sky and stars' (above, p. 96).
6. While I will read *Alton Locke* in such a way as to foreground the circumstances that inhibit poetic activity, and political activism indeed, it should be observed that it is also possible to read Kingsley as actually 'proposing solutions' to 'social and political problems' (p. 52): see, for example, E. M. Gottlieb, 'Charles Kingsley, the Romantic Legacy, and the Unmaking of the Working-Class Intellectual', *Victorian Literature and Culture*, 29:1 (2001), 51–65.
7. Gottlieb offers a more detailed reading of the protagonist's poetic endeavours in the novel than I do, also comparing the role of poetry in *Alton Locke* to Kingsley's own opinions about various poets: see Gottlieb, 'Romantic Legacy'.
8. The other moments in *Alton Locke* that seem to relate to Wordsworth's 'Three years she grew' can be found in Chapter 11, when Alton first leaves the city, and in Chapter 13, in Cambridge. In the former, Alton looks out 'over glittering brooks' and finds the physical parameters of his view replicated in his mental state: 'I felt at that moment a capability of clear, bright meditation, which was new to me … it seemed to me the most delightful life on earth … to study the secrets of the flower world, the laws of soil and climate' (*Alton Locke*, p. 116). In the other of these moments, Alton finds himself entering into an involuntary reverie while staring into the Cam: 'I leaned upon the parapet, and gazed, and gazed, so absorbed in wonder and enjoyment, that I was quite unconscious, for some time, that Lord Lynedale was standing by my side, engaged in the same employment' (*Alton Locke*, p. 147). It is not that these moments, taken on their own, constitute an allusion to Wordsworth's poem, but that, when placed alongside Lancelot's reverie in *Yeast*, and the scenes on Waterloo Bridge and above the Atlantic, Kingsley's writing seems to be punctuated by the motif of the waterside reverie. The direct allusion to Wordsworth that occurs in *Yeast* is thus kept in the reader's mind, even in *Alton Locke*, by the novel's frequent visual references to that episode.
9. John Stuart Mill, *Autobiography*, ed. J. Stillinger (Oxford: Oxford University Press, 1971), pp. 10–11.
10. *Ibid.*, p. 11.
11. *Ibid.*, pp. 35–6.

12. *Ibid.*, p. 37; Mill was invited to stay with Sir Samuel Bentham and his family in the south of France in 1820. Samuel Bentham was the designer of the Panopticon.
13. *Ibid.*, p. 81.
14. *Ibid.*, p. 83.
15. This is also the kind of education Bentham strove to employ in the Panopticon penitentiary and Chrestomathic School, as we saw.
16. Mill, *Autobiography*, p. 84.
17. *Ibid.*, p. 86.
18. *Ibid.*, pp. 88, 89–90.
19. *Ibid.*, p. 86.
20. J. S. Mill, 'Coleridge' in *Mill on Bentham and Coleridge*, ed. F. R. Leavis (London: Chatto and Windus, 1962), p. 101.
21. *Ibid.*, p. 140.
22. Raymond Williams, in this connection, reads Mill's attempt to 'unify', 'by discrimination and discarding' the 'truths alike of the utilitarian and idealist positions' as 'a prologue to a very large part of the subsequent history of English thinking'; see R. Williams, *Culture and Society* (London: Chatto and Windus, 1967), p. 49.
23. J. S. Mill, 'Inaugural Address Delivered to the University of St Andrews' in *Essays on Equality, Law, and Education*, ed. J. M. Robson, Vol. XXI of *Collected Works of John Stuart Mill*, 33 vols. (Toronto: University of Toronto Press, 1984), pp. 217–57 (p. 256).
24. *Ibid.*, p. 255.
25. *Ibid.*, pp. 255–6.
26. See Mill, *Autobiography*, pp. 50–1.
27. For a more complete account of this aspect of *Alton Locke*, see R. Menke, 'Cultural Capital and the Scene of Rioting: Male Working-Class Authorship in *Alton Locke*', *Victorian Literature and Culture*, 28:1 (2000), 87–108. Menke analyses the manner in which Alton's writing serves as an attempt to access a culture from which his status as a tailor debars him.
28. Mill, *Autobiography*, p. 92.
29. Jack Stillinger, connectedly, reads Mill's account of his education alongside first-hand reports of that education from other sources, finding that the *Autobiography* is not as reliable as it seems: see J. Stillinger, 'John Mill's Education: Fact, Fiction, and Myth' in M. Laine (ed.), *A Cultivated Mind* (Toronto: University of Toronto Press, 1991), pp. 19–43.
30. Mill, *Autobiography*, p. 94.
31. *Ibid.*, pp. 144–5.
32. Quoted in M. Filipiuk, 'John Stuart Mill and France' in Laine (ed.), *A Cultivated Mind*, p. 111.
33. See Mill, *Autobiography*, p. 86.
34. *Ibid.*, p. 18.
35. The distinction to be made between the materials of Mill's education leads Williams to read the *Autobiography* as contending that the part of the mind that responds to poetry is 'a special reserve area in which feeling can be

tended and organized'. He goes on to suggest that 'both the practice and the appreciation of art have suffered from art being thus treated as a saving clause in a bad treaty'; see Williams, *Culture and Society*, p. 67.
36. Menke, 'Cultural Capital and the Scene of Rioting', p. 93.
37. In this connection, indeed, one might plausibly read Mill's thought as contending for the truth of what from Kingsley's perspective might be described as the mythic power of the pastoral. Mill's rural retirement renders that genre of aesthetic distance a reality, while Kingsley's novels represent it as ideology fragile enough to crumble under the pressure of social reality and realism.
38. Williams, *Culture and Society*, p. 43.

Bibliography

PRIMARY SOURCES

Bentham, Jeremy. 'Outline of a Work Entitled Pauper Management Improved', *Annals of Agriculture and Other Useful Arts*, 30 (1798), 89–176, 241–96, 393–424, 457–504.
   Panopticon; or, The Inspection-House (Dublin: Thomas Byrne, 1791).
Coleridge, Samuel Taylor. *Biographia Literaria*, ed. N. Leask (London: J. M. Dent, 1997).
   The Complete Poems, ed. W. Keach (London: Penguin, 1997).
   Notebooks, ed. K. Coburn and M. Christensen, 5 vols. (London: Routledge, 1990).
   On the Constitution of Church and State, ed. J. Barrell (London: J. M. Dent and Sons, 1972).
   Poetical Works I, ed. J. C. C. Mays, Vol. XVI of *The Collected Works of Samuel Taylor Coleridge*, 23 vols. (Princeton: Princeton University Press, 2001).
   Untitled sonnet in *Letters*, Vol. I, p. 104.
Ferguson, Adam. *An Essay on the History of Civil Society*, ed. F. Oz-Salzberger (Cambridge: Cambridge University Press, 1995).
   Principles of Moral and Political Science, 2 vols. (New York: AMS Press, 1973).
Kant, Immanuel. *The Critique of Judgement*, ed. J. C. Meredith (Oxford: Clarendon Press, 1978).
   Kritik der Urtheilskraft (Berlin: Druck und Verlag von Georg Reimer, 1913).
Marx, Karl. *Capital: A Critical Analysis of Capitalist Production*, 3 vols. (Moscow: Foreign Languages Publishing House, 1954).
   Economic and Philosophic Manuscripts of 1844 in Marx and Engels, *The Marx–Engels Reader*, pp. 66–125.
   The German Ideology in Marx and Engels, *The Marx–Engels Reader*, pp. 146–200.
Marx, Karl and Friedrich Engels. *The Marx–Engels Reader*, ed. R. C. Tucker (London: W. W. Norton, 1978).
Mill, John Stuart. *Autobiography*, ed. J. Stillinger (Oxford: Oxford University Press, 1971).
   'Inaugural Address Delivered to the University of St Andrews' in *Essays on Equality, Law, and Education*, ed. J. M. Robson, Vol. XXI of *Collected Works*

of John Stuart Mill, 33 vols. (Toronto: University of Toronto Press, 1984), pp. 217–57.
   Mill on Bentham and Coleridge, ed. F. R. Leavis (London: Chatto and Windus, 1962).
Mill, John Stuart and Jeremy Bentham. *'Utilitarianism' and Other Essays*, ed. A. Ryan (London: Penguin, 1987).
Nietzsche, Friedrich. 'On the Uses and Disadvantages of History for Life' in *Untimely Meditations*, ed. J. P. Stern (Cambridge: Cambridge University Press, 1983), pp. 57–123.
Plato. *The Republic*, ed. G. R. F. Ferrari (Cambridge: Cambridge University Press, 2000).
Rousseau, Jean-Jacques. *A Discourse on the Origin of Inequality* in *The Social Contract and Discourses*, ed. G. D. H. Cole (London: Everyman, 2001), pp. 31–126.
   Les Rêveries du promeneur solitaire (Paris: Librairie Jules Tallandier, 1969).
   The Reveries of the Solitary Walker (Dublin: Whitestone, Lynch, Gilbert, et al. 1783), pp. 167–346.
Schiller, Friedrich. *Die Horen, 1795*, ed. Jürgen Kühlne, available online at www.wissen-im-netz.info/literatur/schiller/herausgeber/horen/1795/06/02.htm. Last accessed 10 May 2010.
Wollstonecraft, Mary. *The Female Reader*, Vol. IV of *The Complete Works*, ed. J. Todd and M. Butler, 7 vols. (New York: New York University Press, 1989).
Wordsworth, William. *The Brothers* in W. Wordsworth and S. T. Coleridge, *Lyrical Ballads*, ed. R. L. Brett and A. R. Jones (London: Routledge, 1991), pp. 135–50.
   'Gipsies' in Poems in Two Volumes, *and Other Poems, 1800–1807*, ed. J. Curtis (New York: Cornell University Press, 1983), pp. 211–12.
   '*Home at Grasmere*, MS. B' in *Home at Grasmere*, ed. B. Darlington (New York: Cornell University Press, 1977), pp. 38–106.

SECONDARY SOURCES

Adelman, Richard. 'Idle Thought in Wordsworth's Lucy Cycle', *Romanticism*, 17:1 (2011).
Allen, Peter. 'S. T. Coleridge's Church and State and the Idea of an Intellectual Establishment', *Journal of the History of Ideas*, 46:1 (1985), 89–106.
Bailey, Nathan. *Dictionary English–German and German–English, oder englisch–deutsches und deutsches–englisch Wörterbuch*, 2 vols. (Leipzig and Züllichau: Friedrich Frommann, 1797).
Barrell, John. *English Literature in History 1730–80: An Equal, Wide Survey* (London: Hutchinson, 1983).
   'The Public Prospect and the Private View: The Politics of Taste in Eighteenth-Century Britain' in S. Pugh (ed.), *Reading Landscape: Country, City, Capital* (Manchester: Manchester University Press, 1990), pp. 19–40.

Barry, Peter. 'Coleridge the Revisionary: Surrogacy and Structure in the Conversation Poems', *The Review of English Studies*, 51 (2000), 600–16.
Baulch, David M. 'The "Perpetual Exercise of an Interminable Quest": *The Biographia Literaria* and the Kantian Revolution', *Studies in Romanticism*, 43:4 (2004), 557–81.
Bender, John. *Imagining the Penitentiary: Fiction and the Architecture of Mind in Eighteenth-Century England* (Chicago: University of Chicago Press, 1987).
Bohls, Elizabeth. *Women Travel Writers, Landscape and the Language of Aesthetics, 1716–1818* (Cambridge: Cambridge University Press, 1995).
Bourdieu, Pierre. *Distinction: A Social Critique of the Judgement of Taste*, ed. R. Nice (London: Routledge and Kegan Paul, 1984).
Burwick, Frederick (ed.). *Coleridge's* Biographia Literaria*: Text and Meaning* (Columbus: Ohio State University Press, 1989).
Bygrave, Stephen. *Coleridge and the Self* (London: Macmillan, 1986).
Cohen, Ted and P. Guyer (eds.). *Essays in Kant's Aesthetics* (Chicago: University of Chicago Press, 1982).
Copley, Stephen (ed.). *Literature and the Social Order in Eighteenth-Century England* (London: Croom Helm, 1984).
Copley, Stephen and K. Sutherland (eds.). *Adam Smith's* Wealth of Nations*: New Interdisciplinary Essays* (Manchester: Manchester University Press, 1995).
De Bolla, Peter. *Art Matters* (Cambridge, MA: Harvard University Press, 2001).
— 'Toward the Materiality of Aesthetic Experience', *Diacritics*, 32:1 (2002), 19–37.
Empson, William. *Some Versions of Pastoral* (London: Hogarth Press, 1986).
Favret, Mary A. '*Letters Written during a Short Residence in Sweden, Norway, and Denmark*: traveling with Mary Wollstonecraft' in C. L. Johnson (ed.), *The Cambridge Companion to Mary Wollstonecraft* (Cambridge: Cambridge University Press, 2002), pp. 209–27.
— *Romantic Correspondence: Women, Politics, and the Fiction of Letters* (Cambridge: Cambridge University Press, 1993).
Ferguson, Frances C. 'The Lucy Poems: Wordsworth's Quest for a Poetic Object', *ELH*, 40:4 (1973), 532–48.
Filipiuk, Marion. 'John Stuart Mill and France' in Laine, *A Cultivated Mind*, pp. 80–120.
Fitzgibbons, Athol. *Adam Smith's System of Liberty, Wealth, and Virtue: The Moral and Political Foundations of* The Wealth of Nations, (Oxford: Clarendon Press, 1995).
Fleischacker, Samuel. *On Adam Smith's* Wealth of Nations*: A Philosophical Companion* (Princeton: Princeton University Press, 2004).
Goldsmith, M. M. *Private Vices, Public Benefits: Bernard Mandeville's Social and Political Thought* (Cambridge: Cambridge University Press, 1985).
Goodman, Kevis. *Georgic Modernity and British Romanticism: Poetry and the Mediation of History* (Cambridge: Cambridge University Press, 2004).

'The Loophole in the Retreat: The Culture of News and the Early Life of Romantic Self-Consciousness', *South Atlantic Quarterly*, 102:1 (2003), 25–52.

Gottlieb, Evan M. 'Charles Kingsley, the Romantic Legacy, and the Unmaking of the Working-Class Intellectual', *Victorian Literature and Culture*, 29:1 (2001), 51–65.

Griffin, Dustin. 'Redefining Georgic: Cowper's Task', *ELH*, 57:4 (1990), 865–79.

Guest, Harriet. *Small Change: Women, Learning, Patriotism, 1750–1810* (Chicago: University of Chicago Press, 2000).

Hazlitt, William. 'Coleridge's Literary Life' in *Complete Works of William Hazlitt*, ed. P. P. Howe, 21 vols. (Bungay: Chaucer Press, 1933), Vol. XVI, pp. 115–38.

Holmes, Richard. *Coleridge: Early Visions* (London: Penguin, 1989).

Hont, Istvan and Michael Ignatieff. 'Needs and Justice in the *Wealth of Nations*: An Introductory Essay' in Hont and Ignatieff, *Wealth and Virtue*, pp. 1–44.

   (eds.). *Wealth and Virtue: The Shaping of Political Economy in the Scottish Enlightenment* (Cambridge: Cambridge University Press, 1983).

Howard, John. *An Account of the Principal Lazarettos in Europe* (Warrington: W. Eyres, 1789).

   The State of the Prisons in England and Wales, with Preliminary Observations, and an Account of Some Foreign Prisons (Warrington: W. Eyres, 1777).

Hutcheson, Francis. *A System of Moral Philosophy*, 3 vols. (Glasgow: R. and A. Foulis, 1755).

Ignatieff, Michael. *A Just Measure of Pain: The Penitentiary in the Industrial Revolution, 1750–1850* (New York: Pantheon, 1978).

Kames, Henry Home, Lord. *Sketches of the History of Man*, 4 vols. (Basil: J. J. Tourneisen, 1796).

Kettler, David. *The Social and Political Thought of Adam Ferguson* (Columbus: Ohio State University Press, 1965).

Kooy, Michael John. *Coleridge, Schiller and Aesthetic Education* (Basingstoke: Palgrave, 2002).

Laine, M. (ed.), *A Cultivated Mind* (Toronto: Toronto University Press, 1991)

Leask, Nigel. *The Politics of Imagination in Coleridge's Critical Thought* (London: Macmillan, 1988).

Lukács, Georg. *Goethe and His Age*, ed. R. Anchor (London: Merlin Press, 1968).

Lux, Kenneth. *Adam Smith's Mistake: How a Moral Philosopher Invented Economics and Ended Morality* (London: Shambala, 1990).

Magnuson, Paul. '"The Eolian Harp" in Context', *Studies in Romanticism*, 24:1 (1985), 3–20.

'The Politics of "Frost at Midnight"', *Wordsworth Circle*, 22:1 (1991), 3–11.

Malachuk, Daniel S. 'Labor, Leisure, and the Yeoman in Coleridge's and Wordsworth's 1790s Writings', *Romanticism on the Net*, 27 (2002), available online at www.erudit.org/revue/ron/2002/v/n27/006564ar.html. Last accessed 10 May 2010.

Menke, Richard. 'Cultural Capital and the Scene of Rioting: Male Working-Class Authorship in *Alton Locke*', *Victorian Literature and Culture*, 28:1 (2000), 87–108.
Owen, W. J. B. *Wordsworth as Critic* (Oxford: Oxford University Press, 1969).
Parker, Noel. 'Look, No Hidden Hands: How Smith Understands Historical Progress and Societal Values' in Copley and Sutherland, *Adam Smith's Wealth of Nations*, pp. 122–43.
Phillipson, Nicholas. 'Adam Smith as Civic Moralist' in Hont and Ignatieff, *Wealth and Virtue*, pp. 179–202.
Pocock, John G. A. *Barbarism and Religion*, 4 vols. (Cambridge: Cambridge University Press, 1999).
 The Machiavellian Moment: Florentine Political Thought and the Atlantic Republican Tradition (Princeton: Princeton University Press, 1975).
 Virtue, Commerce, and History: Essays on Political Thought and History, Chiefly in the Eighteenth Century (Cambridge: Cambridge University Press, 1985).
Porter, Roy. *Mind-Forg'd Manacles: A History of Madness in England from the Restoration to the Regency* (London: Athlone Press, 1987).
Priestman, Martin. *Cowper's Task* (Cambridge: Cambridge University Press, 1983).
Reid, Nicholas. 'Coleridge and Schelling: The Missing Transcendental Deduction', *Studies in Romanticism*, 33:3 (1994), 451–79.
Robertson, John. 'The Scottish Enlightenment at the Limits of the Civic Tradition' in Hont and Ignatieff, *Wealth and Virtue*, pp. 137–78.
Ross, Marlon B. 'Naturalizing Gender: Woman's Place in Wordsworth's Ideological Landscape', *ELH*, 53:2 (1986), 391–410.
Semple, Janet. *Bentham's Prison: A Study of the Panopticon Penitentiary* (Oxford: Clarendon Press, 1993).
Sher, Richard B. 'Adam Ferguson, Adam Smith, and the Problem of National Defense', *Journal of Modern History*, 61 (1989), 240–68.
Simpson, David (ed.). *The Origins of Modern Critical Thought* (Cambridge: Cambridge University Press, 1988).
 Wordsworth's Historical Imagination (New York: Methuen, 1987).
Skinner, Andrew S. and T. Wilson (eds.). *Essays on Adam Smith*. Oxford: Clarendon Press, 1975.
Solomon, J. F. 'Annotating the Annotations: A Philosophical Reading of the Primary and Secondary Imagination' in Burwick, *Coleridge's* Biographia Literaria, pp. 138–49.
Spiegelman, Willard. *Majestic Indolence* (Oxford: Oxford University Press, 1995).
Steuart, James. *An Inquiry into the Principles of Political Oeconomy*, 2 vols. (London: A. Millar and T. Cadell, 1767).
Stillinger, Jack. *Coleridge and Textual Instability* (Oxford: Oxford University Press, 1994).
 'John Mill's Education: Fact, Fiction, and Myth' in Laine, *A Cultivated Mind*, pp. 19–43.

Sychrava, Juliet. *Schiller to Derrida: Idealism in Aesthetics* (Cambridge: Cambridge University Press, 1989).
Thompson, Janet. 'An Autumnal Blast, a Killing Frost: Coleridge's Poetic Conversation with John Thelwall', *Studies in Romanticism*, 36:3 (1997), 427–56.
Vogler, Thomas. 'Coleridge's Book of Moonlight' in Burwick, *Coleridge's* Biographia Literaria, pp. 20–46.
Wakefield, Priscilla. *Reflections on the Present Condition of the Female Sex: With Suggestions for Its Improvement* (London: J. Johnson, and Darton and Harvey, 1798).
Wallace, C. M. *The Design of* The Biographia Literaria (London: Allen and Unwin, 1983).
Wellek, René. *Immanuel Kant in England, 1793–1838* (Princeton: Princeton University Press, 1964).
Wheeler, K. *Sources, Processes and Methods in Coleridge's* The Biographia Literaria (Cambridge: Cambridge University Press, 1980).
Williams, Raymond. *Culture and Society* (London: Chatto and Windus, 1967).
Winch, Donald. *Riches and Poverty: An Intellectual History of Political Economy in Britain, 1750–1834* (Cambridge: Cambridge University Press, 1996).
Wu, Duncan (ed.). *Romanticism: An Anthology* (Oxford: Blackwell, 1994).

Index

'Adam Smith Problem', 30–1, 177
aesthetic contemplation, 7, 8, 9, 58–9, 60, 62, 64, 66, 67, 72, 94–5, 97, 126, 130, 135, 136, 137, 138, 139, 140, 141, 147–8, 150, 162, 169, 170, 171, 172
aesthetic education, 7, 37, 38, 52–68, 96–7, 126, 143, 149, 162, 163, 168, 170
Allen, Peter, 189, 190
American Declaration of Independence, 40
Arnold, Matthew, 190
Arnold, Thomas, 190
art, 52–3, 60, 61–2, 63, 188, *see also* poetic labour/composition
avocation, 47–8, 49, 50, 51, 66, 135–6

Bacon, Francis, 127
Barbauld, Anna Letitia, 86–8, 183
Barrell, John, 33, 34, 177, 189, 190, 195
Barry, Peter, 183
Behmen, Jacob, 108
Bell, Andrew, 46
Bender, John, 41
Bentham, Jeremy, 7, 60, 65–7, 99, 127–8, 135, 136, 159, 160, 163, 167, 178, 179, 180, 193
  'Pauper Management', 39
  Chrestomathia, 7, 39, 46–52, 63, 64, 66, 163, 180
  Panopticon Letters, *see* Panopticon Project
  Panopticon Project, 39–46, 179, 180, 193
  Panopticon Writings, *see* Panopticon Project
Bentham, Sir Samuel, 39, 193
Blackburn, William, 41
Blackstone, William, 40, 42, 43, 179
Bygrave, Stephen, 183

Carlyle, Thomas, 144
civic humanism, 177
classical republicanism, 24–8, 134, 176, 177, 191
classical societies, 18–19, 24–7, 34, 38, 61, 134, 176, 177, 181, *see also* classical republicanism

Coleridge, George, 104
Coleridge, Samuel Taylor, 7–8, 67, 86–8, 93, 95–101, 135–6, 138–40, 141, 144, 147, 150, 160, 163, 165, 168, 170, 171, 172, 184, 191
  'Address to a young Jack Ass', 105–6
  Biographia Literaria, 3–6, 7, 8, 102, 108–23, 126, 127, 128, 130, 131–2, 137, 186, 187, 188, 189, 190
  'Effusion XXXV', 7, 79–81, 83–4, 86, 87–8, 95–6, 97–8, 102, 122, 130, 131–2, 134, 137, 138, 144, 147, 183, 185, 187
  'Frost at Midnight', 7, 77–9, 80, 81–5, 88, 90–1, 95–101, 102, 122, 130, 131–2, 134, 147, 151, 170, 183, 184, 185, 192
  On the Constitution of Church and State, 8, 102, 123–32, 133–5, 139, 189, 190
  Pantisocracy, 7, 102–8, 113, 119–20, 131–2, 138, 139, 186, 190
Coleridge, Sara, 80–1, 84, 87–8, 97, 137, 183, 186, 187
Cowper, William, 7, 98–101, 102, 135–6, 137, 138–40, 141, 143, 144, 147, 150, 157, 171, 172, 184, 186, 191
  The Task, 7, 68–77, 81, 82, 83–4, 85–7, 88–9, 90–2, 93–4, 98–9, 100, 138, 139, 140, 143, 184, 185

Disraeli, Benjamin, 190
division of labour, 6, 7, 9, 10–37, 38, 60, 66, 68, 100, 133, 172, 174, 180, 181, 191, *see also* specialization; Smith, Adam; Ferguson, Adam

Eden, William, 40, 42, 179
education, 14, 18–19, 20, 31, 34–5, 38, 40–1, 43, 71–2, 103–4, 131, 134, 136, 152–3, 158–64, 167, 193, *see also* aesthetic education; utilitarian education
Edwards, Thomas, 103
Empson, William, 138

201

Engell, James and W. Jackson Bate, 189
ennui, 47–9, 50, 51, 52, 65–6

fancy, 73, 74, 75, 82, 89, 92, 95, 97, 116, 144
Favret, Mary, 89
Ferguson, Adam, 6, 8, 10, 11, 38, 43, 46, 48, 52, 60, 65, 66, 67, 68, 69, 76, 84, 99–100, 109, 124, 127, 129, 133, 135–6, 137, 140, 175, 176, 181
  Essay on the History of Civil Society, 6, 17–26, 27, 32, 34–6, 37, 135–6, 175, 176
  Principles of Moral and Political Science, 20–1, 23–4, 25
Fleischacker, Samuel, 13–14, 178
Forbes, Duncan, vii, 175, 181
Fox, George, 108
French Revolution, 89, 94
Fruman, Norman, 188

Godwin, William, 102, 184
Goethe, Johann Wolfgang von, 165
Goodman, Kevis, 75–6, 183, 192
Gottlieb, Evan, 192
Griffin, Dustin, 75, 76
Guest, Harriet, 94, 184
guilt, 84–5, 97, 137

habit, 11–12, 13, 35, 41
happiness, 19, 21–2, 23–4, 43, 45, 46, 69, 89, 93, 128, 130, 162, 164
harmony, 53–4, 55, 56, 57, 60, 64, 95, 117, 118, 123, 124, 129, 162, 163, 164, 165, 168, 169, 182, 185, *see also* state of nature
Hartley, David, 102, 108, 110–14, 116, 118–19, 126, 132, 160
  materialist psychology, 40–1
Hazlitt, William, 186
Heath, Charles, 103
Holmes, Richard, 186
Homer, 148, 159
Hont, Istvan & Michael Ignatieff, 174, 178
Howard, John, 40, 41, 42, 44, 45, 178, 179
Humboldt, Wilhelm von, 190
Hutcheson, Francis, 11

Ignatieff, Michael, 40–1, 45, 179
imagination, 19, 114–18, 120, 126, 130, 131, 136, 137, 147, 187, 188
'impartial spectator', 29–30, 36
inspection principle, 40, 41–2, 46

Kames, H. Home, Lord, 12
Kant, Immanuel, 59–60, 181, 187
Kingsley, Charles, 8, 190, 192, 194
  Alton Locke, 8, 141, 150–8, 164–5, 166, 169–71, 172, 192
  Water Babies, The, 192
  Yeast, 8, 141–50, 170–1, 172, 192
Kooy, Michael John, 54, 62, 121, 122, 182, 189

Lancaster, Joseph, 46
Leask, Nigel, 116, 120, 187, 190
leisure, 1, 6, 15–17, 32, 33, 36, 69, 84–5, 89, 103, 104, 105, 107, 108, 119, 138, 139, 140, 157, 164, 172, 175, 186, 190
Locke, John, 75, 108
Lukács, Georg, 181

Magnuson, Paul, 82, 183
Malachuk, Daniel, 186, 190
Malthus, Thomas, 113
Mandeville, Bernard, 16, 174
martial activity, 13, 22, 38, 52
Marx, Karl, 13, 174, 191
Maurice, Frederick Denison, 190
Menke, Richard, 170, 193
mental vacuity, *see* ennui
Mill, James, 61, 158, 160, 167
Mill, John Stuart, 8, 61–2, 135, 141, 168–9, 190, 193, 194
  Autobiography, 8, 61, 158–62, 163, 164, 165–8, 169, 171, 182, 193
  'Inaugural Address', 61, 163–4, 168
  On Bentham and Coleridge, 162–3
monitorial education, 46

Newman, John Henry, 190
Nietzsche, Friedrich, 35

Omai, 76
Oz-Salzberger, Fania, 175, 195

pastoral, 138–9, 149, 171, 172, 174, 194
Paul, George Onesiphorus, 41, 44, 45
Penitentiary Act of 1779, 40, 41, 42, 44, 180
Petrarch, 117
Phillipson, Nicholas, 177
Plato, 11
play, 12, 15, 17, 50, 57, 58, 59–60, 66, 73, 75, 78–9, 97, 99, 106, 116, 135–6, 137, 168
'play-drive', 57–8, 122–3
Pocock, John, 26, 175, 176, 177
poetic capability, 7, 8, 102, *see also* poetic labour/composition
poetic labour/composition, 2, 4–5, 69–70, 74, 98, 102, 109, 110–12, 113–20, 126, 130, 131–2, 136–8, 151, 159, 165
political economy, 6, 9, 38, 65, 99, 100, 124, 128, 135, 136, 139, 162, 167, 180, 185, *see also* division of labour; specialization; Smith, Adam; Ferguson, Adam
Poole, Thomas, 102–3, 105

Pope, Alexander, 159
Priestley, Joseph, 102
Priestman, Martin, 75, 76
promiscuous association, 45, 180

Reni, Guido, 170
reverie, 91, 113, 135, 145, 147, 153, 155, 157, 162, 164, 170, 171, 184, 187, 192,
  see also aesthetic contemplation
Ross, Marlon, 191
Rousseau, Jean-Jacques, 54, 89, 99, 102, 138, 184
Ryan, Alan, 61

Schelling, Friedrich, 120, 121, 122, 187, 188, 189
Schiller, Friedrich, 7, 8–9, 37, 72, 75, 94–5, 97–101, 117, 120–4, 127, 129, 130–1, 133, 135, 136, 138, 139–40, 141, 147, 148, 149, 160, 161, 162, 163, 164, 165, 172, 178, 180, 181, 182, 185, 189, 190
  Horae, 123, 129, 131, 189
  On the Aesthetic Education of Man, 7, 8, 9, 52–67, 121, 122–4, 129, 130–1, 137, 138, 139–40, 162, 163, 168–9, 170, 172, 173, 178, 180, 181, 182, 189, 190
  The Muses' Almanac, 122
Schlegel, Friedrich, 182, 185
Scott, Sir Walter, 159
second nature, 25–6, 40–1, 65, 99–100, 129,
  see also state of nature
self-interest, 11, 12, 15–17, 21, 22, 24–7, 31–2, 33, 35, 43, 45, 46, 176, 179
  as self-involvement, 29–30
Semple, Janet, 44
Seven Years' War, 177
Shakespeare, William, 108
Sher, Richard, 177
Simpson, David, 3, 173
Smith, Adam, 6, 8, 38, 46, 52, 60, 65, 66, 67, 68, 99–100, 127, 133–6, 140, 176, 178, 180, 181, 191
  An Inquiry into the Nature and Causes of the Wealth of Nations, 6, 10–17, 22, 23, 25, 26–8, 30–7, 53, 65, 99, 124, 133–7, 139, 174, 176, 177, 178, 186, 191
  The Theory of Moral Sentiments, 6, 27–31, 32, 36, 177, 178
solitary confinement, 40–1, 43–5

Southey, Robert, 7, 102, 103, 104, 105, 106, 107, 132, 186
specialization, 7, 10, 11, 12–13, 14, 15, 16, 17, 18, 22–3, 32, 33, 35, 36, 37, 45, 52, 53–4, 56, 59, 60–1, 62, 65, 66, 68, 134, 136, 139, 140, 172, 174, 191, *see also* division of labour
state of nature, 10–11, 26, 54, 56, 175, 177,
  see also second nature
Steuart, Sir James, 174, 176
Stillinger, Jack, 193
subjunctive mode, 33–4, 36, 37
Swift, Jonathan, 190
sympathy, 28–30

Thelwall, John, 82, 184
Thompson, Janet, 184
Thompson, Judith, 82
Thornton, William, 167
tranquillity, 17, 29, 30, 32, 162, 164, 166, 175

uncanny, the, 88, 93, 98–9, 131
Utilitarianism, 65, 127–9, 162, 190
  utilitarian education, 7, 39–52, 61–2, 65–7, 128, 129, 178
  utility, 23, 36, 45, 46, 52
  Utility as idol, 53, 56, 62

vacancy, 109, *see also* ennui
Vogler, Thomas, 187, 190

Wakefield, Priscilla, 175
Wilkinson, Elizabeth and Leonard Willoughby, 54, 63, 120–1, 122, 123, 181
Williams, Raymond, 172, 193
Wollstonecraft, Mary, 7, 88–95, 97, 101, 135–6, 138, 139, 140, 141, 143, 145, 150, 170, 171, 172, 184, 185
Wordsworth, William, 158, 162, 165, 166, 172
  'Gipsies', 1, 8, 136–8
  Home at Grasmere, 2
  Lyrical Ballads, 5, 142
  The Brothers, 1, 8–9
  'Three years she grew in sun and shower', 8, 141, 142–8, 150–8, 162, 170, 171, 191, 192
Wu, Duncan, 183

Young, Arthur, 39

CAMBRIDGE STUDIES IN ROMANTICISM

General Editor
JAMES CHANDLER, University of Chicago

1. Romantic Correspondence: Women, Politics and the Fiction of Letters
   MARY A. FAVRET
2. British Romantic Writers and the East: Anxieties of Empire
   NIGEL LEASK
3. Poetry as an Occupation and an Art in Britain, 1760–1830
   PETER MURPHY
4. Edmund Burke's Aesthetic Ideology: Language, Gender and Political Economy in Revolution
   TOM FURNISS
5. In the Theatre of Romanticism: Coleridge, Nationalism, Women
   JULIE A. CARLSON
6. Keats, Narrative and Audience
   ANDREW BENNETT
7. Romance and Revolution: Shelley and the Politics of a Genre
   DAVID DUFF
8. Literature, Education, and Romanticism: Reading as Social Practice, 1780–1832
   ALAN RICHARDSON
9. Women Writing about Money: Women's Fiction in England, 1790–1820
   EDWARD COPELAND
10. Shelley and the Revolution in Taste: The Body and the Natural World
    TIMOTHY MORTON
11. William Cobbett: The Politics of Style
    LEONORA NATTRASS
12. The Rise of Supernatural Fiction, 1762–1800
    E. J. CLERY
13. Women Travel Writers and the Language of Aesthetics, 1716–1818
    ELIZABETH A. BOHLS
14. Napoleon and English Romanticism
    SIMON BAINBRIDGE
15. Romantic Vagrancy: Wordsworth and the Simulation of Freedom
    CELESTE LANGAN

16. Wordsworth and the Geologists
   JOHN WYATT

17. Wordsworth's Pope: A Study in Literary Historiography
   ROBERT J. GRIFFIN

18. The Politics of Sensibility: Race, Gender and Commerce in the Sentimental Novel
   MARKMAN ELLIS

19. Reading Daughters' Fictions, 1709–1834: Novels and Society from Manley to Edgeworth
   CAROLINE GONDA

20. Romantic Identities: Varieties of Subjectivity, 1774–1830
   ANDREA K. HENDERSON

21. Print Politics: The Press and Radical Opposition: In Early Nineteenth-Century England
   KEVIN GILMARTIN

22. Reinventing Allegory
   THERESA M. KELLEY

23. British Satire and the Politics of Style, 1789–1832
   GARY DYER

24. The Romantic Reformation: Religious Politics in English Literature, 1789–1824
   ROBERT M. RYAN

25. De Quincey's Romanticism: Canonical Minority and the Forms of Transmission
   MARGARET RUSSETT

26. Coleridge on Dreaming: Romanticism, Dreams and the Medical Imagination
   JENNIFER FORD

27. Romantic Imperialism: Universal Empire and the Culture of Modernity
   SAREE MAKDISI

28. Ideology and Utopia in the Poetry of William Blake
   NICHOLAS M. WILLIAMS

29. Sexual Politics and the Romantic Author
   SONIA HOFKOSH

30. Lyric and Labour in the Romantic Tradition
   ANNE JANOWITZ

31. Poetry and Politics in the Cockney School: Keats, Shelley, Hunt and Their Circle
   JEFFREY N. COX

32. Rousseau, Robespierre and English Romanticism
   GREGORY DART

33. Contesting the Gothic: Fiction, Genre and Cultural Conflict, 1764–1832
   JAMES WATT

34. Romanticism, Aesthetics, and Nationalism
   DAVID ARAM KAISER

35. Romantic Poets and the Culture of Posterity
   ANDREW BENNETT

36. The Crisis of Literature in the 1790s: Print Culture and the Public Sphere
   PAUL KEEN

37. Romantic Atheism: Poetry and Freethought, 1780–1830
   MARTIN PRIESTMAN

38. Romanticism and Slave Narratives: Transatlantic Testimonies
   HELEN THOMAS

39. Imagination under Pressure, 1789–1832: Aesthetics, Politics, and Utility
   JOHN WHALE

40. Romanticism and the Gothic: Genre, Reception, and Canon Formation, 1790–1820
   MICHAEL GAMER

41. Romanticism and the Human Sciences: Poetry, Population, and the Discourse of the Species
   MAUREEN N. MCLANE

42. The Poetics of Spice: Romantic Consumerism and the Exotic
   TIMOTHY MORTON

43. British Fiction and the Production of Social Order, 1740–1830
   MIRANDA J. BURGESS

44. Women Writers and the English Nation in the 1790s
   ANGELA KEANE

45. Literary Magazines and British Romanticism
   MARK PARKER

46. Women, Nationalism and the Romantic Stage: Theatre and Politics in Britain, 1780–1800
   BETSY BOLTON

47. British Romanticism and the Science of the Mind
   ALAN RICHARDSON

48. The Anti-Jacobin Novel: British Conservatism and the French Revolution
   M. O. GRENBY

49. Romantic Austen: Sexual Politics and the Literary Canon
   CLARA TUITE

50. Byron and Romanticism
   JEROME MCGANN AND JAMES SODERHOLM

51. The Romantic National Tale and the Question of Ireland
   INA FERRIS

52. Byron, Poetics and History
   JANE STABLER

53. Religion, Toleration, and British Writing, 1790–1830
   MARK CANUEL

54. Fatal Women of Romanticism
   ADRIANA CRACIUN

55. Knowledge and Indifference in English Romantic Prose
   TIM MILNES

56. Mary Wollstonecraft and the Feminist Imagination
   BARBARA TAYLOR

57. Romanticism, Maternity and the Body Politic
   JULIE KIPP

58. Romanticism and Animal Rights
   DAVID PERKINS

59. Georgic Modernity and British Romanticism: Poetry and the Mediation of History
   KEVIS GOODMAN

60. Literature, Science and Exploration in the Romantic Era: Bodies of Knowledge
   TIMOTHY FULFORD, DEBBIE LEE AND PETER J. KITSON

61. Romantic Colonization and British Anti-Slavery
   DEIRDRE COLEMAN

62. Anger, Revolution, and Romanticism
   ANDREW M. STAUFFER

63. Shelley and the Revolutionary Sublime
   CIAN DUFFY

64. Fictions and Fakes: Forging Romantic Authenticity, 1760–1845
   MARGARET RUSSETT

65. Early Romanticism and Religious Dissent
   DANIEL E. WHITE

66. The Invention of Evening: Perception and Time in Romantic Poetry
   CHRISTOPHER R. MILLER

67. Wordsworth's Philosophic Song
   SIMON JARVIS

68. Romanticism and the Rise of the Mass Public
   ANDREW FRANTA

69. Writing against Revolution: Literary Conservatism in Britain, 1790–1832
   KEVIN GILMARTIN

70. Women, Sociability and Theatre in Georgian London
   GILLIAN RUSSELL

71. The Lake Poets and Professional Identity
   BRIAN GOLDBERG

72. Wordsworth Writing
   ANDREW BENNETT

73. Science and Sensation in Romantic Poetry
   NOEL JACKSON

74. Advertising and Satirical Culture in the Romantic Period
   JOHN STRACHAN

75. Romanticism and the Painful Pleasures of Modern Life
   ANDREA K. HENDERSON

76. Balladeering, Minstrelsy, and the Making of British Romantic Poetry
   MAUREEN N. MCLANE

77. Romanticism and Improvisation, 1750–1850
   ANGELA ESTERHAMMER

78. Scotland and the Fictions of Geography: North Britain, 1760–1830
   PENNY FIELDING

79. Wordsworth, Commodification and Social Concern: The Poetics of Modernity
   DAVID SIMPSON

80. Sentimental Masculinity and the Rise of History, 1790–1890
   MIKE GOODE

81. Fracture and Fragmentation in British Romanticism
    ALEXANDER REGIER

82. Romanticism and Music Culture in Britain, 1770–1840: Virtue and Virtuosity
    GILLEN D'ARCY WOOD

83. The Truth about Romanticism: Pragmatism and Idealism in Keats, Shelley, Coleridge
    TIMOTHY MILNES

84. Blake's Gifts: Poetry and the Politics of Exchange
    SARAH HAGGARTY

85. Real Money and Romanticism
    MATTHEW ROWLINSON

86. Sentimental Literature and Anglo-Scottish Identity, 1745–1820
    JULIET SHIELDS

87. Romantic Tragedies: The Dark Employments of Wordsworth, Coleridge, and Shelley
    REEVE PARKER

88. Blake, Sexuality and Bourgeois Politeness
    SUSAN MATTHEWS

89. Idleness, Contemplation and the Aesthetic, 1750–1830
    RICHARD ADELMAN